Manage Your Money, Manage Your Mind:

Positive Psychology Skills for Financial Wellbeing

Dr Pradnya Surana

ROBINSON

ROBINSON

First published in Great Britain in 2025 by Robinson

Copyright © Pradnya Surana, 2025

1 3 5 7 9 10 8 6 4 2

A CIP catalogue record for this book
is available from the British Library.

ISBN: 978-1-47214-942-8

Typeset in Bembo by M Rules
Printed and bound in Great Britain by
Clays Ltd, Elcograf S.p.A.

Papers used by Robinson are from well-managed forests and
other responsible sources.

MIX
Paper | Supporting
responsible forestry
FSC
www.fsc.org   FSC® C104740

Robinson   The authorised representative
An imprint of   in the EEA is
Little, Brown Book Group   Hachette Ireland
Carmelite House   8 Castlecourt Centre
50 Victoria Embankment   Dublin 15, D15 XTP3, Ireland
London EC4Y 0DZ   (email: info@hbgi.ie)

An Hachette UK Company
www.hachette.co.uk

www.littlebrown.co.uk

Contents

Section 1: Introduction

Section 2, Part 1: Heart/spirituality/feelings

Section 2, Part 2: Brain/psychology/thoughts

Section 2, Part 3: Hand/financial behaviour/action

Appendices

Acknowledgements

This book is dedicated to the memory of my late father, Dr Kanahaiyalal Surana. His values, his ideas and his extraordinary capacity to love have served as my guiding light throughout my life.

The journey of this book would not have been possible without the help and encouragement of many other wonderful people. To begin, I want to say thank you from the bottom of my heart to my mom and to my three fur babies, Samantha, Sandy and Coco, for always believing in me and for making everything easier by making the difficult things worth doing.

To my brother Nilesh and sister Kirti – ever present through crazy times and reasoned times alike – my heartful thanks for steady hope and abiding love. To Bhumi, Varun and Prachi – for being consistently there, in all phases, believing in me all the way – thank you.

I would like to thank heartily Dr Jolanta Golan for her friendship, generosity and continuous help.

My gratitude goes to my efficient staff, whose dedication to the task is the key reason why I was able to bring this book to reality.

I owe huge thanks to the many clients around the world who have given me the time and space to do this work, and to those who have accepted extra sessions to accommodate my busy schedule.

This book draws upon the tireless efforts and incisive thought of untold numbers of scholars whose work has contributed uniquely to our understanding of wellbeing; to them I am indebted.

With deep gratitude, I wish to thank Andrew, my first-rate editor, whose honesty, acumen, intelligence and tolerance have made this book a reality. I would like to extend my heartfelt thanks to Steve and Rebecca for their incredible efforts in editing this book, and to Jessica Purdue and the Rights team for their efforts in getting the book published in multiple other languages! The entire team at Little, Brown Book Group has transformed it into something far better than I could have ever envisioned or achieved on my own.

On a final note of gratitude, I would like to acknowledge my soul brother, friend and business partner, Mr Kim Stephenson, the man who listened day after day to my waffling thoughts, my constant interruptions, my incessant rewrites, my irritations and frustrations, and was always there to smooth my rough edges and make me shine brighter. You have been a constant sounding board, capable of analysing my ideas, putting them into a workable sequence and making sense of the jumble in order to put it into writing. Thank you for your patience, perseverance and love. Thank you for emphasising what is important. Thank you for listening to every iteration of every chapter or sentence every single day, and thanks again for the final read at the eleventh hour to ensure there were no more hiccups. You make anything seem possible. Thank you for being in my life. Thanks to your beautiful wife Diane and fur baby Demelza.

With the deepest gratitude of my heart, I thank all those who have contributed directly or indirectly to the production of this work: you inspired me to embark on this labour of love.

About the author

I'll share my own story with money – and how it shapes my perspective – briefly for context. I was born and brought up in Aurangabad (now Chatrapati Sambhajinagar) in India and I belong to an upper-middle-class family. My parents have always been advocates for education and modern thinking. They encouraged all three of their children (I have two older siblings) to pursue higher education, and pushed them to think beyond provincial norms.

My dad's embrace of modernity informed my attitude towards the future and the conduct of my affairs, while my mom's religious and socially minded views about the virtue of giving and freeing oneself from the shackles of materialism also shaped my character.

But because the community I was raised in – the Marwari – was traditionally a business class, money was the talk of the town. Business purchases, profits, investments, cuts and cost of products were standard talk Everybody in the community talked about having more respectability, status and power and, obviously, more money. And having less money would mean stress, anxiety and more problems, and give you less leverage in the community dynamics.

I first became interested in money during my college days, when I started to ask myself questions like, 'Why is money so important?' 'Why do so few people have it?' 'Why doesn't everyone earn a lot of money if it is just a matter of changing the way they think and behave?' 'Do these mindsets vary across person and place, and where do people use them?'

Religion and spirituality, too, have had an influence on my thinking about money – I am a practising Jain, so charitable giving forms a fundamental part of our faith. From a very young age, I was brought up to donate some of my income to good causes. My father, a medical practitioner, had at least one consultation day every week where he would see patients free of charge, while the cost of the medicines he prescribed was borne out of his own funds. My mother used to encourage us when we were little to donate any money we received on birthdays and festivals to orphanages. My parents held the belief that nothing was more important than relationships, not even money, and this is how they taught me to think about money.

These views shaped my educational and career choices too. I had always believed that money was a means to follow my own heart and took up the post of assistant to my brother in his software-selling company and other family businesses when I was seventeen; quite young for an Indian girl.

By the age of twenty-one, I had saved up enough money to start a business of my own. This provided me with the financial freedom to learn what I loved while not having to depend on my family. I completed my undergraduate and two master's degrees: MBA (Master of Business Administration) in human resources and MA (Master of Art) in clinical psychology in India while working and studying simultaneously.

But even though I received a decent income and owned material goods, I also knew I was stressed about money. It was not a concern about having enough to survive, but rather an urge somehow to outperform in order to earn more, have more and own more things. I felt like I was on an ever-faster treadmill yet kept running without a clue as to why.

It was at this challenging moment that a new opportunity emerged – I stumbled across a 'positive psychology' (PP) course offered in the UK. Determined to explore this subject further, I embarked on a PhD at the University of East London where I was given a very rare opportunity to explore the theme of money and find answers to the questions that had been haunting me.

My move to the UK shifted my view on money, as access to the academic literature led me to a conscious discovery of money paradigms, including my own, that I'd been blind to before. I came to recognise that 'how much' I had in my bank account wasn't the problem – it was my inclination to worry about money, whether I had it or not, that was causing the stress.

In addition, my own financial situation changed. I switched from being a well-established independent businesswoman to an international student who was only allowed to work up to twenty hours a week. For the very first time, I felt pressure and stress over the availability of money itself – I was working part-time jobs to cover the tuition fees and bills which gave me a real insight into the struggle to earn money.

These experiences opened up whole new areas of discussion and ways of looking at things that I had been unaware of – contenting myself with a small sum of money on holiday and finding creative ways to economise, meeting people running their livelihoods on a shoestring and living happily.

My views on what constitutes 'enough money' changed dramatically. During my PhD, I learned to be grateful for what I had and let go of what I couldn't control or didn't have at the moment. I started to come to terms with the fact that 'more' doesn't always mean 'better', and that money and life satisfaction are correlated but not always in a cause-and-effect relationship. I realised that I could be happy with what I had without constantly comparing myself to others.

While I'm not sure if this is the key to solving all my money-related issues, it's definitely a starting point. After completing my education, I decided to continue researching the topic without the rigid constraints of academia. I've read hundreds of books and thousands of journal articles over the last decade, trying to find solutions for money-related stress and help others find relief.

What I've discovered is that the meaning of money is a constant inquiry, a journey of discovering truth rather than arriving at a single, final answer. This book is just one attempt to find those answers, to share what I've learnt, and hopefully to help others navigate their own relationships with money in a healthier, more fulfilling way.

Why this book?

Money is a profound and emotionally charged aspect of our lives, yet it remains one of the most neglected topics in psychology.

Let's start with an honest observation – earning more money isn't always the solution to our financial woes. Many books out there offer theoretical knowledge but lack practical guidance. That's where this workbook differs – it's designed to be an interactive companion, empowering you to take action and create meaningful change in your relationship with money.

While we live in an age of 'information oversupply', the real action occurs when our attitudes, dispositions, perceptions and behaviour change as a result of this exposure to information. This workbook is not a passive, academic collection of knowledge. It is designed as an interactive tool for those who want to experience a change in their life outcomes, and will guide you through the world's most well-researched self-help techniques and interventions, designed with the objective of real consequences.

Now, a disclaimer: this is not a self-help book with a new-age aura and inspirational prose. It is organised on a scientific basis and provides one intervention at a time. For each intervention, you should read about it, try out the techniques suggested to help with your psychological issues around money, and then measure the change to see if you have solved them. If not, it is time to try the next intervention. You will not only read about the most recent research but work through several activities, learning how to apply the findings. You can measure your progress by completing pre- and post-intervention assessments, providing you with quantifiable results.

While the financial field has been dominated for years by economic theories that oversimplify our money worries as mere cognitive or rational decisions, this workbook takes a holistic approach and acknowledges that money issues are often a result of many influences, including your age, gender and culture; your marriage, friends and family; your beliefs; and your life experience.

Picture it this way. We have a herd of expert advisers – researchers, philosophers, economists, financial planners, motivational speakers, spiritual gurus, sociologists, religious leaders and more. All these experts are well intentioned and genuinely want to help people with their money problems. However, their advice is rarely ideal because they often lack a holistic view. Most of them focus narrowly on their specific area of expertise without considering the broader picture. They seldom take into account the complex psychology behind our relationship with money, including the emotional, social and cultural factors that deeply influence our financial behaviours and decisions.

Without this holistic perspective, their advice might address a part of the problem but fail to provide comprehensive solutions that resonate with people's real life experiences. For instance, financial planners may give sound budgeting advice, but if they don't understand the emotional triggers that lead to overspending, their advice might not be effective. Similarly, motivational speakers might inspire action, but without understanding underlying fears or beliefs about money, their guidance could fall short of creating lasting change. True financial wellbeing requires an integration of these diverse perspectives, considering not just the economic and practical aspects of money, but also the psychological and emotional dimensions that drive our financial decisions.

That's why this workbook incorporates perspectives from clinical, positive and organisational psychology along with insights from spiritual wisdom. By recognising the interrelatedness of our financial, physical, emotional, social and spiritual health, you can create holistic solutions for your life.

Most of us struggle with money issues on a daily basis. From advertisements to news stories, books to television shows and movies, we're exposed to a constant stream of narratives about irrational or self-destructive financial behaviour – from acquiring products and objects to hoarding and committing crimes for money, and to the negative effect of wealth on relationships and mental health. Then there are the real-life anecdotes, sometimes from our own family and friends, of struggles with money. Yet our stories about why we don't know how to spend, save or share don't often come with recommendations on how to address these issues using empirically supported therapies or interventions.

Most self-help books promise shortcuts and easy processes to get rich, frequently relying on positive thinking, affirmations, visualisation and 'authoritative' and unsubstantiated claims.[1] Although they are typically well intentioned, such books often lack even basic empirical research to support their methods.[2]

I want to help you bridge that gap with this workbook, which translates the science from jargon to layman's terms so you can understand and begin applying what the science shows will work to promote financial wellbeing.

I'm drawing on more than a decade of research into stress and anxiety about money, which I've written about both academically and in the real world during my career as a researcher, consultant and author. I'm not an expert in every subject I'm going to talk about, and I won't pretend to be. But I've completely immersed myself in these topics, and I'll send you off with a few places to explore if you want to deepen your knowledge.

However, let me reiterate that this workbook is not a cure-all. It won't solve your future money problems immediately, but it will provide you with access to scientific and evidence-based ways of managing financial and psychological problems. Perhaps you will like some of the interventions and not others ('this is not for me'). Or, perhaps, you will like a few, or one or two ('this one is good'). Again, that's fine. Not all the interventions will work for you, and that's perfectly OK. The tools and exercises provided are designed to cater to a wide range of people with different experiences, backgrounds and financial mindsets. It's possible that you might only find one or two strategies that truly resonate with you or fit into your life. The key takeaway is not to use every single intervention, but rather to gain access to a new way of thinking. Even if just one tool helps you overcome a limiting belief or enhances your relationship with money, that can be a significant breakthrough.

Just like you, I'm on a continuous journey of learning and self-discovery. If you have insights, experiences or knowledge that could contribute to our collective understanding, please reach out to me at www.positivepsychologyofmoney.com. Together, we can embark on a transformative path towards financial wellbeing, free from the shackles of stress and anxiety.

Using this book effectively

This book aims to provide practical knowledge and interventions for enhancing your financial wellbeing. It is designed for those who are willing to take action and apply the concepts in their daily lives. The activities I present are scientifically tested and proven to be effective in reducing stress and anxiety related to money matters.

Participation is the key. The focus is on your active participation in the psychological intervention activities. Each chapter includes a questionnaire to assess your current state, scientific research on the specific intervention, and the latest findings on how it can help reduce financial stress and anxiety.

The book's structure

The book is divided into two main sections:

Section 1: Introduction

This section is theoretical in focus and comprises three chapters that explore the following:

- The relationship between money and overall wellbeing;
- the impact of money on mental health issues;

- the importance of financial wellbeing and its various aspects.

Section 2: How to improve your financial wellbeing

This more applied section is further divided into three parts: heart, brain and hand. Achieving financial wellbeing requires aligning your personal values, emotions and actions with your financial goals. This coherence fosters conscious spending, saving and investing decisions. The heart sets intentions, the brain devises strategies and the hand takes action. Each psychological intervention follows this structure:

- **Pre-questionnaire:** an initial assessment to gauge your starting point, emotional state and financial habits.
- **Intervention overview:** detailed information about the specific intervention, including its theoretical background, scientific evidence and how it can help enhance financial wellbeing.
- **Activity sheet:** Practical exercises or tasks aligned with the intervention's principles, designed to be completed step by step.
- **Post-questionnaire:** A follow-up assessment to measure changes in your emotional state, financial habits and overall insights gained post-intervention.
- **Supplementary resources:** Recommendations for additional materials like books, podcasts, websites and applications to further support your understanding and implementation of the intervention.

Section 2.1 focuses on interventions related to the heart/spirituality/feelings, such as:

- Gratitude: Cultivating a sense of appreciation for what you have;

- Savouring: Mindfully enjoying positive experiences;
- Meditation: Calming the mind and reducing stress;
- Self-compassion: Treating yourself with kindness and understanding;
- Meaning therapy: Exploring your values and finding purpose.
- Best possible self: Envisioning your ideal future self.

Section 2.2 addresses interventions related to the brain/cognition/thoughts, including:

- *Cognitive behavioural therapy (CBT):* Identifying and reframing unhelpful thought patterns;
- *Rational emotive behaviour therapy (REBT):* Challenging irrational beliefs;
- *Acceptance and commitment therapy (ACT):* Developing psychological flexibility;
- *Expressive writing:* Processing emotions through writing;
- *Psychological emergency toolkit:* Strategies for managing intense emotional states.

Section 2.3 focuses on interventions related to the hand/behaviour/actions, such as:

- *Money habits:* Developing healthy financial routines;
- *Financial literacy:* Improving knowledge and skills in money management;
- *Money diary/journalling:* Tracking and reflecting on financial decisions;
- *Goal setting:* Defining and working towards financial goals;
- *Charitable giving/pro-social spending:* Finding fulfilment through generosity;
- *Financial hygiene and maintenance:* Maintaining financial organisation and wellbeing.

Guidelines for effective learning

- **Don't believe a word of it:** Between now and the end of the book, don't assume any of the material is true or assertable until you're certain that you can reach the same conclusion yourself from your own experience. Be a healthy sceptic.
- **Practise:** To really learn and internalise the practical skills that are presented in this book, it is essential that you actually do the exercises; holding the intellectual position or trying to intellectualise the material will not make a difference in the long term. So, practise, practise, practise!
- **Sequence or focus:** You can either go through the book in the recommended sequence or take one section at a time, whichever approach resonates with you better. However, it is strongly advised to read the entire book first, to gain a comprehensive understanding, and then revisit individual interventions as needed.
- **Open-mindedness:** As you go through the book, at least for now, try not to compare or judge the various information and insights you are exposed to. Try not to pre-emptively decide that something you are reading is of no value, relevance or use. Instead, experience multiple possibilities and perspectives as distinct and coexisting, even if they seem to contradict some knowledge you may have about yourself or the world. This will give you a much clearer picture of how the insights can be applied.
- **Take note of your insights:** Create a working journal or notebook where you record the insights, initiate troubleshooting, observe the breakthroughs, and measure the progress. This practice works two ways: you track your progress and reinforce the learning.

- **Be easy and playful**: Treat yourself and your practice with an easy and playful attitude. Take each exercise as an opportunity to be curious and compassionate towards yourself and your body. Remember that every change takes time and effort, and expect to have hiccups in the process.
- **Redoing and rereading**: When you find it particularly resonant or fruitful, don't hesitate to return to the interventions or even to a single page. Think of the book as a lifetime companion. The real benefits come through application over time, integrating the practices into your life.
- **Don't make comparisons**: While reading the book, don't compare it to other methods or modalities that you've encountered in your life. Suspend your intellect, and put aside your opinions or judgements, if only temporarily, so that you can wash yourself in the substance of this material and come to your own conclusions.

Remember, this book is a comprehensive tool to enhance your financial wellbeing, and its true value lies in your active participation and application of the concepts in your daily life. Consistent effort, an open mindset and a gentle approach will lead to lasting positive changes in your relationship with money.

Frequently asked questions

1. **Should I read this book in one go and do exercises later?**
   Answer: It is recommended that you read the book in the given sequence and complete all activities, or the activities you find relevant, as you progress through it. Actively engaging with the material and exercises is crucial to obtain the best possible results.

2. **Are the concepts from this book inspired by any particular religion or thought process?**
   Answer: No, the book is not inspired by any specific religious beliefs. Instead, it is an attempt to integrate principles from spirituality, finance and psychology, providing holistic solutions to the financial issues people commonly face.

3. **Will this book really change my financial condition?**
   Answer: The book can help you develop a healthier mindset about money, enabling you to take appropriate actions towards achieving your financial goals. In my experience as a financial wellbeing consultant, most individuals experience financial gains, which can be significant, when they overcome their limiting beliefs about money and take positive steps forward.

4. **Will this book help me have more money immediately?**
   Answer: Perhaps, but it depends on your specific issues, how long you've been dealing with them, and what beliefs you need to change or actions you need to take. The book is not a quick fix or self-help solution; it requires commitment and effort on your part.

5. **Does this book provide financial advice?**
   Answer: No, it primarily focuses on developing a healthier mindset around money, which can lead to improved financial wellbeing. The primary emphasis is on the psychology of the individual concerning money, rather than providing specific financial advice.

6. **Can strong attitudes or long-held beliefs towards money be changed?**
   Answer: Yes, it is definitely possible to change or overcome long-held limiting beliefs about money, but it requires dedicated work. In my experience, shortcuts do not work for chronic issues; you need to put in consistent effort to change your mindset.

7. **Can the exercises really reduce stress and anxiety about money?**
   Answer: Yes, all the interventions included in this book are scientifically tested, and there is evidence that they can effectively reduce stress and anxiety related to money and help to flourish in relation to money.

8. **How can I improve my knowledge about a particular intervention?**
   Answer: Each intervention is accompanied by a resource list that includes books, websites, apps,

podcasts and journal articles. These resources can help deepen your understanding of the specific intervention. Additionally, the research used to support the claims about the intervention's effectiveness is provided in the endnotes.

9. **What if the money issues are caused by factors beyond my control, such as government policies, societal or cultural circumstances, or unavoidable situations?**
   Answer: I understand that some situations are unavoidable, but how we respond to them is always our choice. This book can help you develop a different mindset and response that can lead to reducing stress and anxiety, and ultimately achieving greater financial wellbeing, despite external circumstances.

Remember, the path to financial wellbeing requires dedication, an open mind and a willingness to implement the strategies and exercises presented in this book. Approach the material with kindness towards yourself and a commitment to personal growth.

SECTION 1

Introduction

In this section you will gain basic information regarding financial wellbeing and its relationship with overall wellbeing and mental health issues.

SECTION I

Introduction

CHAPTER 1

The relationship between money and wellbeing

Keep cash in your brain, not in your veins

Introduction

Money and happiness: it's an enduring puzzle, made all the more intriguing by the unexpected ways that income and consumption can facilitate or inhibit our health and wellbeing. It seems intuitive to suppose that having money will make you happier, helping you to get what you need in life and open new opportunities. But, in practice, how the pursuit of material gain appeases – or inflames – us is dizzyingly complex. Figuring out what's really going on in this relationship is vital – not only for individuals and their psychological wellbeing, but also for communities and policymakers, as it helps us understand how to lead a good life. More than that, it can show us what we should care about as a society, and how best to help everybody thrive. By engaging with the details of the relationship between money and mental health, we better understand the subtle yet powerful ways that these two 'currencies' cut across each other – often in unexpected ways – which may help to lay the foundation for a healthier and more humane approach to leading our lives.

This chapter explores the various intricate ways money impacts wellbeing and plays a crucial role in shaping identity. Financial resources, of course, clearly contribute to wellbeing, in enabling people to take care of basic needs and to have opportunity. But money and wellbeing are also affected by many other inter-related factors, such as the notion of 'diminishing returns' – the idea that when it comes to cash contributions to happiness, once basic needs are met, more money does not reliably make us much happier. Above a certain 'threshold' the addition of more income will add relatively little happiness.

The chapter also addresses the importance of what researchers call 'financial literacy', where managing money wisely can be helpful. Importance is given to spending money on experiences rather than on too many material possessions, and to the emotional and psychological benefits of healthy social connections, especially when people are having problems with money.

The theoretical background

Subjective wellbeing is often used, more or less, as another term for happiness. It refers to life satisfaction as a state of mind in which we have plenty of positive feelings (also known as positive affect) and not too many negative feelings (negative affect).[1] There are different philosophical and social scientific theories of happiness and wellbeing. The *hedonic* approach holds that wellbeing is fundamentally about taking pleasure in experiencing positive stimuli and avoiding the unpleasant experience of negative stimuli.[2] This can be contrasted with the stoical, *eudaimonic* life that finds its roots in Aristotle's philosophy, which emphasises living a true-to-self and self-realising life – not simply chasing happiness.

Some believe that it is money itself that is responsible for much human misery – for lack of wellbeing.[3] On the other hand, there are those who argue that without an adequate amount of money one cannot be happy.[4] What these opposite views show is that there are very strong opinions about the linkages between money and wellbeing, and that the current thinking about connections fails to capture some of the important nuances involved.

Income and subjective wellbeing

Researchers have found that the higher your income and that of the country in which you live, the higher your levels of self-reported happiness.[5] This makes sense given that money can supply the most basic needs and provide access to a portfolio of things that promote wellbeing, including healthcare, education and opportunities for leisure.

But it's not just like that, and we see dwindling returns on happiness once a certain level of income is reached. This is sometimes referred to as the Easterlin paradox, after the decades-long empirical findings of the economist Richard Easterlin, who observed, first, that people in richer countries inside a culture tend to report higher satisfaction, but that, second, economic growth for a whole society does not seem to make that society much happier over time. As a result, the easing of poverty in a culture does increase a sense of wellbeing for people inside it but, past a certain point, the effects of increased income on widely shared happiness show diminishing returns.

Once your basic needs are met and you're comfortable, more income doesn't significantly improve your happiness or life satisfaction. According to classicist Barry Schwartz and economist Beam Durchholz, this is known as the 'satiation point' or 'diminishing marginal utility of income'.[6]

One possible explanation is the 'hedonic treadmill', which suggests that people quickly adapt to better conditions, making the initial boost in happiness temporary.[7] As income rises, people adjust their comparison levels to match others, leading them back to their previous levels of satisfaction. Another factor is 'adaptive preferences', where people adjust their goals based on their circumstances.[8] As income increases, people raise their expectations and material goals, but this doesn't necessarily lead to greater wellbeing.

Additionally, people often compare their wealth and income to that of their peers. While higher income might itself not boost happiness much, not keeping up with the income of one's reference group can feel like falling behind. Even at higher income levels, people may feel less satisfied if others around them earn significantly more.

This paradox has sparked many studies and debates, with evidence both supporting and challenging it across different countries and time periods.[9]

Financial management and wellbeing

Even if the link between income and wellbeing follows the standard 'diminishing returns' pattern, where continuing to add more money does not improve your wellbeing as much as it previously did, being financially literate and managing your money well still contribute substantially to overall wellbeing. Having the knowledge, skills and confidence to make informed financial decisions and manage money well is defined as financial literacy.[10]

The more financially literate a person is, the more able they are to make sense of increasingly complex financial situations, to make good decisions about how to spend, save and invest, to balance debts and also to reduce the uncertainty that can lead to stress.[11] Being in control of our financial affairs and feeling we are adept at meeting our financial needs can reduce stress and financial uncertainty – leading to feelings of wellbeing.

Good money management habits, such as budgeting, saving for emergencies and long-term goals, and investing intelligently, can also contribute to greater financial security and wellbeing.

By cultivating and sticking to wise financial habits, people can soften the economic blow of surprising financial shocks, build up resources in the face of future expenses, and feel greater stability and control over their finances.[12]

Research also shows that being financially literate improves people's ability to make good financial decisions, such as budgeting, saving and investing, increasing their financial security and reducing financial stress. People with financial literacy also have greater ability to cope with economic hardship, and to make informed decisions about their money.

A person's sense of control over their life can influence how income affects their wellbeing. People who focus on personal growth, creativity and living a purposeful life (intrinsic orientation) often find that income has less impact on their happiness. On the other hand, those who are motivated by external rewards like money or recognition from others (extrinsic orientation) tend to feel a stronger connection between income and wellbeing.[13]

Spending patterns and life satisfaction

Income can play a role in buying things, but economic research has consistently shown that spending money on experiences and things that matter to you – buying too many material goods aside – is likely to increase life satisfaction.[14] Indeed, when people spend money on experiences, such as travel, cultural events or educational goods, they tend to report greater increases in subjective wellbeing compared with those who buy material goods. This might be because experiences are more likely to build social networks, help us to grow as individuals, and provide enduring memories, all of which are more strongly linked to our emotional happiness than material goods.

There are several possible explanations for this. Experiences relate more strongly to eudaimonic development: the process of becoming your whole, true self; the fulfilment of personal potential; the feeling of living purposefully; and to deeper, more meaningful, self-defining memories that may have greater long-term impact and personal significance.[15] Furthermore, experiences are more likely to be enjoyed with others – fostering positive, supportive relationships. This may be why social relationships, and participation in them, are so strongly linked to wellbeing and are found to contribute more to the experience of high life satisfaction than do material possessions.

Conversely, materialistic striving, or continuously chasing material goods, has been related to reduced wellbeing and life satisfaction.[16] A lot of materialism can lead us to a vicious circle of striving for more, ultimately being dissatisfied with the results as the hedonic adaptation process quickly takes hold. Moreover, if it keeps us in a constant cycle of social comparison and envy, it may be harmful to both wellbeing and social relationships.

Again, this is not to say that materialism leads ineluctably to unhappiness. Much depends on how a person sets priorities and runs their life, and on their personal values and cultural group. A balanced approach is likely to be best both for the environment and wellbeing: spending resources in line with one's broader values and life priorities.[17]

There's some evidence that if workers are paid hourly, as distinct from, say, weekly or monthly, they focus on income more and are less willing to do things for free.[18] This information shows that the structures we use for compensation can actually affect how people feel about doing things and how they think about their jobs more broadly.

Social connections and financial wellbeing

Support and social networks contribute to wellbeing, especially when it comes to financial stressors. Strong social ties have been shown to predict good physical and mental health, greater life satisfaction, and resilience in the face of adversity.

When money is tight or times are tough, social support can take the form of mental comfort, material aid and a feeling of attachment. Having a close-knit network of family and friends or broader community can cushion the psychological toll of financial stressors, thereby limiting their adverse effects on our wellbeing.

Social relationships that make it easier to share resources, information and coping strategies can support people to better manage the financial challenges they face.[19] Possessing social capital and access to collective resources can act as a buffer against financial shocks and contribute to feeling more secure and flourishing.

What's more, social connections bring meaning and purpose, which are major ingredients of wellbeing.[20] Engaging in meaningful relationships and in the flourishing of others can provide deep levels of fulfilment and life satisfaction independent of material resources.[21]

These processes include providing instrumental assistance, social support, access to resources, and promoting adaptive behaviours and coping strategies – all of which help to alleviate the harmful effects of financial challenges on wellbeing.[22] Promoting a focused effort to nurture social ties and community can help reduce the harmful effects of financial insecurity.

Societal factors and policy implications

The relationship between having money and wellbeing depends as much on each person's context as on the larger society and the policies that govern it. Improving people's economic lives, through such things as education, employment opportunities and financial inclusion programmes, can be a vital step towards improving individual and community wellbeing.[23] When financial resources and opportunities are provided so that people and communities can live and work, then the cycle of poverty can be broken and lives can be improved.

Finally, social policy – and in particular, initiatives promoting close social relationships, civic participation and even measures that reduce inequity – can also help sustain this wellbeing.[24] For instance, policies encouraging work–life balance, community development and social safety nets can reduce financial strain and boost life satisfaction through stronger social cohesion and security. 'Financial capability' programmes aimed at promoting informed financial decision-making and helping people manage their finances in economically enabling ways can empower people to be more in control of their finances, and so lead to better flourishing.[25] These may include such things as financial literacy programmes, consumer protection laws and policies and various financial planning programmes.

Conclusion

Money and wellbeing are connected through a complex web of factors, including individual and household choices, attitudes, traits and broader social policies. Research shows that household financial behaviours, like saving and spending habits, play a significant role, but they are also shaped by many social influences. It is important to view individuals' and families' lives within a broader context of social and financial networks, values and interdependencies. Effective policies should acknowledge these interactions, as people's lives are too diverse and complex for a one-size-fits-all approach to wellbeing. To achieve sustainable wellbeing and prosperity in developed societies, we need a combination of financial responsibility, value-driven decisions, and a focus on nurturing social connections and relationships.

CHAPTER 2

The relationship between money and mental health

If getting rich breaks you, is it really worth the bill?

Introduction

Let's start with the relationship between financial wellness and mental health. There's a reason why the two go hand in hand: they often feed off one another, for better or for worse. When we're in good financial stead, our stress levels tend to go down. But when we're constantly worried about money, or falling behind on our bills and overdue notices, stress can lead to mental health problems like anxiety, emotional distress and burnout.

The link between financial wellbeing and mental health is crucial, because it affects pretty much everything. Psychological distress in the form of depression, anxiety disorders and substance use disorders can all result from financial hardship. And mental health problems, such as impulsivity, are well known to interfere with the ability to effectively manage one's finances, creating a vicious circle of financial struggles and psychological distress.[1]

Financial stability and stress reduction

Let's explore how financial stability can improve our mental wellness by taking away stress. When we are financially stable, we are better prepared for financial shocks. A study showed that when people experience some form of financial or economic shock such as getting laid off, or missing a mortgage payment, or being on food stamps, their mental health suffers.[2]

Conversely, when we stop worrying about money, we have space in our mind to pay attention to other important things in life.[3] We take better decisions, we work harder and, essentially, we feel happier. That same weight will be lifted from our shoulders; we will be able to breathe better, and focus on the things we love in our much-improved life.

Autonomy and independence are also related to our financial security. Greater financial stability is associated with greater self-determination, meaning our ability to advance worthwhile goals and live out meaningful values. Greater financial security can help to make people feel more self-directed and enable them to pursue the things that will lead to greater life satisfaction and psychological health.[4]

The pursuit of wealth and its psychological consequences

However, the constant chase for money and the associated materialistic attitude does not always lead us along the golden path to success. Sometimes it backfires on those who try it. Studies show that people for whom money holds a higher priority than happiness, authenticity, meaningful work and relationships are more susceptible to burnout and lower self-esteem.[5]

Feeling that we'll never have enough, that we must constantly keep up with the Joneses, can add real stress to our lives – and all for very little in the way of payoffs. Stress induced in this way – from trying desperately to make enough money to conform to an artificial lifestyle – is clearly absurd. We could find ourselves working ever harder, without reward, just to have things. Yet our very humanity is damaged by this type of stress, as we can become increasingly disconnected from those we love.[6] In extreme cases, we may develop the unhealthy symptoms of psychosomatic collapse, such as nausea, night sweats, emotional detachment and stress responses that impair our judgement.

That's where the compulsion for money – driven by psychological motivations, including fear of scarcity, desire for power and control, and the need for recognition and status – can step in.[7] Such forces can cause us to act contrary to our own good, both financially and emotionally.

It's not just about the money, though. Having a healthy bank account doesn't guarantee good mental health. Sometimes, it's the attitudes, ideas or habits that often accompany financial success that can cause problems. We know that chasing external rewards can come at the expense of putting our effort towards intrinsic goals, such as interpersonal connection, personal growth or the forging of purpose. In giving up valued living for the sake of being rich, we might also be giving up on what is truly worthwhile. And so, loneliness can follow.[8]

Overspending, debt and emotional distress

Before I dive into the dark side of spending and debt, let's first consider how overspending can lead to depression, anguish and resentment. The American Psychological Association conducted a study which reported that financial problems are the leading source of stress amongst adults in the United States.[9]

Thinking only about how to make enough money to live,

how to pay bills and debts, to secure our future, can monopolise our attention. It is difficult to think about other things when you are in this position. Anxious, worried and restless, you feel burdened, always at the edge of a breakdown. The stress can cause psychological problems such as insomnia and irritability, as well as many physical health problems.[10]

The shame and stigma that often accompany financial stress can leave you feeling isolated and alone, too scared to ask for help.[11] You feel like your suffering is unique to you and that something must be wrong with you as a human being. You easily give in to despair. The disappointment brings about a sense of hopelessness. Researchers describe despair as an existential threat that feels unbearable, and speaks to your personal limitations: 'You have taken a hammer to your own dreams and beliefs in your ability to cope.' Researchers explain that 'feeling hopeless is like feeling trapped in one's feelings, thoughts and behaviours'.

Money problems can mess with your emotions and mental health in several ways. When you're stressed about finances, your body might react by releasing stress hormones like cortisol or by raising your blood pressure.[12] If this stress keeps up for a long time, it can lead to anxiety and depression. Furthermore, the mental strain of ongoing financial distress may not only impair our ability to make important decisions but also exacerbate other mental health conditions. When you live with constant thoughts of bills, debts and financial insecurity, it can be difficult to focus your mind on anything else. It is all debilitating.

The impact of money on self-esteem, life satisfaction and inequality

Money also plays a pivotal role in shaping self-esteem and personal identity. Individuals may seek financial success as a means of compensating for feelings of low self-worth or detachment.[13] Many people, for instance, chase financial success in an effort to feel good about themselves. 'If I can just make more money, or buy more stuff,' they think, 'then I'll finally like myself.'

However, this approach is risky. Basing self-worth on external factors is unstable and can lead to disappointment when those external elements disappear or diminish. Genuine self-esteem is an inner feeling of self-acceptance and value, no matter what we have or lack. This behaviour underscores the intricate relationship between money, self-esteem and mental health, highlighting the need for holistic approaches to promote financial wellbeing and emotional resilience.

And when we compare ourselves favourably to others financially, it briefly makes us feel happier,[14] but only momentarily. It's a shot of satisfaction that quickly wears off, leaving us no better off than when we started. In any case, there will always be people who make more money, have nicer stuff or live a more luxurious life than us – ultimately nagging at our happiness. Comparing ourself to others is the surest and fastest way back to a dark and miserable state.

Research on inequality underscores how growing disparities contribute to feelings of unfairness and reduced wellbeing in society. Inequality is also a part of the money/happiness equation; the larger the gap between rich and poor, the less equitable are the economic conditions and the lower average levels of wellbeing in a society.[15] It's harder to feel good when we have vivid awareness of how vastly rewarded others are relative to us, especially when they have the resources and opportunities available to them solely because of their unearned social status.

Even unearned riches such as lottery wins do not necessarily buy happiness and freedom from anxiety in the long term. There might be a burst of happiness following the win, but outcomes in the medium to long term depend upon the individual and how they use their new-found riches.[16] Relationships, purpose in life and wellbeing are often damaged by lottery wins.

The two-way relationship between money and mental health

The relationship between money and mental health operates in both directions. Financial hardship can lead to mental health problems, sure, but mental health problems can also make it harder to manage money. It's a chicken and egg situation.

Someone with depression, anxiety or a substance use disorder, might struggle with budgeting and saving, or with making smart financial decisions.[17] When we are struggling with mental illness, we may not be able to direct enough motivation and cognitive focus to responsible financial management. Issues with poor decisions, lack of focus and inability to behave consistently can impair our finances, causing increased anxiety. The two-way nature of the relationship can create a vicious cycle that perpetuates both financial and emotional distress.

And some conditions, like bipolar disorder, or attention deficit hyperactivity disorder (ADHD), can raise the risk of impulsive spending or poor financial management.[18] Bipolar disorder's manic highs can line you up for reckless spending sprees, while the impulse control and focus issues inherent in ADHD might make it hard to stay on budget too.

This two-way street can set up a cycle in which the spiralling financial and emotional consequences keep piling on. We might make bad financial choices when we're having a bad mental health day and then exacerbate our mental health problems when we're running low on money.

It's important to acknowledge this complex feedback and to intervene on both fronts – financial wellness and mental wellness – at the same time. Treating one without treating the other is like putting a bandage on a bullet wound. We must approach the individual from a multifaceted perspective, not as a bank account or a diagnosis, but rather as a whole person.

Promoting financial literacy and healthy money mindsets

So, how can we foster financial literacy and healthy money mindsets? It isn't too much of a surprise that the answer is education. Comprehensive programmes to promote financial literacy, delivered in school, at work or in the community, can build budgeting, credit-management, investing and other financial skills and help us set financial goals.[19] People build that foundation when they have the knowledge and ability to make informed financial decisions for their families. We can flourish when we learn about the psychology and emotions behind money.

Working with a financial counsellor or coach who has specialised knowledge in your area can be equally helpful as these professionals can provide personalised support and direct, role-model advice that caters for individual skills and brains. Such professionals can help you identify your personal financial triggers, reframe negative money voices, and build healthy coping mechanisms for financial stress.[20]

Mindfulness and CBT techniques could become very helpful tools for the development of a healthy money mindset.[21] By learning practices such as observing our thoughts and emotions about money without feeling the need to reject or change them, we can start to separate our relationship to money from the whirlpool of stress and anxiety, and reframe negative beliefs about money that we might be holding on to, such as: 'My net worth equates to my self-worth' or 'I am a "bad" person if I don't have money saved.'

Access to resources and support networks, such as budgeting tools, consumer credit counselling and support groups, are critical for gaining greater control over our financial lives.[22] As important as what we encounter is the assurance of being among others who have experienced the same struggles, and knowing there are people and resources to help us get back on our feet – and ultimately allow us to feel emotionally restored.

The role of professional support and advice

Of course, when we're experiencing stress or pain where money and our mental health are involved, it's important to look to qualified professionals for financial or mental health support. An approach that addresses the dual problems of money and our minds can help to resolve issues effectively.[23]

Financial planners and mental health professionals can work together to create a plan that takes into account both our financial context and our mental health needs, as well as the values that matter most to us. This kind of financial planning acknowledges that our private inner experiences and our working life, including money issues, are intermingled, and that we need help in both areas to live fulfilling and secure lives.

But not everyone can access these services and there are many reasons why not. A lack of funds, of available resources or of time can be obstacles, as can the stigma that may be involved. We need to find ways to remove these obstacles, through policy reform, increased funding and public awareness campaigns.[24]

In so doing, we could make financial and mental health services more accessible and affordable, thereby bolstering support for the many people who need help to develop and maintain healthy money habits. Things such as expanding mental health insurance coverage, establishing low-cost/no-cost financial counselling, and fostering goal-based financial literacy curricula in schools and community groups could help everyone sustain good money habits and allow them to suffer less stress overall.[25]

Conclusion

To sum up, mental health and financial wellbeing are integral to one another, and they have complex interconnections. Higher levels of financial literacy, healthier relationships with money, and getting professional help when needed are all key ways to better balance the money in our lives with our minds.

Fundamentally, happiness and flourishing comes from living in ways that are intrinsically valuable to you, *not* from having large amounts of money. If you cultivate good mental health and build good relationships with others, and otherwise focus your efforts on meaningful and valuable goals, you might find practical happiness and flourishing regardless of your wealth.

But ultimately, our long-term relationship with money will only be governed by the balancing act between our financial stability and emotional wellbeing. We want to be relatively sure of our financial security, but it would be easy to forget that there is more to life than money; and it will be wise to give more meaning to our bank accounts instead of just more meaningless-ness to our lives.

CHAPTER 3

What is financial wellbeing and why is it important?

Life's real flex? Living it your way, not payday to payday

Introduction

Little wonder that financial wellbeing has been a hot topic of late. It encompasses more than just money; it's the intersection of two domains of life – the financial and the psychological – with feelings of financial security and satisfaction, of control and autonomy, of being able to make decisions that fit with your values and your idea of who you are. In fact, Brüggen and her colleagues had an excellent go at capturing what financial wellbeing meant in their 2010 study; the team described it as 'a state of being wherein the individual can fully meet current and ongoing financial obligations, is psychologically comfortable with their current and future financial situation, and is able to make trade-offs that afford a satisfaction of life's novelties, treats, and experiences'.[1]

Knowing what financial wellbeing means so you can achieve it makes sense because it may influence your mental and emotional wellbeing, your quality of life, and the ability to feel fulfilled by your existence. When your financial wellbeing is in good shape, there's a greater likelihood you will be able to withstand the challenges life hurls your way, pursue what you want, and feel more at ease about money. In the long run, making a focused effort to embrace financial wellbeing is important to resiliency, higher-quality life and ease of survival.[2]

The finer details of financial wellbeing will be covered in this chapter. The ways in which it is related to wellbeing more broadly will be considered. Also, some of the predictors of financial wellbeing will be discussed. Importantly, some suggestions for increasing financial wellbeing will be provided.

Defining and understanding financial wellbeing

However the term is defined and explored, it becomes increasingly clear that financial wellbeing has many facets. Brüggen and her team, for example, propose a framework consisting of four components: meeting financial obligations, financial security, financial freedom of choice and financial freedom of mind.[3] And Kempson and their team assert that financial wellbeing has similarly been defined as having four elements: financial control, financial security, financial freedom and financial future security.[4]

Vlaev and Elliott have a broader view of financial wellbeing. They define it as 'a state where people have the financial resources, knowledge, skills and confidence to meet their responsibilities, achieve their goals and enjoy life'.[5] This definition stresses the role of financial knowhow, decision-making ability and psychology, as well as cash flow.

Each study yields different definitions, but there are key elements and dimensions of financial wellbeing that recur across the literature:

- managing current expenses;
- avoiding excessive debt, while being able to afford credit;
- having financial flexibility;
- feeling satisfied with your purchasing power and overall wealth;
- securing goods and services for your family's needs;
- feeling financially secure (the expectation of having enough money to meet future goals or life stages);
- experiencing mental and emotional wellbeing due to financial wellness.

Here are some key components and dimensions of financial wellbeing:

1. **Financial security:** having sufficient income or savings to cover your current and future financial needs, to pay bills, and to provide a stable and secure foundation for you and your family. You have enough money or other resources to get by and, if necessary, weather emergencies, such as a recession in your industry.[6]
2. **Financial satisfaction**: feeling content and happy with your financial situation, including being able to pay bills and meet other goals.[7]
3. **Financial control:** understanding that you have control of your money and feel able to navigate your financial situation and make good decisions.[8]
4. **Financial agency:** having the financial capability and flexibility to act in a way that aligns with your values and priorities, and having the freedom from money-limiting beliefs.[9] Financial agency focuses on having the financial capabilities and flexibility that enable you to engage in the activities that you value or hold important, being in control of your autonomous pursuits, and thereby being in a position to flourish.

5. **Financial literacy and decision-making:**
   Understanding and applying basic financial knowledge
   and skills, with the confidence to make informed
   decisions across a range of financial needs and
   circumstances.[10]

These aspects all contribute to form the 'total financial wellbeing' of an individual, and serve to illustrate how it's a multidimensional construct.

How financial and overall wellbeing are connected

Financial wellbeing is related to several other aspects of wellbeing, including mental and emotional health, quality of life and life satisfaction. Numerous studies have shown the reciprocal relationship between financial wellbeing and mental health.

Jaggar and Lovaii note that financial flourishing and 'mental thriving' have 'a two-way relationship',[11] in that financial stress or anxiety can affect our mental wellbeing, while mental health problems such as depression or anxiety can make it harder for us to manage our money well. Tackling the connection between financial and mental health in a synergistic way highlights just how deeply the two are intertwined.

Zemtsov and Osipova consider financial wellbeing as a type of 'human wellbeing', a significant and necessary dimension of life satisfaction and a meaningful measure of quality of life.[12] From this perspective, the presence of financial wellbeing enables various goods, such as housing, which in turn enables certain life projects, such as schooling, healthcare and leisure activities, all of which are linked to overall wellbeing.

Other research suggests that financial wellbeing can be a protective factor against stress and aids our ability to be more psychologically resilient.[13] First, when we have a solid sense of financial wellbeing, we are more likely to be able to roll with the punches and face uncertainty in life because we have a greater sense of control and security about our finances.

There are many routes by which financial wellbeing impacts (and is impacted by) wellbeing more broadly. Financial stress and worry can directly result in poor physical health (e.g. headaches, poor sleep patterns, obesity) and mental health (e.g. depression). Poor mental health, in turn, can affect our ability to make good financial decisions, which in turn puts us under more financial stress and exacerbates the stress and worry cycle.[14]

Financial wellbeing confers on individuals the means and the freedom to aim for their personal goals, to engage in leisure activities, and to maintain social relations, all of which are conducive to a higher level of life satisfaction and happiness.[15]

Positive psychology and money

Positive psychology has some important insights about money, encouraging people to aim high while staying grounded. Positive psychology emphasises that the absence of negative experiences does not necessarily mean the presence of positive experiences. Aspects of wellbeing are inherent in theories like the PERMA model (Positive emotions, Engagement, Relationships, Meaning, Accomplishment), illustrating a network of elements that influence each other to produce positive experiences. Money has the potential to fuel wellbeing by providing opportunities for positive emotion and pleasure, engagement in activities, fostering relationships and providing meaning. In addition, the feeling of autonomy and mastery of money enhances feelings of accomplishment.[16]

Dimensions of financial wellbeing

Financial wellbeing is a multi-faceted concept that reflects the various ways in which money contributes to personal wellbeing:

- **Positive emotions and flow:** when people are in charge of their money and know how to manage it well, they feel in control and effective, resulting in positive emotions and a state of flow.[17]
- **Strengthening skill development:** When we engage in learning financial management skills, it may help the development of a sense of accomplishment and self-efficacy, thus improving overall wellbeing.[18]
- **Purpose and goals:** Establishing and meeting financial goals can provide a sense of purpose and meaning to life which in turn enhances overall wellbeing.[19] It may also lead to positive relationships and contribute to society.[20]
- **Good financial habits:** Building good habits around money like budgeting, saving or simply being mindful of how we spend it can help a great deal with feelings of control and security.[21]
- **Challenging negative money mindsets:** through addressing the negative thought patterns and beliefs we have around money, we are able to finally make the healthy financial decisions that will bring financial wellbeing back into your lives.[22]
- **Resilience:** An ability to bounce back in the face of financial adversity can limit the likelihood of experiencing poor mental health.[23]
- **Improving objectivity:** Staying objective and rational with your choices can improve your finances but also your life as a whole.[24]
- **Gaining skills:** As you learn how to manage debt, how to budget and invest wisely, your financial wellbeing increases, and therefore your life satisfaction is improved.[25]

Why financial wellbeing matters

Financial wellbeing means having the resources to freely pursue our goals, care for ourselves and others, prepare for the future and connect to our community. Achieving this means greater health, prosperity and joy for individuals and for our society. It allows us to live without the consequences, usually nasty ones, that come from financial stress.

Having greater financial wellbeing is also associated with greater empowerment – the feelings of being able to handle what life throws our way, and of having greater resilience in responding to life's financial knockdowns and setbacks.[26] When we have more financial wellbeing, we're less likely to get thrown to the mat by the stress and anxiety that money worries can induce.

But financial wellbeing can also enable your dreams and ambitions. When we feel we have enough and that we're in charge of our financial lives, we can direct our resources to the things that are valued or meaningful to us – a college education for our children, or the trip of a lifetime, or simply the chance to pursue a passion. It is this sense of choice that can really enhance your life satisfaction.[27]

Besides, being financially well adds to our sense of resilience, and resilience is good for mental and emotional health. Financial stress and anxiety are major contributors to mental health disorders, such as depression and anxiety disorders, and use of substances including alcohol and drugs.[28] Improving our financial wellbeing can lower these risk factors and create a better life for those who have them.

However, the flip side is that lack of financial wellbeing can result in some very real personal and social consequences. Financial stress can damage relationships, exacerbate marital problems and hurt family life.[29] Financial difficulties can also limit access to fundamental resources, such as healthcare and education, which further entrenches patterns of inequality and keeps the cycle of poverty and disadvantage in play.

Factors that influence financial wellbeing

Our financial wellbeing can be affected by financial literacy, by money mindsets, by budgeting skills, and by the availability of access to free and helpful resources.

Being financially literate is central to gaining a sense of financial wellbeing. Overall, those who have high levels of financial literacy are more likely to make responsible financial choices about budget planning, saving, investing, starting a business or using debt.[30] They have overall more effective financial behaviours, such as creating and sticking to a budget, and are better at navigating complicated financial issues.

Financial wellbeing is also influenced by money mindsets, which refers to the attitudes, feelings and beliefs that people have about money. For example, individuals prone to a scarcity mindset – the fear of not having enough – may overindulge in impulsive spending, shopping or saving behaviours. In contrast, feelings of abundance and gratitude are related to better financial behaviours and stronger perceived financial control.

Budgeting skills refer to a person's ability to track their income and expenses, to allocate spending based on priorities and needs, and to set aside savings for future goals. Those with strong budgeting skills are more likely to attain financial wellbeing, and feel secure and satisfied about their finances.[31]

Access to resources – including courses in money management, credit counselling and other financial education, as well as access to social support networks – can contribute to financial wellbeing by opening up access to information and confidence in dealing with financial matters. People who are growing up in resource-constrained environments or those who are dealing with economic hardship may be deprived of this important source of support.

Furthermore, spending money to attain purposeful objectives – such as supporting others, building social ties, or pursuing spiritual and self-transcendent goals – can also promote wellbeing by enhancing a person's material and social resources.[32] Syncing financial choices with core values and a sense of purpose may boost the role of financial wellbeing in improving our lives.

Strategies and interventions for promoting financial wellbeing

Responding to these insights, researchers and practitioners increasingly focus on developing and implementing strategies and interventions that enhance people's financial capability and financial wellbeing, including financial education or counselling programmes, and policy interventions.

The aim of financial education programmes is to help people acquire the knowledge and skills to make informed financial decisions. Their content is often limited to relatively simple financial topics such as budgeting, saving, investing and managing debts. Research evidence shows that financial education programmes can improve financial literacy and financial wellbeing.[33] However, they can be effective only to a certain extent, depending on their context – the target audience, the way they are delivered or their content.

Financial counselling services offer personalised guidance and support to people who can benefit from new skills or are on the lookout for guidance with their finances. They can help clients to develop new strategies to manage their finances, whether it be a budget, getting out of debt or looking to the future.[34] A financial counsellor can also address the psychological hurdles to financial wellbeing such as money mindset issues.

Financial wellbeing policy programmes might involve any number of interventions. For instance, policies that expand access to low-cost deposit accounts and credit can help individuals establish a vital stock of financial resilience.[35] Protections against predatory lending and opacity in the selling of financial products can help people feel they have more control over their lives and more reason to trust financial institutions.

Positive psychology coaching, which helps people use money to thrive rather than just to be better off, also has a role in enhancing financial wellbeing.[36] It helps people to link savings and spending goals with what really matters to them – their values, passions and character strengths – in order to promote and maintain meaning, purpose and engagement in their relationships with money.

Though hailed as helpful for many people, these strategies and interventions can be fool's gold, and improving financial literacy may pose challenges and limitations of its own. Financial education programmes can be ill-equipped or unable to reach and influence some populations, including poor people or other groups who haven't benefited from traditional banking or the formal economy, and people who face discrimination for any reason, such as LGBTQ people or people of colour, to name just some who may well be underbanked and routinely denied financial services.[37] Even if financial literacy is improved, this may fail to expand financial inclusion when people don't have access to the appropriate financial products or services.

Such services can also be costly and may not be available at all in areas where there's a need for them. In addition, the effectiveness of financial counselling will depend on the expertise of the counsellor, the receptiveness of the client and the complexity of the financial situation of the individual.

Besides those political and economic impediments, policies face entrenched interest groups, upstream polluters, downstream beneficiaries and a whole series of other players who might prefer to delay or even evade enacting or implementing them. Those charged with oversight and enforcement can be as meagre in number, funding and agility in the application of sanctions as the groups being monitored. In areas with inadequate resources and low regulatory capacity, implementation is commonly hapless at best.

Future research directions and limitations

Although there are already good results from this line of research, including a few promising definitions of financial wellbeing, the factors that contribute to it, and its connection with other components of wellbeing, there are also gaps to fill:

- **Long-term studies:** An area that was missing from the literature was studies on the long-term effects of financial wellbeing on broader life outcomes, including physical and mental health, and trajectories for jobs and careers, as well as intergenerational wealth transfer. These studies could help clarify the broader implications of financial wellbeing and help to tailor interventions and policies to have a wider impact.
- **Disparate populations:** More work is required to appreciate the specific difficulties and practical barriers that hamper access to decent work for disadvantaged groups (such as low-income or disadvantaged communities, people with disabilities or people in precarious employment arrangements such as gig workers). Specific strategies and solution mechanisms might be required to accommodate the particular needs and circumstances of these groups.
- **Technology and digital platforms:** Related to this is the study of how access to technology and digital platforms contributes to financial wellbeing, as financial transactions become increasingly digital, and the impact of financial wellbeing on one's digital capabilities, for example, the importance of digital literacy and technology access. Additionally, digital platforms are increasingly serving as the space where people engage with matters relevant to their financial wellbeing. Research on how these platforms can be used to build

financial capability and provide social support is another exciting and important growth area.

- **Cross-disciplinary research:** Additionally, we need more cross-disciplinary research to harness the perspectives offered by the social sciences, such as psychology, behavioural economics and sociology, in order to fill gaps in our knowledge about how financial wellbeing is coupled with different facets of human behaviour, decision-making and social structures.
- Self-reports of financial wellbeing are commonly used in studies, but they can be influenced by biases and mistakes. Sometimes, the groups or situations being studied may not apply to everyone. Also, because financial wellbeing has many different aspects, it's hard to define or measure it the same way across all studies.

Conclusion

As I have outlined in this chapter, financial wellbeing encompasses security, satisfaction, control and autonomy, and the making of effective decisions that are consistent with our values and goals. Overall wellbeing and financial wellbeing are connected, influenced by a common set of factors.

Financial wellbeing is connected to many other aspects of wellbeing, such as mental and emotional health, life satisfaction and quality of life. Those with greater financial wellbeing can cope better with life's challenges, pursue the things that matter to them, and experience less stress and its negative consequences.

Various things contribute to a person's financial wellbeing, for example their financial knowledge, attitude to money, money management ability and financial resources. There are several potential strategies and interventions to improve financial wellbeing, such as financial education programmes, counselling or other psychological interventions, and policy interventions, although there are several potential issues and pitfalls.

Further research can fill in the gaps – for example, there is still much we don't know about the long-term consequences of having a sense of financial wellbeing, the distinct challenges that can affect particular groups of people, the different role that technology might play, and even how this concept fits into a broader interdisciplinary perspective on subjective and objective wellbeing. There are also limitations with the state of knowledge on financial wellbeing. We need more cross-cultural comparisons; studies that rely more on archival data or richly detailed interview information, since much of the existing research uses self-reported measures or financial and demographic records from known beneficiaries; and studies that address bias caused by the self-selection of volunteers in the existing research.

Positive financial wellbeing can also free people from the burdens of debt, allowing them to invest in their communities and making them more resilient. Coming to terms with our finances, having the capability to manage them and the confidence to pursue what matters to us, gives individuals a new sense of power – a sense of emotional resilience, the ability to set and achieve goals, and the strength to cope with adversity. Financial wellbeing can help to build wellbeing in the round: reducing stress, promoting mental and emotional health, and creating a basis for a settled and positive future.

SECTION 2

How to improve your financial wellbeing

Finding true wellbeing is a journey that involves harmonising different aspects of ourselves – our emotions, thoughts and actions. Countless studies have shown that aligning these three interconnected domains (heart/spirituality/feelings, brain/cognition/thoughts, and hand/behaviour/actions) is crucial for achieving a state of holistic wellbeing.

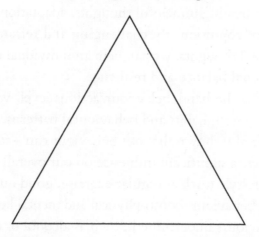

Brain/cognition/thoughts

Heart/spirituality/feelings   **Hand/behaviour/actions**

At the centre of this idea is the recognition that our thinking, emotional states or behaviour can impact our wellbeing, that they're also intricately intertwined and influence each other in profound ways. For example, our emotions – as products of our values, beliefs and spiritual orientations – shape the way we think and behave. At the same time, our thinking and cognitive functioning influence our emotional states and therefore how we behave. In light of this interaction between emotion, reasoning and behaviour, the need for balance among these domains becomes clearer and is certainly a key to flourishing.

First, the heart/spirituality/feelings part. This encapsulates our emotional state, ethos or sense of value and meaning – our motivational forces that bring focus and meaning to our activities. Research shows that fostering our emotional intelligence, and increasing our (self-) awareness and spirituality safeguard our wellbeing. Whether it's mindfulness, gratitude or compassion, there's abundant proof that all these practices work to reduce stress, enhance emotional responsivity and bring a feeling of flourishing.

Next, the brain/cognition/thoughts domain, which encompasses thought processes, beliefs and the way we think. Cognitive behavioural therapy (CBT) and rational emotive behaviour therapy (REBT) are widely accepted therapeutic models that are excellent at addressing unhelpful thoughts, adaptation to change and patterns of cognition. By challenging and reframing negative or irrational thoughts, we can help an individual experience greater emotional balance and resilience.

Then there is the hand/behaviour/actions level, which is associated with action, habits and behavioural patterns. A number of studies have also shown that our behaviour can – for better or for worse – have a significant influence on our overall wellbeing, as a healthy lifestyle (such as regular exercise, good nutrition and goal-oriented behaviour) boosts physical and mental health, while negative behaviours undermine it, such as alcohol or drug abuse or procrastination.

When emotions, thoughts and actions are consistent and aligned, people feel more life satisfaction, more resilience, more empathy for self and others, and greater life-enhancing growth. When they are not aligned, life can be marred by inner dissidence, turbulence, emotional upset – and poor wellness.

This also factors in the back-and-forth relationship between these domains. For example, feeling positive through behaviours such as exercise or mindfulness can impact how we feel on an emotional level and how we think and perceive certain scenarios on a cognitive level. At the same time, negative thought patterns or emotional states can influence what we do, potentially leading us to certain behaviours or habits that may not be healthy.

Many therapeutic approaches and interventions have been designed to encourage this integrative approach to wellbeing. For instance, acceptance and commitment therapy (ACT) focuses on facilitating psychological flexibility and mindfulness, while also promoting a values-based way of living, targeting all three wellness domains. The broad and well-studied field of positive psychology has developed and researched several interventions designed to improve wellbeing through values-based identities, such as gratitude journalling (emotion), savouring (thought) and strength-based practices (action).

In essence, the data supports coherence – across heart, brain and hand – as being key to wellbeing. That makes sense. When these three interconnected arenas of being are aligned, we feel better emotionally. We think more clearly. And we act more consciously in the world. Support for such an approach in clinical practice has consistently been positive. Individuals experience increased emotional regulation, greater cognitive clarity and more behavioural alignment. This means more life satisfaction, paired with greater resilience and adaptability.

Heart/spirituality/feelings

This section focuses on improving financial wellbeing through spirituality, emotional connection and heartfelt approaches.

CHAPTER 4

Gratitude

*Forget the wallet – measure wealth
by hugs, laughs and naps*

Practising gratitude can have a profound impact on your financial situation. When you shift your attention from what you don't have to what you do have, you set yourself up for a more abundant mindset, which leads to better decision making about money and how you treat it, and ultimately makes you happier. Practise gratitude every day and watch your relationship with money and your overall happiness shift.

Before delving further into the relationship between gratitude and money, let's start with a brief survey to gauge your current understanding of money and wellbeing.

Money gratitude questionnaire

This survey is designed to help you track and assess your personal growth. For each of the ten statements, circle the number below which corresponds with how much you agree with it. Total up the scores for an initial sense of your gratitude level. Once you've gone through the chapter and engaged in the suggested exercises, revisit the survey. You don't need to disclose your answers to anyone; it's simply a tool to gauge any shifts or improvements in your outlook.

1. **I am grateful for the amount of money I have right now.**
   Strongly disagree – 1
   Disagree – 2
   Somewhat disagree – 3
   Neither agree nor disagree – 4
   Somewhat agree – 5
   Agree – 6
   Strongly agree – 7

2. **I appreciate the freedom money provides to me.**
   Strongly disagree – 1
   Disagree – 2
   Somewhat disagree – 3
   Neither agree nor disagree – 4
   Somewhat agree – 5
   Agree – 6
   Strongly agree – 7

3. **How often do you feel grateful for the money you have?**
   Never – 1
   Once a year – 2
   A few times a year – 3
   Once a month – 4
   A few times a month – 5
   Once a week – 6
   More than once a week – 7

Daily – 8
More than once a day – 9

4. **When I look at my bank balance and assets, I don't see much to be grateful for.**
Strongly agree – 1
Agree – 2
Somewhat agree – 3
Neither agree nor disagree – 4
Somewhat disagree – 5
Disagree – 6
Strongly disagree – 7

5. **I am grateful for the variety of things I can experience because of money.**
Strongly disagree – 1
Disagree – 2
Somewhat disagree – 3
Neither agree nor disagree – 4
Somewhat agree – 5
Agree – 6
Strongly agree – 7

6. **I have a long list of the things/experiences that I am grateful for because of money.**
Strongly disagree – 1
Disagree – 2
Somewhat disagree – 3
Neither agree nor disagree – 4
Somewhat agree – 5
Agree – 6
Strongly agree – 7

7. **When I look at the people who have less money than me, I feel thankful.**
Strongly disagree – 1
Disagree – 2
Somewhat disagree – 3
Neither agree nor disagree – 4
Somewhat agree – 5
Agree – 6
Strongly agree – 7

8. **I don't have the amount of money that I desire but I am thankful for what I have.**
Strongly disagree – 1
Disagree – 2
Somewhat disagree – 3
Neither agree nor disagree – 4
Somewhat agree – 5
Agree – 6
Strongly agree – 7

9. **People with more money than me make me feel bad about myself.**
Strongly agree – 1
Agree – 2
Somewhat agree – 3
Neither agree nor disagree – 4
Somewhat disagree – 5
Disagree – 6
Strongly disagree – 7

10. **When someone loses a large amount of money, I feel grateful for the money I have.**
Strongly disagree – 1
Disagree – 2

Somewhat disagree – 3

Neither agree nor disagree – 4

Somewhat agree – 5

Agree – 6

Strongly agree – 7

My total score:

Let's now explore what research has discovered regarding the connection between gratitude and money.

Introduction

Gratitude and money – two words that at first glance seem not to have much in common. But think about it – there's a lot more going on here than meets the eye. To express gratitude is like a kind of cuddle for your soul. It helps you see things in a certain way; to appreciate what you have. And what you 'have' can turn out to matter in all sorts of ways, not the least of which include what you think, to whom you're connected, and even where you belong in the world.[1] Money, meanwhile, is what you do with the gratitude. You use it to get the things you (think you) want. So, how do all these things hang together?

Gratitude and wellbeing

Gratitude and wellbeing are closely linked. An attitude of gratitude equates to higher levels of happiness and lower levels of stress and sadness.[2] Money matters here, too. Thankfulness may help you cope with financial stress more successfully.[3] When you take the time to write down the things you're grateful for, you have an easier time appreciating what you already have rather than constantly coveting what you don't.[4] And gratitude may help you feel more comfortable and confident about your finances.

Money and happiness

Now, let's talk about money and happiness. It's no surprise that we feel happier when we have more money. But here's the thing – after a certain point, having more money doesn't make us that much happier. As mentioned in Chapter 1, this is called the Easterlin paradox.[5] The Easterlin paradox states that while people with higher incomes within a country tend to report higher levels of happiness, increases in a country's income per capita over time do not necessarily lead to increased happiness among its citizens. This suggests that once a country reaches a certain level of economic development, further increases in income do not significantly improve overall wellbeing. According to the Easterlin paradox, countries (for example, the USA) report that happiness goes up with increasing income, meaning that happiness should theoretically increase as average income and wealth increases. In fact, over time, average incomes increase, countries and individuals become wealthier and have more income, but their average happiness does not rise. The paradox highlights the importance of relative income and other factors, such as social relationships and personal values, in determining an individual's happiness.

So, what's the key to being happy without being rich? Gratitude! When you're thankful for the non-material things in life, like your relationships and experiences, you can find joy without needing a ton of cash. It's all about appreciating the simpler things.

Gratitude and materialism

Materialism nowadays is a very common mindset in society – the more you have, the more you want. There seems to be the notion that you can always make yourself happier by buying stuff. However, the research says that expecting material things to be conducive to a happy and stable existence is not only unrealistic, but can also be detrimental to you.[6]

Luckily, there is a cure for materialism-induced problems that has been proven to work: gratitude. Gratitude makes people focus less on people or gadgets or other things that they can touch, and more on non-material sources of meaning. It might be the pleasure of spending time with loved ones, your personal accomplishments, the wonders of nature, or a host of other things. As you start to appreciate these things, you also build up a solid foundation of gratitude.[7]

People who practise gratitude report greater satisfaction with their lives, even when they aren't rich.[8] It's because health or wealth comes from valuing what you have, not wanting more.

What's more, you'll be less susceptible to the commercial forces that nudge us to buy more things in the vain pursuit of happiness. In a consumer culture where a 'good life' is equated with a life full of material possessions, gratitude can bring focus and help you keep sight of what's most important: being fulfilled in the here and now by what you already own.[9]

This shift in outlook can instil a more thoughtful society. A grateful person is more likely to think carefully about what to buy, and be less prone to impulse shopping.[10] And that is great for your wallet and the planet.

Work and relationships: Developing a relationship with gratitude

Gratitude functions as a force that binds and bolsters your relationships. As a verbal expression, 'thank you' acts as cement between you and your associates. Likewise, you can use the power of money as your vehicle for expressing gratitude, buying someone lunch or contributing to a more generous state. When under the sway of gratitude, you use your money to strengthen bonds and fortify your relationships.[11]

Reflect on the fact that, in most of your everyday lives and relationships, one way people might try to express care for you is by spending money. Perhaps this is yet another way in which commerce and romance work hand in hand, by tying your heart and your wallet together.

Money, status and gratitude

The amount of money you have can influence how you see yourself and how others perceive you in society. And how you feel about your financial success or social standing can also be shaped by gratitude. It might help you stay humble and appreciate what you have, or it could lead you to believe you're entitled to special treatment.[12]

Researchers have also found that feeling gratitude can help offset some of the negative side effects of high status, such as arrogance.[13] Grateful people are also likely to be more helpful and make a bigger positive difference in the world. Gratitude, in this way, can be a really potent antidote for destructive feelings about money and status.

Societal implications

Step back a bit, and look at the bigger picture. We find that gratitude declines when the rich get richer and the poor get poorer.[14] Meanwhile, prosocial behaviour (charitable giving) is highest when greed and inequality are low. But, if we create a more grateful culture, things might start to change. It could improve communication and strengthen the social bonds that tie us together.[15]

One way to do this is to come up with programmes of charitable funding and patronage that help to foster this kind of thinking about money as a form of gratitude from the outset. They demonstrate the way in which putting money in the context of gift-driven reciprocity can help to produce a new kind of gift – and a happier, better-connected society in the process.[16]

Financial decision-making and gratitude

Gratitude fundamentally changes your relationship with money and the way you think about it, influences your decisions about money, how you spend it, how you save it, and where you invest. Here are some of the ways in which it can do so:[17]

- *Foresight:* Grateful individuals think more about the future. They consider how financial choices today will affect them in years to come and make decisions conducive to their long–term wellbeing and life goals.[18]
- *Values and meanings:* Gratitude helps you align your life with what's most important to you. People who are grateful for what they have are more likely to do what's important for them financially. For example, because you care more about experiences and time with your loved ones, you'll be less impulsive in how you spend.[19]
- *Less impulsive spending:* Gratitude can protect you from impulsive shopping. When we see something we think we should buy and it's a good deal, most shoppers will have an immediate urge to just buy it. Grateful people are more likely to pause and reflect instead, and make sure that it is really something they want or need. This, in turn, leads to more deliberate spending.[20]
- *Greater financial security:* People who feel grateful are more likely to develop good financial habits in their lives, such as establishing good credit, setting up emergency funds, contributing to retirement savings, investing for the future, and working to reduce their debt load. In the longer term, they feel more financially secure.[21]

Money, stress and gratitude

Often the stress of managing money can sneak up on you and undermine your emotional and physical wellbeing. The research indicates that gratitude could be an antidote. When you feel that you have enough and are grateful for what you have, desires for what you do not have no longer immediately stress you.[22]

When people are grateful, financial hardships stimulate them to start tapping their ingenuity instead of feeling helpless. Gratitude can be a secret weapon in helping people endure financial shocks and setbacks – a source of resilience that can lead to better mental health.[23]

The neurobiology of gratitude and money

Recent findings in neuroscience have begun to fill in the picture of how gratitude works in the brain and how it is related to our personal finances and emotional lives. Brain scans indicate that the experience of being grateful activates brain regions involved in reward processing and social bonding.[24] Perhaps even more strikingly, these same neural pathways also seem to light up when you contemplate positive outcomes related to money, or when you use money to be generous.[25] This means that at some level, the biological mechanisms behind gratitude and money may be linked, and both may be key drivers of human behaviour.

How gratitude around the world will lead us to money

Attitudes towards both gratitude and money also differ across cultures. Gift cultures value giving and sharing, being together and looking after one another. Citizens of such cultures are grateful for what they give away, and these acts of giving engender feelings of abundance and community.[26]

But in other parts of the world, people are often left more on their own, and expected to become financially independent through their own efforts. This can affect their way of being grateful towards others.[27] Adaptation to these differences can help in recognising what each group values, or how it treats gratitude and money as reflective of core concerns. The move towards seeing gratitude as a commodity enables a grasp of what really matters.[28]

Education and making a positive impact

Learning about the relationship between gratitude and money makes sense because education is part of personal development. By teaching aspects of gratitude as part of financial literacy classes and school curriculums, you help people acquire the tools they need to be mindfully responsible for their money decisions, helping them engage meaningfully and effectively without having to feel guilty or cheap.[29] It is a way to help people figure out how to use money in ways that they find meaningful and lead to a better world. You can do a lot of this in schools. But you can also do it in your workplace and communities. The more you can seed gratitude, the more you are making the case that gratitude is just as important as money.[30]

Conclusion

The relationship between money and gratitude is complex, but looking at the two together provides much insight into yourself and society at large. Gratitude can fundamentally alter your behaviour with respect to money; likewise, money can provide a tangible pathway for gratitude, using it to do good for yourself and others. We simply cannot overestimate the role of gratitude in our use of money. Looking at the connection between the two allows people to see how they can work in tandem. If you can fuel the force of their combined power, you will create a happier, richer human world.[31]

Now that you've gained some insight into how gratitude impacts your financial outlook, let's engage in a few activities to put this understanding into practice and observe its real-life effects on your relationship with money.

Activity 4.1: Money gratitude journal

There's no specific method that's right or wrong for maintaining a gratitude journal. You can use pen and paper, a computer, a tablet or a phone – whatever suits you. But here are some tips for how to do it:

1. Set a regular schedule: Choose a specific time each day or week to sit down and write in your money gratitude journal. Consistency is key to forming a habit.
2. Take a moment to reflect on the financial blessings and abundance in your life. This can include your income, savings, investments, possessions or any financial support you receive.
3. Write down grateful thoughts: Jot down in your journal what you are grateful for regarding your financial situation. Be specific and heartfelt in your expressions of gratitude. For example, you can write about how grateful you are for having a steady job, being able to pay your bills, or the opportunities you have to save and invest.
4. Focus on positive aspects: Try to shift your focus away from financial stress or worries and instead concentrate on the positive aspects of your financial situation. This can help you build a more positive relationship with money.
5. Review and reflect: Periodically review what you've written in your money gratitude journal. This can help

you track your progress, see patterns in your thinking and remind yourself of the positive aspects of your financial life.

Please do this activity for **twenty-one** days. Then take the money gratitude questionnaire from the beginning of this chapter again and see if your results have changed.

Activity 4.2: Gratitude for bills

Rather than resisting your bills and treating them as if they're evil, there's enormous benefit to expressing gratitude and even seeing them as an opportunity. Here are some examples, to get the ideas rolling:

- **Electricity bill**: My home is comfortable and well lit. Making my home more comfortable means providing my family with a safe and cosy place.
- **Water bill**: Here in the house we can use water, as we have enough clean water, which is very important because it helps us in our health and our daily needs.
- **Internet/cable bill**: Keeps me in touch with the world, provides valuable information and entertainment, relaxes me.
- **Rent/mortgage payment**: I'm thankful for the shelter and security my home provides. Each payment is an investment in a space where my family can live, grow and create lasting memories. It's more than just a house – it's a place of belonging and comfort.
- **Phone bill**: I can communicate with people, keeping in touch with friends, family and colleagues, so I can work, maintain family relationships and social relationships.

- **Insurance premium**: I keep myself away from the effects of bad luck by paying to protect myself and my loved ones against life's uncertainties.
- **Payment by credit card**: I am personally responsible for my general financial situation, for securing a good credit history and for organising to fulfil my financial goals.

Please do this activity for **twenty-one** days. Then take the money gratitude questionnaire from the beginning of this chapter again and check if your results have changed.

Activity 4.3: Money gratitude jar

A money gratitude jar is a low-cost and fun way to create thankfulness for the money blessings in your life. It can be a jar or container of any kind, physical or digital, into which you deposit notes or items that represent your money blessings. Here's how to create and use one:

- **Financial gratitude notes:** Every time you experience a cash blessing, receive money unexpectedly or simply feel grateful for your financial situation, write a gratitude note: date, description, feelings and any additional notes.
- **Be specific and heartfelt**: When you write your gratitude notes, get specific about what you're thankful for and why. Express your feelings heartily and try to keep your writing positive – while congratulating yourself on financial 'wins', use the notes as an opportunity to be thankful for the delightful things in your life.
- **Put into the jar:** Put the notes or digital entries into the jar or box. For a digital version, enter your items and save them in a file.

- **Stick to a schedule**: Set a day or a timeframe for writing your gratitude notes. It can be daily, weekly or in sync with your inspiration. The important part is to schedule it. Doing it as a habit will help a lot.
- **Review and reflect**: Spend some time once in a while to read back your money gratitude notes. This will bring back feelings of appreciation of your financial life and serve as a reminder of your financial successes and blessings.

Please do this activity for **twenty-one** days. Then take the money gratitude questionnaire from the beginning of this chapter again and check if your results have changed.

Resources

Here are some additional resources to improve your understanding about gratitude and its impact on overall wellbeing.

Books

Thanks! How the New Science of Gratitude Can Make You Happier by Robert A. Emmons, Houghton Mifflin Harcourt, 2007
Emmons explores the psychological and scientific benefits of gratitude, showing how it can increase happiness and wellbeing.

The Gratitude Diaries: How a Year Looking on the Bright Side Can Transform Your Life by Janice Kaplan, Dutton, 2015
Kaplan documents her year-long experiment of practising gratitude and demonstrates how a positive outlook can lead to a more fulfilling life.

The Little Book of Gratitude by Robert A. Emmons, Gaia, 2016
A concise guide to understanding and practising gratitude,

based on Emmons' research, to improve emotional and
mental health.

The Gifts of Imperfection by Brené Brown, Hazelden
Publishing, 2010
Brown encourages embracing vulnerability and
imperfections, offering strategies for cultivating
authenticity, compassion and gratitude.

The Book of Joy by the Dalai Lama and Desmond Tutu, with
Douglas Abrams, Avery, 2016
A profound conversation between two spiritual leaders on
finding joy and gratitude in the face of adversity.

Gratefulness, the Heart of Prayer by David Steindl-Rast, Paulist
Press, 1984
Steindl-Rast explores the spiritual practice of gratefulness
and how it can transform prayer into a deeper experience of
connection with the divine.

*365 Thank Yous: The Year a Simple Act of Daily Gratitude
Changed My Life* by John Kralik, Hachette Books, 2010
Kralik shares how writing daily thank-you notes
transformed his life, leading to greater personal and
professional success.

Apps

Grateful
Presently
Gratitude
365 Gratitude Journal
My Gratitude Journal

Websites

Positive Psychology: positivepsychology.com
Gratitude Jar: gratitudejar.org
Mindful: www.mindful.org/
   an-introduction-to-mindful-gratitude

Blog/Journal Articles

'Gratitude and well-being: A review and theoretical
   integration', Wood, A. M., Froh, J. J., & Geraghty, A. W.
   A. (2010). *Clinical Psychology Review*, 30(7), 890-905. DOI:
   10.1016/j.cpr.2010.03.005.
Gratitude in practice and the practice of gratitude, Emmons,
   R. A., & McCullough, M. E. (2003). In C. L. M. Keyes
   & J. Haidt (eds.), *Flourishing: Positive psychology and the
   life well-lived* (pp. 377–89). Washington, DC: American
   Psychological Association. DOI: 10.1037/10594-016.
Gratitude, like other positive emotions, broadens and builds,
   Fredrickson, B. L. (2004). In R. A. Emmons & M. E.
   McCullough (eds.), *The Psychology of Gratitude* (pp. 145–66).
   New York, NY: Oxford University Press.

Videos

Want to be happy? Be grateful by David Steindl-Rast
The Power of Vulnerability by Brené Brown
The happy secret to better work by Shawn Achor
Nature. Beauty. Gratitude. by Louie Schwartzberg
The Science of Gratitude by Robert Emmons
Are you biased? I am. by Kristen Pressner
The Science of Gratitude by UC Berkeley's Greater Good Science
   Centre
The Power of Gratitude by Oprah Winfrey

Podcasts

Gratitude Podcast by Georgian Benta
Why Gratitude Works by Christine Carter and Rona Renner
The Gratitude Diaries by Janice Kaplan
'The Science of Gratitude & How to Build a Gratitude
    Practice' by *Huberman Lab Podcast*: www.youtube.com/
    watch?v=KVjfFN89qvQ

CHAPTER 5

Savouring

Life's too short – savour the coffee, sunsets and awkward dance moves

Savouring, the act of consciously appreciating positive experiences, plays a significant role in improving our overall wellbeing. Before learning more about it, let's first take this brief survey.

Money savouring questionnaire

This survey is intended to help you track and reflect on your personal development. Using the scale below, circle one number for each of the ten statements based on how much you agree with it. Add the numbers up and you'll get a rough sense of your financial wellbeing. Please repeat the survey after reading the chapter and doing the suggested activities. The only purpose is to see what changes you have made in the way of dealing with this aspect of your life.

1. **I enjoy taking time to appreciate and savour money when I acquire it.**
   Strongly disagree – 1
   Disagree – 2
   Neither agree nor disagree – 3
   Agree – 4
   Strongly agree – 5

2. **Savouring money improves my mood and emotional wellbeing.**
   Strongly disagree – 1
   Disagree – 2
   Neither agree nor disagree – 3
   Agree – 4
   Strongly agree – 5

3. **My enjoyment of money is enhanced when I take time to reflect on how I earned it.**
   Strongly disagree – 1
   Disagree – 2
   Neither agree nor disagree – 3
   Agree – 4
   Strongly agree – 5

4. **I admire people who use their wealth to stop and enjoy the moment.**
   Strongly disagree – 1
   Disagree – 2
   Neither agree nor disagree – 3
   Agree – 4
   Strongly agree – 5

5. I find joy in reflecting on past financial successes
   and accomplishments.
   Strongly disagree – 1
   Disagree – 2
   Neither agree nor disagree – 3
   Agree – 4
   Strongly agree – 5

6. I take the time to savour the experience when
   achieving a financial goal.
   Strongly disagree – 1
   Disagree – 2
   Neither agree nor disagree – 3
   Agree – 4
   Strongly agree – 5

7. I make a conscious effort to enjoy the present
   instead of constantly worrying about future financial
   concerns.
   Strongly disagree – 1
   Disagree – 2
   Neither agree nor disagree – 3
   Agree – 4
   Strongly agree – 5

8. I find pleasure in small financial victories, even if
   they are not significant in the long run.
   Strongly disagree – 1
   Disagree – 2
   Neither agree nor disagree – 3
   Agree – 4
   Strongly agree – 5

9. **I believe that enjoying the journey of managing money is essential for overall wellbeing.**
Strongly disagree – 1
Disagree – 2
Neither agree nor disagree – 3
Agree – 4
Strongly agree – 5

10. **Even in the hardest times, I have the grace to see the better things about my financial state.**
Strongly disagree – 1
Disagree – 2
Neither agree nor disagree – 3
Agree – 4
Strongly agree – 5

My total score:

Now let's learn some theory about savouring and how it can be a useful tool in developing financial wellbeing.

Introduction

It's no surprise that savouring and money are linked to everyday wellbeing. A term from positive psychology, savouring involves being completely engaged in the present moment – and taking note of positive emotions and experiences in our body.[1] And while we might have a thousand plans and dreams for enjoying the money we make, money itself is a critical asset that helps us access opportunities, fulfil our basic needs and get closer to the experiences we want. Savouring behaviours are especially interesting when it comes to financial wellbeing because they can help us identify what motivates people to pursue certain types of financial and experiential rewards rather than others.

Savouring: An overview – the definition and the dimensions

Savouring has cognitive, affective and behavioural components. It can be considered 'the capacity to attend to, appreciate and enhance the positive experiences in one's life'.[2] Researchers have identified four types of savouring: (1) *sate-focused savouring*, which involves the experience of heightened attention to the fullness of one's present-moment experiences; (2) *past-focused savouring*, which involves experiencing positive memories and reflecting on past events with positive emotions; (3) *future-focused savouring*, which involves the anticipation and vivid imagining of pleasurable future events to help motivate behaviour; and (4) *life-focused savouring*, which involves savouring life as a whole.

Savouring has been measured in psychological research using self-report instruments, such as the Savouring Beliefs Inventory (SBI) and the Ways of Savouring Checklist (WOSC).[3] Both measures address individual differences in dispositional tendencies to savour as well as various strategies people use to savour positive experiences.

Psychological theories about savouring

Savouring draws from the research of positive psychology, the scientific study of subjective experiences, personality traits and institutions that help people and communities to flourish.[4] The theory that underpins work on savouring is informed by empirical research into the *broaden-and-build theory*[5] and the *meaning maintenance model*.[6] Both theories help us explain the health and wellbeing benefits of savouring.

Based on observations of hundreds of children, the broaden-and-build theory posits that positive emotions, such as happiness and gratitude, broaden a person's repertoire of thought-action

79

patterns, and build enduring resources over time.[7] Savouring can be an important avenue to amplify and sustain pleasure, translating into greater wellbeing and resilience.[8]

According to the meaning maintenance model, people participate in activity to imbue their lives with meaning and purpose. By doing so, positive events have more force for people who have a more balanced mindset, and make it possible for individuals to savour their blessings above and beyond ordinary situations that they take for granted.

Savouring in everyday life

Research has shown that savouring in daily life is related to a group of activities and behaviours, such as paying attention to enjoyable sensory experiences (like eating a delicious meal or appreciating a beautiful landscape), reflecting on positive memories, and looking forward to future positive events.

Sometimes, just the anticipation of a good experience is a good experience in and of itself, and other research shows that such anticipation also predicts life satisfaction and positive emotions in general.[9] Still another way that savouring increases happiness is that, when one savours physical sensation, it helps calm down the amygdala. Calming this small structure in the brain is essential because the amygdala plays a key role in processing emotions, particularly those related to fear, stress and anxiety. When the amygdala is overactive, it can trigger heightened stress responses, leading to increased cortisol levels and long-term effects on both physical and mental health. This can result in chronic anxiety, difficulty in focusing, sleep disturbance and impaired decision-making. When all your attention is focused on the good feelings associated with touch, say, or with eating, your attention can't be focused at the same time on all the possible threats to your survival in this very moment. In the short run, this will lift your mood, but in the long run, it will also improve psychological and physical health. Finally, savouring is a focus and emphasis on the good, pleasant things associated with the here and now.

Savouring and financial decision-making

Recent research is attempting to understand how savouring can affect financial behaviours and decision-making. Researchers have begun looking at how savouring experiences can impact finances by affecting our decisions, spending and investing behaviours.

The idea of 'experiential purchase' (the notion that experiences are more 'satisfying' than products) is closely related to savouring. It has been demonstrated that experiences make people happier and more satisfied[10] than material goods.[11]

Furthermore, much research on savouring and consumption practices has been dedicated to the question of whether savouring experiences can mitigate conspicuous consumption. Bryant and Giorgia (2016) found that savouring practices have the potential to reduce what they call non-deliberate consumption patterns (i.e. impulse purchases) by changing the context of use for a product into more enjoyment. Consumers who savour are more satisfied, because these practices further increase purchasing satisfaction and, consequently, decrease non-deliberate purchasing, resulting in higher levels of financial wellbeing.

Savouring and financial wellbeing

Numerous studies have explored the link between savouring, financial goals and overall contentment with money. Research indicates that the enjoyment of financial experiences, such as the joy of saving or the satisfaction of seeing net worth grow, has a direct positive impact on financial wellbeing.[12]

This kind of relish for financial experiences (as opposed to non-financial experiences) has been shown to bring about greater satisfaction with life, as shown in studies by Koh and Kim.[13]

Savouring and technology in financial context

Researchers are looking into how technology-based programs and mobile apps can be used to help people savour financial experiences, considering the close relationship between technology and many aspects of our lives. For instance, Kuppelwieser and Finsterwalder, in their empirical research of a mobile app to help users savour financial experiences, found that users of the app had elevated levels of financial savouring and flourishing.[14] Flow experiences – when you become fully immersed and focused on an activity – can lead to happy feelings; typically, people in today's distracted world take longer to finish things than previous generations of workers, and some rarely feel as though they are rested enough. Yet while people are immersed in a flow experience, they generate positive feelings that benefit their relationships and the rest of their lives. Playful pursuits can also provide them with escapes from everyday stressors and increase their perceived control.

Savouring and money: Cultural and demographic impacts

People have different attitudes towards money and different abilities to enjoy it i.e savouring. Everyone's relationship with these concepts is unique. To truly understand consumer behaviour and the emotions tied to financial experiences, it's essential to consider each person's individual financial situation. Research shows that factors like age, gender, socioeconomic status and cultural values significantly influence consumer behaviour and emotional responses to financial experiences.[15]

Challenges and barriers to savouring in the financial context

Although savouring can be an important tool in the journey to financial health, researchers have also noted that barriers to savouring, such as financial stress, can make it hard for many people to incorporate savouring financially, even when it's effective. There are other psychological barriers as well, including materialistic values or extrinsic goals that can inhibit the magnitude or intensity of savouring financial experiences.[16]

Financial stress, economic instability and low levels of financial literacy[17] are possible external barriers, which can impair our ability to experience positive aspects of financial life or life experiences, and to maintain positive financial wellbeing.

Implications for financial counselling and education

Research on behavioural economics offers insights about consumers' complex and often surprising attitudes and behaviours, which should better equip policymakers and financial education designers to improve the nature, usability and outcomes of financial tools and information. Evidence regarding the relationship between savouring behaviours and financial wellbeing might help to direct interventions aimed at increasing financial literacy or improving consumers' financial attitudes and behaviours.

Therefore, financial education programmes might target savouring strategies, such as mindful savouring of financial progress (e.g. enjoying the gradual accumulation of savings or savouring the process of saving for a vacation, relishing each deposit made), and enjoying more meaningful purchases (e.g. investing in a hobby like photography, where the enjoyment rests in the learning and personal growth).

Likewise, savouring could be used by financial counsellors and financial advisers to promote a more positive – and appreciative – perspective towards a client's financial hardships, which in turn should foster enhanced motivation and long-term commitment to the completion of their financial goals.[18]

Conclusion

In this chapter I've shown why it is so important to think of savouring behaviours in relation to financial wellbeing. Savouring has been shown to be positively related to life satisfaction more generally, and this may very well influence the extent to which experiencing happiness when making a financial decision makes a difference, how much spending in relation to money brings us happiness, and to what extent we remember and savour experiences with money in the moments after they have occurred.

What are the lessons for all of us? The first is that conscious savouring shapes people's feelings about and management of money. Experiencing money in positive ways can link the brain activity related to pleasant feelings with thoughts about money. By spreading the experience of pleasant feelings across time, thinking about one's money in positive, rather than negative, ways should increase our sense of overall wellbeing, as well as the soundness of our spending, saving and investment choices.

But savouring our financial lives is harder yet when we're confronted with real-life barriers, such as financial stress or financial illiteracy. Given these obstacles, it's critical that financial education programmes and counsellors embrace savouring strategies as a way not only to increase savouring but to foster a stronger and more positive relationship to money as well.

Ultimately, when savouring itself, and what it is doing – or how it maps in your financial life – is understood, you can begin to move towards greater financial wellbeing, and satisfactory life more generally. Altogether, it will likely help to start bringing those smile-inducing money moments. And who knows where it'll take you from there!

I hope you learned a bit about savouring in the previous section. Let's try some practical activities that explore savouring.

Activity 5.1: Celebrate the win in financial goals

This activity is designed to acknowledge the accomplishment of a money goal and to celebrate the positive behaviours used to make this objective happen, in order to help maintain motivation to keep pursuing your money objectives.

1. **Identify your financial goal**
   Objective: _____
   _____
   Date: _____
   Date you achieved the objective: _____

2. **Look at the effort and discipline you are putting out**
   What challenges did you face? How did you
   overcome them?

3. **Choose a reward**
   What simple pleasure can you afford to treat yourself to?

4. **Plan a time and place**
   Where and when will you experience and enjoy your reward?

5. **Share your achievement**
   Who will you tell about your accomplishment? How
   will you celebrate together?

6. **Document your success**
   Think how you felt, reflect on the subject of that day
   and what you have learned, then fill in your journal
   entry for the day.

Activity 5.2: Mindful spending

This activity will help you to grow the muscle of mindful spending, which in turn produces more informed, value-based purchases, higher levels of satisfaction and better alignment with your financial goals.

- **Set your intention**
  Financial goals? What can you blow on whatever you want?
- **Reflect before purchasing**
  That item is just a want, versus a need.
  How does this spending decision relate to my financial objectives?
  Does it truly provide a sense of value or fulfilment over time?
- **Decision-making**
  Don't rush it: if in doubt, wait twenty-four hours before purchasing (that is, wait until you're completely sure).
- **Appreciate your purchase**
  What value does this product or service bring to your life?

Activity 5.3: Money memories

This exercise helps you reflect on positive money moments by revisiting some of the best financial moments in your life, in order to build confidence, reinforce lessons learned and guide future financial decisions. Reflecting on your past can provide valuable insights to shape your future relationship with money.

Step 1: Remember the good times with money

For each memory, recall a specific positive money experience. Write down the challenges your faced, the actions you took to overcoming it and the outcomes that followed. For instance, perhaps you faced a large medical bill but negotiated with the provider for a payment plan, or perhaps, when dealing with credit card debt, you created a strict repayment plan and stuck to it. This will help you see how past experiences have shaped your financial journey.

Memory 1:
Describe a positive financial moment from your past.
   Prompts:

   • What challenges did you face during this time?
   • What went wrong, if anything?
   • What actions did you take to overcome these challenges?
   • What was the final result?

Memory 2:
Describe another significant money moment.
   Prompts:

   • What obstacles came up?
   • How did you address them?
   • What results did you achieve after taking action?

Memory 3:
Recall one more impactful financial experience.
   Prompts:

   • What problems did you face during this time?
   • What actions did you take to resolve them?
   • What outcomes resulted from these actions?

Step 2: Identify lessons learned

Reflect on each memory and extract the key lessons you learned from these experiences.
Prompts:

- How have these lessons influenced your current financial behaviours?
- In what ways have they impacted your decision-making process?

Step 3: Revisit your financial path

This is a moment to acknowledge your achievements and growth.
Prompts:

- What successes or progress can you celebrate from your financial journey?
- How have these experiences built your confidence in managing your finances?

Activity 5.4: Reflection on previous battles

This activity is designed to help you reflect on the biggest financial challenges you've faced, identify your strengths in overcoming them, and find lessons that can guide your future financial behaviour. The prompts under each section remain consistent to help you explore your experiences fully.

Step 1: Recall financial challenges

Think back to specific financial challenges you've encountered. Describe what the challenge was, how you approached solving it, and the outcome.

Challenge 1:
Describe a financial challenge you faced.
  Prompts:

- What was the challenge?
- What solutions or actions did you attempt?
- What was the outcome of your efforts?

Challenge 2:
Describe another financial challenge.
  Prompts:

- What obstacles did you encounter?
- What steps did you take to address the challenge?
- What were the results?

Step 2: Identify coping strategies

Consider the tools, resources or methods you used to overcome these challenges.
  Prompts:

- What strategies or resources helped you tackle these hurdles?
- Did you receive assistance from others (financial advice, tools, or emotional support)?

Step 3: Reflect on your resilience

Recognise the strength and growth you demonstrated during these experiences, and think about how these strategies can help you in future situations.
  Prompts:

- How can the coping strategies you used be applied to future challenges?
- What lessons have you learned that can help you manage your finances more effectively in future?

Step 4: Celebrate your progress and plan ahead

Take a moment to acknowledge your successes and resilience in overcoming financial challenges.

Prompts:

- What progress have you made in your financial journey?
- How can you continue to develop healthy spending habits and improve your financial wellbeing?

After completing all the activities in this setion, please go back to the money savouring questionnaire and see if your results have changed.

Resources

Here are some extra resources to deepen your knowledge of savouring and how it enhances overall wellbeing.

Books

The Art of Savouring: Simple Pleasures for Everyday Life by Joe Linehan, Wellness Press, 2018
This book offers practical tips on embracing mindfulness and finding joy in the small moments of everyday life.
Savor: Mindful Eating, Mindful Life by Thich Nhat Hanh and Dr Lilian Cheung, HarperOne, 2010
A guide to applying mindfulness to eating and lifestyle

choices, helping readers cultivate healthier relationships with food and overall wellbeing.

The Joy of Missing Out: Finding Balance in a Wired World by Christina Crook, New Society Publishers, 2014
This book explores the benefits of disconnecting from digital devices and finding fulfilment through intentional living.

Hygge: The Danish Art of Happiness by Marie Tourell Søderberg, Penguin Life, 2016
A beautifully illustrated guide on the Danish concept of hygge, focusing on creating warmth, cosiness and contentment in everyday life.

Living in the Moment: Understanding the Science of Mindfulness by Daniel J. Siegel, Mindful Books, 2017
This book delves into the science behind mindfulness and its benefits for mental and emotional health, offering tools for integrating mindfulness into daily life.

Apps

Stop, Breathe & Think – Guided meditations and reminders to check in with yourself throughout the day. Allows you to assess your mood and emotions. www.stopbreathethink.com

Oak – Designed for breathing exercises, reflection, and savouring positive emotions in bite-sized daily sessions. www.oakmeditation.com

Moov – Personalises recommendations for mindful movement sessions to appreciate the present. moov.cc

I Am – Collection of affirmation and savouring-based audio tracks. www.iamaffirmations.app

Websites

Greater Good Science Center – Research studies, articles, and videos on the science behind living meaningful, happy lives. Lots on mindfulness and savouring pleasures: greatergood.berkeley.edu

Mindful – Nonprofit news site publishing thoughtful, in-depth stories illuminating mindfulness, contemplative wisdom and teaching savouring techniques: www.mindful.org

The Art of Simple – Blog focuses on embracing simplicity, decluttering life to appreciate meaningful moments rather than chasing the next thing: theartofsimple.net

Zen Habits – Top articles on implementing mindfulness, focusing on the present through meditation, decluttering and lifestyle design conducive to savouring: zenhabits.net

Positivity Blog – Science-based articles for living a more positive life. Content on gratitude, happiness, self-care and reducing stress: www.positivityblog.com

Psych Central – Trusted mental health site with mindfulness exercises and worksheets for teaching savouring skills: psychcentral.com

Blog/journal articles

Does savouring increase happiness? A daily diary study. P. Jose, B. Lim, F. Bryant
Available at: journals.sagepub.com/doi/10.1177/0146167212455301

The Language and Social Psychology of Savouring: Advancing the Communication Savouring Model. M. Pitts. Journal of Language and Social Psychology
Available at: journals.sagepub.com/doi/10.1177/0261927X14561470

Developing Savouring Interventions for Use in Multicultural

Contexts: Bridging the East-West Divide. Jennifer L. Smith, Soyeon Kim, Fred B. Bryant
Available at: link.springer.com/article/10.1007/ s11469-018-0021-7

Effects of a Savouring Intervention on Resilience and Well-Being of Older Adults
Jennifer L. Smith, Agnieszka A. Hanni
Available at: journals.sagepub.com/ doi/10.1177/0733464816672046

Videos

Savouring Small Moments: The Benefits of Mindfulness
The Japanese Concept 'Wabi Sabi'

Podcasts

10% Happier with Dan Harris: 10percenthappier.com
The Art of Happiness with Arthur Brooks: arthurbrooks.com/ podcasts-and-videocasts
The Mindful Mom Podcast: themindfulmompodcast.com
Mindrolling: www.mindrollingpodcast.org
Live Inspired Podcast: theliveinspiredpodcast.com/podcast
On Being with Krista Tippett: onbeing.org
Mindful Living Podcast: beherenownetwork.com/ mindful-living-podcast
The Mindfulness Mode Podcast: mindfulnessmode.com/ mindfulness-mode-podcast
Steady Mind, Steady Body: steady202.com
Happier with Gretchen Rubin: gretchenrubin.com/podcast

CHAPTER 6

Meditation

*Shut your brain up for a minute –
your soul has something to say*

Meditation is our pause button in a world of constant information overflow. It is simple, but profound; you just sit down and tune into yourself, let go of all the thoughts and become more aware of what is happening inside you. By practising meditation, you have a tool that can help you deal with stress, anxiety or sadness. It helps you stay grounded, centred and focused in the reality you're in, instead of constantly escaping it. You can also just enjoy the experience, seeing what comes up for you. In this chapter we will focus on how meditation can be an effective tool to improve financial wellbeing.

Meditation and money questionnaire

This questionnaire assesses the effectiveness or impact of meditation practices to improve financial wellbeing. For each of the ten statements, indicate your level of agreement by circling the corresponding number. Calculate the total score to gain an initial understanding of your financial wellbeing. Once you have gone through the chapter and engaged in the recommended exercises, revisit the survey. You need not disclose your responses; it is merely a tool to assess any changes or improvements in your perspective. For each question, consider how much meditation – or the idea of meditation if you haven't tried it – helps you with:

1. **Reducing financial stress and anxiety**
   Not at all – 1
   Slightly – 2
   Moderately – 3
   Quite a bit – 4
   Extremely – 5

2. **Increasing awareness of spending habits**
   Not at all – 1
   Slightly – 2
   Moderately – 3
   Quite a bit – 4
   Extremely – 5

3. **Avoiding impulsive or unnecessary purchases**
   Not at all – 1
   Slightly – 2
   Moderately – 3
   Quite a bit – 4
   Extremely – 5

4. **Sticking to a budget or financial plan**
   Not at all – 1
   Slightly – 2
   Moderately – 3
   Quite a bit – 4
   Extremely – 5

5. **Making more mindful and well-thought-out financial decisions**
   Not at all – 1
   Slightly – 2
   Moderately – 3
   Quite a bit – 4
   Extremely – 5

6. **Clarifying and staying focused on financial goals**
   Not at all – 1
   Slightly – 2
   Moderately – 3
   Quite a bit – 4
   Extremely – 5

7. **Feeling more confident in managing finances**
   Not at all – 1
   Slightly – 2
   Moderately – 3
   Quite a bit – 4
   Extremely – 5

8. **Building healthier attitudes and relationships around money**
   Not at all – 1
   Slightly – 2
   Moderately – 3
   Quite a bit – 4
   Extremely – 5

9. **Achieving a more balanced perspective on financial matters**
   Not at all – 1
   Slightly – 2

Moderately – 3
Quite a bit – 4
Extremely – 5

10. **Experiencing greater peace of mind about financial situation**
Not at all – 1
Slightly – 2
Moderately – 3
Quite a bit – 4
Extremely – 5

My total score:

Introduction

Meditation, an ancient practice that dates back centuries in many philosophical and religious traditions, is garnering more attention than ever before as a tool for boosting effective performance, such as financial outcomes. This chapter will explore aspects of these dynamics from the perspective of meditation practices and their effects on financial health, guided by key theories and observational studies. Given that our cognitions, feelings and financial behaviours are so entangled,[1] it stands to reason that mindfulness-based interventions that utilise meditation practices[2] have been found to facilitate self-control and self-regulation[3] – qualities that are themselves crucial factors for sound decision-making. Self-regulation and self-control models[4] provide a useful starting point to understand how meditation can change our financial behaviour and outcomes.

Overview of meditation practices

There are many different kinds of meditation and each offers its own particular opportunities to develop mindfulness, attentional focus and relaxation. Meditation techniques can influence our mental and emotional states in divergent ways, which can potentially impact our financial wellbeing through different mechanisms.[5]

Here are some of the different types of meditation:

- **Mindfulness meditation:** Focuses on bringing awareness to the present moment, observing thoughts and sensations without judgement. Mindfulness meditation often involves paying attention to the breath or bodily sensations.
- **Transcendental meditation (TM):** Involves silently repeating a mantra to achieve a state of relaxed awareness. TM is typically practised for 15–20 minutes twice a day.
- **Loving-kindness meditation (Metta):** A form of meditation that emphasises cultivating feelings of love and compassion, starting with oneself and extending to others.
- **Zen meditation (Zazen):** Rooted in Zen Buddhism, Zazen involves sitting in a specific posture and focusing on the breath or a koan (a paradoxical question or statement).
- **Vipassana meditation:** An ancient form of meditation that involves observing bodily sensations to gain insight into the impermanence of sensations and the nature of suffering.
- **Guided meditation:** Led by a teacher or recorded audio, guided meditation provides instructions and imagery to help the practitioner relax and focus.
- **Body scan meditation:** Involves directing focused attention to different parts of the body, often starting from the toes and moving up to the head.
- **Chakra meditation:** Based on the concept of energy

centres in the body (chakras), this meditation involves visualising and balancing these energy points.

- **Mantra meditation:** Involves repeating a word, phrase or sound (mantra) to help focus the mind and promote a sense of calm.
- **Walking meditation:** Incorporates mindfulness into walking, where each step is taken with awareness and attention to the sensations of movement.
- **Breath awareness meditation:** Focuses on the breath, observing its natural rhythm and sensations. This type of meditation is common in many traditions.
- **Body movement meditation (Tai Chi, Qigong):** Integrates movement with meditation, promoting mindfulness and relaxation through slow and intentional physical activity.
- **Trataka meditation:** Involves gazing at a fixed point, such as a candle flame, to enhance concentration and develop inner focus.
- **Silent meditation:** Practised in complete silence, allowing individuals to turn inward and observe their thoughts without external guidance.
- **Religious meditation:** Rooted in religious contemplative practices, this form of meditation may involve focusing on a passage, prayer or repeating a sacred word.
- **Visualisation meditation:** Involves creating mental images to promote relaxation, enhance concentration or achieve specific goals.
- **Sound meditation (Nada Yoga):** Focuses on the perception of internal or external sounds, such as chanting, singing bowls or other musical instruments.
- **Mindfulness-based stress reduction (MBSR):** A structured programme that incorporates mindfulness meditation to reduce stress and improve overall wellbeing.

Meditation interventions for financial wellbeing

Meditation interventions may be aimed at wellbeing, including financial wellbeing, such as mindfulness-based stress reduction (MBSR) and mindfulness-based cognitive therapy (MBCT).[6] These interventions typically include mindfulness practices, cognitive restructuring and strategies for acceptance and non-judgement. Focused attention meditation and open monitoring meditation are also used in interventions for financial behaviours and decision-making.[7] In focused attention meditation, you maintain your focus on a single object, such as your breath. In contrast, in open monitoring meditation, you maintain an open awareness of your internal and external states of experience as they unfold within you.

The relationship between meditation and financial wellbeing

Empirical investigations of the effect of meditation on financial behaviours and outcomes have begun to clarify how these practices may improve financial wellbeing. Studies show that meditation can mitigate financial stress,[8] improve financial decision-making[9] and cultivate positive financial habits.[10]

There are numerous pathways by which meditation may influence financial wellbeing. Higher levels of self-awareness and emotional regulation, enhanced by meditation practices, may facilitate more mindful financial decision-making and improved reactions to stressors.[11]

Moreover, meditation can reduce cognitive biases and improve reasoning processes. This can enhance the quality of your financial decisions, as the data suggests.[12]

Empirical evidence about meditation interventions and financial wellbeing

Some studies have looked at the effects of meditation interventions on the psychology of finance, including risk perception, risk aversion, spending impulses and self-control.[13] Such mindfulness-based interventions have been found to change financial outcomes by altering our attitude to risk and reducing impulsive spending.[14] Moreover, some uses of meditation have been designed specifically to address different aspects of financial awareness – for example, mindful spending and budgeting, problematic or compulsive spending, gambling and savings.[15] These interventions seek to promote greater awareness, self-control and positive habits around money management.

Mechanisms and potential pathways

Several mechanisms have been proposed to explain how meditation may improve financial wellbeing. Meditation practice can be helpful for emotion regulation and stress reduction, thus improving our ability to make financial decisions in a clear and balanced manner.[16] Furthermore, greater self-regulation and associated 'insight' – cultivated through meditation – can lead to more disciplined spending and the management of impulses in general.[17] Pathways through which meditation may affect financial wellbeing include states of mindfulness, acceptance and non-judgement.[18] Furthermore, enhanced self-regulation and self-control, facilitated by meditation practices, might act as a mediator between healthier financial habits and decisions.[19]

Below, various types of meditations are described along with how they have been useful in improving financial wellbeing:

Mindfulness meditation and financial wellbeing

Mindfulness meditation has been a prominent focus in the literature exploring the relationship between meditation and financial wellbeing. Studies have been conducted to examine the extent to which mindfulness meditation can promote awareness about finances, decrease impulsive spending, and lead to more balanced management of money.[20] The practice of non-judgemental and present-moment awareness can allow people to keep a check on their financial behaviours and patterns, and enhance their psychological flexibility, thus making it more likely that they will choose and enact the behaviours that are aligned with their values and goals. Through regular practice of mindfulness meditation, people can become better attuned to their current experiences, improve at observing their behaviours, and ultimately make more conscious and autonomous choices.[21] Moreover, mindfulness can boost self-control and reduce automatic or impulsive responses – both of which bode well for sensible financial choices.[22]

Loving-kindness meditation (Metta) and financial wellbeing

Loving-kindness meditation has also been studied in relation to attitudes and behaviours around money. Evidence suggests that it can foster compassion for ourselves and others, and may ultimately lead to healthier financial relationships and decisions. Encouraging generous attitudes and goodwill, loving-kindness meditation can help people approach monetary matters with more empathy and a greater awareness of the stakes involved in financial decisions, both for themselves and those around them.[23] That in turn encourages more humane and sustainable economic behaviour, more honest and constructive dialogues, and more reasonable ways to resolve financial disputes.[24]

Visualisation meditation and financial wellbeing

Visualisation meditation involves using mental imagery with intentional focus. Research findings suggest that visualisation techniques can be beneficial for financial goal setting and achievement.[25] Visualising and rehearsing in your mind the monetary outcomes you desire can also boost your motivation and commitment to achieve your financial goals.[26] Visualisation practices can even be used to identify and overcome financial 'blocks' or beliefs that might be hindering success.[27]

Gratitude meditation and financial wellbeing

Gratitude meditation focuses on the cultivation of a positive attitude by encouraging you to feel grateful and thankful towards life's experiences and circumstances. Studies have examined the effects of gratitude meditation on financial satisfaction and wellbeing.[28] When individuals hold a grateful perspective with regard to moneymaking and spending, they are likely to develop higher financial satisfaction and resilience.[29] It's possible that gratitude meditation helps to shift people out of feelings of scarcity or dissatisfaction towards feelings of abundance, which in turn helps them to adopt more positive attitudes and behaviour towards money.[30]

Breath awareness meditation and financial wellbeing

Breath awareness meditation involves focused attention on the sensations of breathing. Research has explored the relationship between breath awareness meditation and reduction in financial stress.[31] As you develop your breath awareness, you may find yourself becoming more relaxed and vigilant in your decision-making – which might help make your financial decisions more prudent and less vulnerable to the effects of stress or anxiety.[32] In addition, breath awareness practices enhance emotional regulation and self-control, both important when tackling harmful financial impulses and behaviours.[33]

Coherence meditation

Achieving financial wellbeing requires alignment between heart, brain and actions. It's crucial to bring your personal values in line with your financial goals. This coherence encourages conscious spending, saving and investing decisions. The heart sets intentions, the brain creates strategies, and actions make them a reality. Emotions influence financial choices, so developing a positive relationship with money is key. To help achieve this coherence, I've designed a special meditation. But before we dive into practising this meditation, let's take a quick look at the science behind it.

Understanding heart and brain coherence

The phenomenon of coherence between cardiac and brain rhythms has been studied in the context of meditation research. Coherence is technically defined as synchronous interaction or harmonisation between the heart's rhythmic nature and the brain's electrical activity.[34] This coherence state is considered to promote greater health and wellbeing by fostering physiological and psychological homeostasis.[35] Heart rate variability (HRV) and brain wave frequencies (alpha, beta, theta, delta) are important concepts in understanding the physiological and neurological parameters of meditation and wellbeing. HRV, which is a measurement of the beat-to-beat interval variation in the heart, is used as a bio-marker of autonomic nervous system health.[36] Brain wave frequencies, on the other hand, are linked to our psychological states and modes of thinking.[37]

Techniques for achieving heart and brain coherence

Various meditation techniques and practices have been used to achieve heart and brain coherence. These include practices such as concentrated breathing, heart-based meditation and biofeedback (or real-time electronic feedback on the mobile or computer screen of HRV and other physiological measures).[38] A growing body of experimental evidence shows that such coherence is effective in increasing physiological and psychological resilience.[39]

Benefits of heart and brain coherence meditation
Scientists have also discovered why heart–brain coherence works, how to attain it, and point to the many physical and mental benefits of practising heart and brain coherence meditation:[40]

- *Better cardiovascular health:* Heart–brain coherence regulates heart rate variability, a marker of cardiovascular health and risk of heart disease.[41]
- *Improved immune system function:* Coherence between the heart and brain builds the immune system's capacity to recognise and neutralise threats from infectious microbes, materially improving health.[42]
- *Enhanced resilience:* Heart–brain coherence enhances the ability to be emotionally and psychologically resilient in bouncing back from challenges and adversity.[43]
- *Improved problem-solving and decision-making:* Having faced and worked through challenging feelings or states such as those described above, coherence meditation can help a practitioner to metabolise their experiences of fear or insecurity better, and develop greater cognitive clarity and creativity that allows for better problem-solving and decision-making.[44]
- *Better sleep quality:* general relaxation techniques performed just before bed can lengthen sleep duration and enhance sleep quality; all of which can improve one's overall wellbeing and performance.[45]
- *Increased social connectedness:* Heart–brain coherence enhances empathy, compassion and social connection, making for richer, more meaningful relationships and social interactions.[46]
- *Better mental health:* Studies have found a correlation

between heart–brain coherence and reduced symptoms of anxiety, depression and post-traumatic stress disorder (PTSD), with a better state of overall mental health.[47]

Neurobiological mechanisms underlying heart and brain coherence

Neuroscientific research has mapped out the neural pathways and mechanisms that underlie the connection between the heart and the brain, as well as coherence between the two organs. The vagus nerve, part of the autonomic nervous system, works via the heart–brain axis to regulate the physiological and emotional responses of the body.[48] Neuroimaging studies have explored the brain regions associated with heart and brain coherence during meditation practices. These studies documented activation patterns in brain regions, including the prefrontal cortex, anterior cingulate cortex and insular cortex, that are respectively involved in emotional regulation, self-awareness and interoceptive processing.[49] The neurobiological mechanisms underlying heart and brain coherence are believed to involve complex interactions between the central nervous system, autonomic nervous system and various neurohumoral pathways (when the nervous system and hormones work together to regulate various physiological processes).[50] The synchronisation of heart and brain rhythms may enable a more coherent state of physiology and psychology, including better functioning and wellbeing.

Practical considerations and implementation strategies

Practical factors, such as duration, frequency and individual differences, may play a role in how effective heart–brain coherence meditation practices are for people. Even if there is a 'sweet spot' for the total duration and frequency of practice, that would be shaped by the needs of the person practising, and their goals. The pattern that matters most of all, however, seems to be one of regular and frequent practice for achieving and maintaining coherence between the beats of the two rhythms.[51] A daily practice of heart and brain coherence meditation can be more easily integrated into life when it's done within an established time-frame and setting. Possible examples for beginners could include starting with short sessions and gradually lengthening them; or seeking a trained professional or group of engaged meditators as support or guidance.[52] Biofeedback devices, HRV monitors and other technology-assisted approaches work well with practices that utilise heart and brain coherence meditation. Such tools provide feedback about internal physiological parameters in real time, and thus allow meditators to view their output and tweak their practice in response to changes.

Conclusion

This chapter has outlined the connection between meditation practices and financial health, integrating theoretical perspectives, empirical findings and neuroscientific research. Findings have begun to point towards various types of meditation that can lead to improved financial behaviour and outcomes. Both mindfulness and loving-kindness meditation, and also visualisation, gratitude and breath awareness practices, as well as coherence meditation (a form of meditation that often integrates other types of meditation practices with specific breathing), appear to be beneficial by increasing self-awareness, improving emotional regulation or enabling more effective decision-making. Examples of meditation-based interventions that have been developed to improve financial behaviour include mindful spending, budgeting, debt management, saving and pro-social spending. Moreover, the experience of heart and brain coherence, achieved through particular meditation techniques, has been shown to correlate with physiological and psychological benefits that might be related to greater overall wellness, including financial wellness.

A logical response to this is to see the integration of meditation practices with financial education and counselling programmes as a way of cultivating better states of mind – and thus, healthier financial attitudes and behaviours. In enabling greater self-regulation, emotional resilience and a more accurate, deeper and more balanced perception of oneself and the world, meditation can act as a useful tool for financial wellness and can aid in exerting appropriate control over our actions and behaviour in the world of money.

Activity 6.1: Aligning mind and heart: A meditation on money and abundance

Please download this meditation from https://overcoming. co.uk/715/resources-to-download, or you can use the following meditation script to record the meditation in your own voice.

Meditation Script

Welcome to the meditation. This meditation will help you to create alignment in your heart and mind about money. We will try to create a new perspective about problems or issues you have about money.

I invite you to be curious, kind and accepting as you are guided through this process.

There is no right or wrong way to meditate ... simply relax and observe.

Take a deep breath in ... and breathe out.

To begin meditating I would like to invite you to sit comfortably. Please do not listen to this meditation when driving. Adjust your posture so that you are sitting in any upright position with your spine straight.

Let your eyes close.

Relax your shoulders, soften your jaw and let go of any tension in your body.

Today we are going to tap into your heart intelligence for the wider and more extensive view of the situation.

Bring your hand to the centre of your heart. Pay attention to your breath. Pay attention to your heart.

Take a couple of deep breaths.

Inhale fully and exhale fully, releasing all of the stale air from your lungs.

Inhale fresh oxygen, and exhale fully.

Do that a few more times.

Focus your awareness on the centre of your heart.

As you inhale, allow your awareness to follow your breath, moving into the heart.

As you exhale allow your body to relax. Inhale awareness, exhale relaxation.

As you inhale, feel the air coming in touch with your nostrils, nose, throat, chest, lungs, and, as you exhale, soften your body. Soften your muscles while maintaining a straight spine.

As you watch your breath, continue to concentrate on the sensations in your heart.

If you find your mind wandering, simply notice that it has wandered, let the thoughts go; and gently bring your mind back to the breath.

Now that you are aware and relaxed, breathe into the area at the centre of your heart. Bring your full awareness to this area at the centre of your heart. Allow your awareness to ride your breath as it goes down into this area of your heart. Observe your sensations in this area. Can you recognise any of them? Is there tension or is there openness? Do you feel any movement? Whatever you recognise is perfectly fine. There is nothing for you to do with the sensations you find – simply bring your awareness to the area and observe. You may feel nothing, which is perfectly fine as well; focus on the feeling of nothing. Any sensation may shift and change as you observe it. For a few more breaths, keep on focusing on the area at the centre of your heart.

As you continue to increase your awareness, breathing and observing, remember to bring an attitude of kindness and acceptance to anything you may be feeling . . .

Breathe into it, observe it, notice any sensations and emotions you experience there.

Now identify a problem or issue about money that you would like to see from a new perspective.

Be really specific about it.

Identify how you feel about it.

What is your attitude about it?

Breathe in . . . breathe out.

Imagine your breath is flowing in and out of your heart area.

As you are breathing from your heart space, imagine yourself easing up. Ease up.

Let go.

Create space within yourself.

Continue focusing on and breathing through your heart.

Take your time.

Now I invite you to activate a heart feeling about money.

A positive heart feeling of appreciation about money.

A positive heart feeling of gratitude about money.

Feel your heart expand and open.

In that heart-centred space, ask yourself what would be an effective attitude about money that would help in this issue?

What can be effective action about money that would help in this issue?

What can be a solution that would help in this issue that you are facing?

Quietly observe any thoughts, perceptions or feelings that are surfacing.

Be gentle, take this time to listen within.

Don't judge yourself or the way you are feeling.

Breathe in . . . breathe out . . .

I invite you now to deepen your breath and bring your

awareness to your whole body, feel the environment around you, the sound of my voice, your presence, my presence, our presence.

Take as much time as you want, and when you feel ready, you can slowly open your eyes.

End

Note: Practise this meditation for fifteen days and notice the changes in your perspective about money. After practising this meditation, please take the meditation and money questionnaire again to notice any changes.

Resources

To boost your understanding of meditation and its effects on wellbeing, here are some additional materials.

Books

Radical Acceptance: Embracing Your Life with the Heart of a Buddha
    by Tara Brach, Bantam, 2003
    A guide to using mindfulness and self-compassion to
    overcome emotional suffering and embrace one's true self.
The Three Pillars of Zen by Roshi Philip Kapleau,
    Anchor, 1989
    A foundational text on Zen practice, introducing the
    principles of teaching, practice and enlightenment.
Encouraging Words: Zen Buddhist Teachings for Western Students by
    Robert Aitken, Pantheon, 1993
    A collection of Zen teachings designed to inspire and guide
    Western students in the practice of mindfulness.
The Joy of Living: Unlocking the Secret and Science of Happiness
    by Yongey Mingyur Rinpoche with Eric Swanson,
    Harmony, 2007

Rinpoche blends traditional Buddhist wisdom with modern science to explain how meditation can cultivate happiness.

Abundance: The Inner Path to Wealth by Deepak Chopra, Rider, 2022
Chopra explores how to cultivate inner abundance and align one's consciousness with the flow of wealth.

Total Meditation by Deepak Chopra, Harmony, 2020
A guide to achieving a heightened state of awareness and mindfulness through daily meditation practice.

How to Practice: The Way to a Meaningful Life by His Holiness the Dalai Lama, Atria, 2002
A step-by-step guide to practising mindfulness, compassion and ethical living from the Dalai Lama.

The Art of Meditation by Matthieu Ricard, Atlantic Books, 2010
Ricard presents an accessible and practical approach to the practice of meditation and its benefits for the mind.

The Heart of Who We Are: Realizing Freedom Together by Caverly Morgan, Sounds True, 2022
Morgan explores how contemplative practices and collective awakening can bring about personal and societal transformation.

Full Catastrophe Living by Jon Kabat-Zinn, Piatkus, 2013
A comprehensive guide to mindfulness-based stress reduction, using mindfulness to face challenges like stress, pain and illness.

The Mindfulness Solution: Everyday Practices for Everyday Problems by Dr Ron Siegel, Guilford Press, 2009
A practical guide to using mindfulness to address everyday mental health issues such as stress and anxiety.

Altered Traits: Science Reveals How Meditation Changes Your Mind, Brain, and Body by Daniel Goleman and Richard J. Davidson, Avery, 2017
Goleman and Davidson explore scientific research on the long-term benefits of meditation on the brain and body.

Unwinding Anxiety by Jud Brewer, Avery, 2021
    Brewer offers insights into breaking the cycle of anxiety
    using mindfulness and neuroplasticity.
Mindfulness in Eight Weeks by Michael Chaskalson,
    HarperThorsons, 2014
    A structured eight-week course in mindfulness meditation,
    designed to enhance mental wellbeing and clarity.

Apps

UCLA Mindful – has multiple languages: www.uclahealth.org/
    marc/ucla-mindful-app
Waking Up: www.wakingup.com
Healthy Minds: hminnovations.org/meditation-app
Headspace: www.headspace.com
The JKZ Meditations App: www.jkzmeditations.com
Calm: www.calm.com
10 Percent Happier: www.tenpercent.com
Smiling Mind: www.smilingmind.com.au
Insight Timer: www.insighttimer.com
Simple Habit: www.simplehabit.com

Websites

Tergar community – courses, resources: tergar.org
Banyan – meditation community, with guided meditations:
    banyantogether.com/free-meditation-library
Massachusetts General Hospital Lazar Lab – researches the
    impact of meditation: www.massgeneral.org/psychiatry/
    research/lazar-lab-for-meditation-research
Transcendental Meditation (TM) – organisation sites around
    the world: usa.tm.org/choose-your-country
Peter Russell – meditation course and articles: www.
    peterrussell.com/index.php

Vipassana – worldwide resources: www.dhamma.org/
   en/index
Vipassana fellowship: www.vipassana.org
Diana Winston: Guided meditations and resources:
   dianawinston.com/meditations
Tenpercent: courses, meditations, podcasts, app: www.
   tenpercent.com
Boundless way Zen Temple: information on Zen, courses,
   retreats: boundlessway.org
Upaya Zen Centre: www.upaya.org/about
Dr Tony Nader Institute – research in neuroscience and
   transcendental meditation: dtni.miu.edu
Craig Hamilton – blog, podcast, courses:
   craighamiltonglobal.com
Caverly Morgan courses, teachings, combines Zen and non-
   dual approaches: www.caverlymorgan.org
Jon Kabat-Zinn teachings, resources: jonkabat-zinn.com
Dr Ron Siegel teachings, books, resources: drronsiegel.com
Richard Davidson books, videos, healthy minds app: www.
   richardjdavidson.com
Dr Jud Brewer resources, mindfulness mediations: drjud.com
Kristin Neff mindful self-compassion meditations and
   resources: self-compassion.org
Rick Hanson rickhanson.com

Blog/journal articles

You Yourself Are Oatmeal – interview with
   Enkyo O'Hara Roshi PhD: tricycle.org/article/
   roshi-pat-enkyo-ohara-interview
What is the best type of meditation: www.medicalnewstoday.
   com/articles/320392
What meditation can do for your mind, mood, and
   health: www.health.harvard.edu/staying-healthy/

what-meditation-can-do-for-your-mind-mood-and-health

Mindfulness meditation: A research-proven way to reduce stress: www.apa.org/topics/mindfulness/meditation

How to Meditate: www.nytimes.com/article/how-to-meditate.html

The Benefits of Meditation for Stress Management: www.verywellmind.com/meditation-4157199

Neuroscience Reveals the Secrets of Meditation's Benefits: www.scientificamerican.com/article/neuroscience-reveals-the-secrets-of-meditation-s-benefits

Meditation: A simple, fast way to reduce stress www.mayoclinic.org/tests-procedures/meditation/in-depth/meditation/art-20045858#

Meditation www.psychologytoday.com/us/basics/meditation

Five Ways Mindfulness Meditation Is Good for Your Health greatergood.berkeley.edu/article/item/five_ways_mindfulness_meditation_is_good_for_your_health

Videos

What is mindfulness?

20-Minute Guided Vipassana Meditation for Beginners: Discover Inner Peace and Mindfulness

10 Minute Guided Meditation for Beginners on Awareness – Yongey Mingyur Rinpoche

Meditation is easier than you think: series of 7 meditations – Yongey Mingyur Rinpoche

An introduction to Transcendental Meditation – Tony Nader MD, PhD

Mindfulness with Jon Kabat-Zinn

30 Minute Guided Meditation: Sitting Together in Presence – Eckhart Tolle

Daily Calm: 10 Minute Mindfulness Meditation for
    Self-Soothing
20 Minute Mindfulness Meditation for Being Present –
    Mindful Movement
Guided Meditation – Chakra Balancing, Chakra Alignment

Podcasts

Deepak Chopra: Science and Spirituality www.deepakchopra.com
The Science of Happiness greatergood.berkeley.edu/podcasts
Mindfulness for Beginners www.mindful.org/
    mindfulness-for-beginners-video-series
Craig Hamilton www.craighamilton.org
Being Well Podcast with Rick Hanson www.rickhanson.net/
    being-well-podcast
Rubin Museum rubinmuseum.org
Tara Brach Podcast www.tarabrach.com/podcast
10 Percent Happier www.tenpercent.com
I Should Be Meditating ishouldbemeditating.com
Mindfulness in Eight Weeks www.mindfulness8weeks.com
Positive Psychology positivepsychology.com
Mind & Life Institute www.mindandlife.org

CHAPTER 7

Self-compassion

Be kind to yourself – second chances don't grow on trees!

Self-compassion, the practice of treating oneself with kindness and understanding during difficult times, is emerging as a powerful tool for enhancing financial wellbeing. Before we learn more about self-compassion, though, let's try this questionnaire.

Self-compassion and money questionnaire

Please note: this survey is intended to assist you in monitoring and evaluating your personal development. For each of the ten statements, mark the number that best reflects your level of agreement. Add up your scores for an initial assessment of your progress. After completing the chapter and participating in the recommended exercises, revisit the survey. Your responses are private; it's merely a tool for measuring any changes or enhancements in your perspective.

1. **I tend to judge myself harshly when I make poor financial decisions.**
   Strongly disagree – 1
   Disagree – 2
   Somewhat disagree – 3
   Neither agree nor disagree – 4
   Somewhat agree – 5
   Agree – 6
   Strongly agree – 7

2. **I find it difficult to accept myself when I'm experiencing money problems.**
   Strongly disagree – 1
   Disagree – 2
   Somewhat disagree – 3
   Neither agree nor disagree – 4
   Somewhat agree – 5
   Agree – 6
   Strongly agree – 7

3. **I try to be understanding towards myself when I don't save or budget as much as I'd like.**
   Strongly disagree – 1
   Disagree – 2
   Somewhat disagree – 3
   Neither agree nor disagree – 4
   Somewhat agree – 5
   Agree – 6
   Strongly agree – 7

4. **I tend to feel like a failure when I don't earn or achieve as much financially as my peers.**
   Strongly disagree – 1
   Disagree – 2

Somewhat disagree – 3
Neither agree nor disagree – 4
Somewhat agree – 5
Agree – 6
Strongly agree – 7

5. **When faced with an unexpected expense, I catastrophise rather than treating myself with kindness.**
Strongly disagree – 1
Disagree – 2
Somewhat disagree – 3
Neither agree nor disagree – 4
Somewhat agree – 5
Agree – 6
Strongly agree – 7

6. **I give myself encouragement and praise for positive financial behaviours rather than focusing on shortcomings.**
Strongly disagree – 1
Disagree – 2
Somewhat disagree – 3
Neither agree nor disagree – 4
Somewhat agree – 5
Agree – 6
Strongly agree – 7

7. **I approach my finances with understanding and patience, even when facing difficult money situations.**
Strongly disagree – 1
Disagree – 2
Somewhat disagree – 3
Neither agree nor disagree – 4
Somewhat agree – 5

Agree – 6
Strongly agree – 7

8. **When money is tight, I acknowledge my feelings without judgement and focus on doing my financial best.**
Strongly disagree – 1
Disagree – 2
Somewhat disagree – 3
Neither agree nor disagree – 4
Somewhat agree – 5
Agree – 6
Strongly agree – 7

9. **While pursuing financial goals, I remember money struggles are a shared human experience.**
Strongly disagree – 1
Disagree – 2
Somewhat disagree – 3
Neither agree nor disagree – 4
Somewhat agree – 5
Agree – 6
Strongly agree – 7

10. **Despite occasional money struggles, I appreciate my efforts and avoid harsh self-judgement.**
Strongly disagree – 1
Disagree – 2
Somewhat disagree – 3
Neither agree nor disagree – 4
Somewhat agree – 5
Agree – 6
Strongly agree – 7

My total score:

Introduction

When it comes to money, we can be our own harshest critic. We feel guilty over our financial blunders, ashamed of our debts, stressed about not having enough saved up. But what if you could give yourself the same empathy that you'd give to a friend?

It's about kindness, rather than punishment, in the face of hardship: instead of telling ourselves we're stupid when we blow our budget, self-compassion encourages us to speak gently to ourselves.[1] Emerging evidence in personal finance literature suggests that being kind to ourselves is linked to better money habits and more resilient finances.

Emotions and money are bound up with each other. Being stressed about your finances can translate into feelings of guilt, shame and depression.[2] These negative emotions in turn can lead us to do unhealthy things when it comes to finance, such as spending too much money, racking up bills on credit cards, or taking foolish risks. Or not opening our bills, because we're scared to face the consequences. Simply practising self-compassion can break this cycle and promote healthier relationships with money.

Understanding self-compassion

So, what is self-compassion? The most comprehensive model comes from Kristin Neff, one of the flagship researchers in this emerging field, who conceptualises it as having three components: self-kindness, common humanity and mindfulness.[3]

Self-kindness is defined as responding to yourself with care and understanding rather than harsh self-criticism when you fail or make mistakes. Self-kindness entails being as warm and understanding to yourself as you would be to a good friend.[4]

Common humanity means acknowledging that everyone suffers and sometimes fails to live up to their own standards. It means bearing in mind that no one goes through life untouched by struggle, which means that there is no need to suffer on your own.[5]

Mindfulness is about the shift from being trapped by painful thoughts and feelings to observing them, without trying to block or change them; and the transition from being overwhelmed by financial fears and past failures to greeting them with balanced acceptance.[6]

Higher levels of self-compassion are associated with greater resilience when it comes to dealing with stress and adversity.[7] Individuals who are more self-compassionate tend to bounce back from stressful events more quickly than those with lower levels of self-compassion, can better manage the challenges of life, and have greater optimism. And, comparable to the realm of health, those benefits extend to personal finance.

The emotional landscape of money

Money is a highly emotional subject. It relates to the very core of who we are, our identity at a very basic level. It signifies our assessment of how we're doing, how secure we feel, and our hopes and expectations for the future. When we don't feel we're doing well with our money, it can trigger intense levels of anxiety, shame and self-judgement.

For example, it's common to feel shame about being in debt – some might even view it as a personal failing.[8] Shame can be powerful enough to prompt individuals to go to great lengths to conceal their financial issues from family and friends. Some avoid bills and bank statements. Others lie about their spending. Similarly, financial upsets such as job loss or unexpected financial expenses might cause our self-worth to plummet: we feel we're failing as a provider, or believe we're incompetent when it comes to money management.

As such, these emotions can spiral into a cycle of detrimental financial behaviours. We might fill a void with shopping, or spend too much to avoid anxiety. We might become reactionary, panic-selling investments or pawning possessions. Or take to denying the issue altogether, ignoring bills, accumulating debt and allowing problems to proliferate.

By practising self-compassion, we're better able to break this cycle: rather than experiencing a wave of shame and self-recrimination, we begin to see our financial situation in a way that's less distorted – we can deal with it in a clearer headspace.

Cultivating self-compassion in financial matters

So, how might we begin to make ourselves a little more financially self-compassionate? Here are a few ideas:

1. *Treat yourself kindly.* When you make a mistake with your money or suffer some kind of financial loss, respond as you might to a friend who has just done the same. Yes, acknowledge any negative emotions, but try to speak to yourself in a voice of soothing and encouragement, not condemnation and denunciation.[9]
2. *Remember it is OK to struggle.* Managing money problems is a normal part of life and we all make the occasional mistake. You do not have to be perfect and you don't have to get everything right.[10]
3. *Take a few deep breaths and teach yourself some mindfulness.* Notice the financial fears and worries you're having: acknowledge that you're having them, without allowing them to sweep you away.[11]
4. *Ask for help.* Confide in a sympathetic friend or family member or a professional adviser who offers the right support; it helps to talk to someone about our financial challenges.
5. *Start small.* Changing your financial path can feel overwhelming, but it's perfectly fine to start with a few

simple steps. Set yourself up for realistic, achievable goals and then continue to make just a little bit of headway when you reach each benchmark – even if it is a super-tiny baby step.[12]

After all, self-compassion isn't about making excuses or avoiding responsibility. It's about giving ourselves the emotional support and understanding required to put forth our best efforts in the face of our money challenges.[13]

Breaking the cycle: Overcoming financial guilt and shame

Perhaps the most powerful use of self-compassion for our relationship with money is to break the cycle of financial guilt and shame. When we're stuck in that cycle, we'll beat ourselves up no matter what in a money-related situation. And from there, we'll start saying to ourselves, 'I am not good enough/smart enough', etc.

After all, shame is not a good behavioural motivator for long-term change – rather the opposite, in fact – and it usually leads to more of the very behaviours we don't want to encourage, such as ramping up spending or financial avoidance.[14] Compared with self-criticism, research suggests that self-compassion is associated with greater motivation and persistence in the face of failure.[15] If we treat ourselves with compassion and understanding after a blunder with our finances, we're more likely to get back up and try again.

Here are a few ways to start overcoming financial guilt and shame:

1. *Accept your feelings.* You may feel guilty or ashamed about the money mistakes you've made. Allow yourself to feel these feelings with compassion rather than pushing them away or ruminating on them.[16]

2. *Forgive yourself.* We've all made some money mistakes. Give yourself permission to forgive yourself for those you made yesterday and focus on what you can do differently tomorrow.[17]

3. *Counter negative self-talk.* Catch your self-talk when you blame and beat yourself up over money and flip it into a more benign, nonjudgemental mode.[18]

4. *Get professional assistance.* If your financial shame is deep-seated or your money behaviours are compulsive, schedule a consultation with a financial therapist or counsellor to help you develop a positive and compassionate money relationship.[19]

But remember, banishing financial shame can also be a work in progress. Be kind to yourself. Celebrate milestones.

Mindful money management

Another way in which self-compassion can enhance our financial wellbeing could be to help ourselves think about our money more mindfully, arriving at better money habits. Mindfulness is the state of attentiveness, characterised by awareness and non-judgemental acceptance of what's presently happening.[20] It turns out that you can apply the skill of mindfulness to your financial life. The more mindful you become with money, the better you'll be able to track your spending triggers and emotional states. It means being able to take a step back from the act of buying itself, and make more finance-related choices that will align with your values and desires in the future.

Here are a few tips for practising mindful money management:

1. *Check in with yourself before spending.* Before you buy something, intercept the urge with some

self-questioning: 'Am I stressed? Bored? What need is this purchase trying to fill?'[21]

2. *Journal your spending without judgement.* Keep a non-judgemental ledger of your income and spending. Spot those patterns and triggers without beating yourself up for them.[22]

3. *Create a values-based budget.* Think about what is most important for you. Put your money where it is important. Split your spending plan so that there's room for pleasure and self-care.[23]

4. *Cultivate gratitude.* Pay attention to what you have, not what you're missing. Feeling satisfied with what you have is an effective antidote to compulsive buying and fosters greater financial satisfaction.[24]

Mastering mindful money management is a daily practice. By bringing mindfulness into our finances through a spirit of curiosity, acceptance and self-compassion, we'll make wiser choices and gain greater peace of mind.

The connection between self-worth and net worth

Perhaps the most significant hurdle to financial self-compassion is the assumption that self-worth equals net worth, and we are all too often situated this way in a culture that puts a premium on translating success into wealth.

However, the truth is, no matter our financial means, we each have intrinsic value as a person that does not depend on having money. We are worthy of love, respect and compassion because we are human beings, not because of what we have accomplished or what we own.

When we use our financial picture as the barometer for how we feel about ourselves, we set ourselves up for emotional swings. With every rise and fall of income or expenses, our self-worth drifts up and down. When we peg how we feel about ourselves to a number, even a positive one, we create a trap for our self-esteem. We become anxious about being worthy and depressed about how our worth compares to other people's, and we live with the feeling that we're just a little bit less than we should be.

Self-compassion, by contrast, provides us with a reliable and unconditional source of self-worth.[25] The essence of being kind to ourselves involves reminding ourselves that we are worthy human beings whatever the state of our bank balances.

Here are a few ways to start decoupling your self-worth from your net worth:

1. *Be compassionate towards yourself.* Remember that you are worthy of being loved and respected, regardless of how much or how little you have. It is not the amount of money you make, how much or how little debt you have, or what kind of house or car you drive that makes you a good or bad person. Values such as honesty, kindness and generosity are far more important than wealth.[26]

2. *Re-evaluate your definition of success.* Think about what success means to you, independent of financial measures. What characteristics, experiences and relationships can lead to a feeling of satisfaction and purpose in your life?[27]

3. *Develop non-monetary sources of self-esteem.* Put time and energy into things you do for non-monetary rewards – a hobby, volunteering, spending time with your family and friends.

4. *Cultivate gratitude.* Bring attention to the abundance that's already present in your life, rather than to its lack. Appreciation of those good things, no matter how modest they may be, can contribute to an improvement in self-esteem and wellbeing.[28]

Remember, your financial portfolio might move up and down, but your inherent value is as solid as a rock. By grounding your sense of self in self-compassion, you can face life's challenges with more endurance and clarity.

Building resilience: Financial challenges and setbacks

No matter how prudently we plan, or how hard we stash away our cash, there will always be financial troubles that come our way. We might lose our jobs. Things might break. Walls might need repainting. The economy might hit a slump.

At these times, self-compassion becomes a source of resilience. Meeting financial adversity with kindness and acceptance allows us to better cope with stress, rebound from challenges and remain optimistic about what lies ahead.[29]

Here are a few ways self-compassion can help us navigate financial challenges:

1. *Recognise the pain.* Being financially cut off or drastically downsized can break your heart. Give yourself permission to feel your sadness, fear or anger, but try not to judge or push away from your feelings.[30]
2. *Soothe yourself.* Be as generous to yourself as you would to a friend having trouble in similar circumstances, and find ways to self-soothe, be it by taking a warm bath or listening to relaxing music.[31]
3. *Turn setbacks into set-ups.* What can you learn from your fiscal failure? What lessons or growth opportunities can you find in your seemingly tragic circumstances or overwhelming, hopeless situation?[32]
4. *Ask for help.* Call on friends or relatives for emotional support, practical suggestions or a different view on what's happening to you. Remember, you don't have to face financial hardships alone.[33]

5. *Chip away one pixel at a time.* Speaking from experience, the most effective way to avoid succumbing to the despair that typically accompanies a financial crisis is to break down the tragic dimensions of your hardship into bite-size problems you can tackle step by step, day by day.[34]

Self-compassion isn't going to miraculously make your financial woes go away; however, it will help you develop the emotional strength to keep your head above water. With self-kindness and understanding, you can endure the present and take action to secure a more promising future for yourself.

Empowering your financial future

In the end, self-compassion is about encouraging ourselves to manifest the financial life we want. We're more likely to make money choices that are true to our nature, and benefit us for the long haul, when we speak to ourselves with kindness and compassion instead of condemnation and judgement.

Here are a few ways to support a thriving financial future using self-compassion:

1. *Set realistic goals* – financial goals that ring true for you. Ambitious although realistic. Within reach, based on what is reasonable given your current circumstances and resources. Tweak your goals, if necessary. Give yourself a break when things go wrong. Made a mistake? Recalibrate and start again, without putting yourself down.[35]
2. *Forgive yourself.* If you've blown your budget or repeated a previous money mistake, do your best to forgive your old self and then do something different in future. Recognise that missteps are learning opportunities, not causes for shame.[36]

3. *Prioritise self-care.* Include room in your budget for activities and experiences that nourish your physical, emotional and mental wellbeing. Remember, taking care of yourself is not a luxury, but a necessity for long-term financial health.[37]

4. *Pat yourself on the back.* Recognise and appreciate the successes – both big and small – in your financial journey. Notice the progress you're making, rather than the ways that you might be falling short.[38]

5. *Develop a growth mindset.* Believe that you can get smarter at managing money, and that your financial circumstances can also improve with practice and effort. Find ways to develop your financial literacy, perhaps through books, workshops or mentorships.[39]

Case studies and personal stories

The best way to understand the power of self-compassion with money is to explore a few examples. Rachel, a thirty-five-year-old teacher, was in debt: a lot of it, sitting on various credit cards. Every time she looked at her balance, she felt deep shame and self-loathing; self-judgements flooded her mind: 'I'm so bad with money. Look at how awful I am. I have such low self-control – I'm a failure.' But when Rachel started to speak to herself in a kinder, more supportive manner, she started accepting her humanity and reality as a human being, and recognised that lots of people can get into debt, it wasn't just her. She began to feel compassion for herself and explored a self-compassionate plan to pay off her debt slowly.

Or consider Mark, a small business owner who was experiencing burnout from his financial stress – specifically, worrying too much about paying his employees and paying his bills and doing so to the detriment of his own self-care. After practising self-compassion for a few weeks, Mark began taking 'minibreaks' for mindful self-care. He engaged a financial adviser and a therapist. He began to feel better about his financial situation and was able to make more effective decisions about his business.

These examples show that, rather than encouraging excuses and poor choices, self-compassion is a prerequisite for seeing the truth about our financial problems, and another fundamental skill required to overcome them.

After all, developing a compassionate relationship with money is a gradual process that will continue to teach us and reorient us over the course of our lifetime. When we learn to treat ourselves with kindness, respect and curiosity in this area, we will build the resilience and energy to develop financial practices that actually contribute to a life well lived.

Conclusion

In a culture where net worth too often becomes self-worth, practising self-compassion in our financial lives is a radical act of self-care. For example, we might approach our own embarrassing story with the same kindness and patience with which we approach a dear friend.

Self-compassion doesn't dwell on excuses or denial. Far from us getting off the hook, it's the antidote to blame, an injection of emotional nutrition to bolster our efforts to confront our financial problems with integrity and balance.

When it comes to money, this applies as well, and by drawing on self-compassion, we have a tool that enables us to actively and harmoniously engage with our challenges around money – setting realistic but difficult goals, and recovering quickly from setbacks – all with a view towards making the right choices with money for ourselves, in ways that better live up to our true values.

In the end, the road to financial wellbeing runs through self-compassion. And the more we can embrace ourselves with kindness, the more resources we have for our personal growth – not just in financial terms, but in all the varying rhythms of our humanity.

And so, when the twists and turns of our financial lives bring pain, may we demand of ourselves the same kindness and honest compassion we give to others. May we bring courage to what frightens us, wisdom to what confounds us, and gentle mercy to ourselves, in all our imperfections.

It's about being kind to yourself, as Kristin Neff, one of the leading voices in the field of self-compassion research, puts it: 'Self-compassion means being willing to ... treat ourselves with the kindness, care and respect we'd devote to a beloved friend.'[40] Let us be good friends to ourselves as we build a better, kinder financial future together.

Activity 7.1: Financial mistake letter

The objective here is to treat yourself with warmth and kindness when you make a financial mistake, just like you would for a friend.

Materials needed: Paper and pen or a digital writing device.

Instructions:

1. *Set the scene:* Find a quiet, comfortable space where you can reflect without distractions. Take a few deep breaths to centre yourself.

2. *Identify a financial mistake:* Recall a financial mistake you regret making. Perhaps you wish you hadn't spent so much recently, or feel like you've made a bad investment, or aren't saving as much as you'd like.

3. *Write a letter to yourself:*
   - Opening: Introduce your letter with an affectionate greeting, as you would to a good friend. You could also follow up with some useful facts about the studies, which are listed below. Example: 'Dear [your name],'
   - Acknowledge the mistake: Describe the financial mistake clearly and concisely. For example: 'I know you feel bad that you spent a fortune on all that junk last month.'
   - Express understanding: Show empathy and understanding for yourself. You are able to show empathy without criticisms or being swayed: for example, 'I understand your state of mind (it's normal and understandable to feel stressed enough to think that shopping could calm you)' rather than, for example, 'I understand why you were feeling stressed.'
   - Offer support: Let the benefit of doubt reassure you that it's OK to make mistakes, good enough, it doesn't have to be perfect; it does not define you. For example: 'Everyone makes mistakes, and it's okay. You are learning and growing every day.'
   - Provide constructive advice: Offer practical advice to help yourself move forward. For instance: 'Well, perhaps next time you have the urge to stimulate yourself, you could try going for a walk or reading a book instead.'
   - End the letter with a positive, supportive note. You can end your letter with a helpful hint, like the one included here. Example: 'Remember, you are doing your best, and I believe in you.'

4. Reflect:
   - Read the letter back to yourself slowly.

- Notice what it's like to offer this kindness to yourself.

Time required: 20–30 minutes

Activity 7.2: Forgiveness practice

The objective here is to practise self-forgiveness and recognise that financial mistakes are opportunities for learning and growth.

Materials needed: Paper and pen, or a journal.

Instructions:

1. *Set the scene:*
   Find a quiet, comfortable place to sit and reflect. Close your eyes and take a few deep breaths to relax.

2. *Reflect on financial mistakes:*
   Think about financial mistakes or decisions that you regret. Write down a list of these mistakes in your journal.

3. *Acknowledge the mistakes:*
   Take a moment to acknowledge each mistake without judgement. Example: 'I admit that I bought a stock blindly, and lost my money.'

4. *Practise self-forgiveness:*
   For each mistake, write a forgiveness statement. Example: 'I forgive myself for that stock purchase. I did my best with the information I had.' Repeat this process for each mistake on your list.

5. *Reflect on learning and growth:*
   Learn from each mistake: write down what you learned and how you've benefited.

   From this we can identify five key milestones of self-growth: (i) Questions about purpose; (ii) moments when you have realised your definitions for success were incorrect; (iii) mistakes you made that led to significant learning; (iv) people who have helped and motivated you to achieve, maybe against the odds; (v) times you had to work through challenges that tested your values and ambitions. Example: 'I was wrong and shouldn't have bought those shares. As a result, I now do more research before I invest.'

6. *Closing:*
   Conclude with a self-compassionate statement acknowledging your efforts and progress. Example: 'I am proud of myself and how I acted; I faced my mistake and learned from it and moved on. I am developing into a better person every day.'

Time required: 30–40 minutes

Activity 7.3. Self-appreciation practice

Here you will practise self-compassion and acknowledge and appreciate your progression through your financial setbacks.

Materials needed: Journal or a digital device for writing.

Instructions:

1. *Set the scene:*
   Find a quiet place where you can reflect daily without

distractions. Close your eyes and take a few deep breaths to centre yourself.

2. *Daily reflection:*
   Each day, spend a few minutes reflecting on the following:

   - **Past financial successes:** Write down at least one financial success you've achieved in the past. Example: 'I successfully paid off my credit card debt last year.'
   - **Progress made:** Reflect on the progress you've made towards your financial goals. Example: 'I have consistently saved 10 per cent of my income each month.'
   - **Lessons learned:** Identify lessons learned from both successes and challenges. Example: 'I learned the importance of having an emergency fund.'
   - **Efforts recognised:** Acknowledge your efforts and hard work. Example: 'I am proud of myself for sticking to my budget even during difficult times.'

3. *Write it down:*
   Record these reflections in your journal daily. Use a positive, supportive tone as you write.

4. *Weekly summary:*
   At the end of each week, review your daily reflections. Summarise your overall progress and celebrate your achievements. For example: 'This week I saved more than last week AND learned what amortisation means.'

5. *Closing:*
   Conclude with a statement of self-appreciation and
   encouragement. Example: 'I appreciate my dedication
   and am excited to continue growing financially.'

Time required: 10–15 minutes daily

After completing all these activities, don't forget to retake the
self-compassion and money questionnaire to check the changes
in the score and in your level of self-compassion.

Resources

These resources will help you gain further insight into self-
compassion and its positive impact on your overall wellness.

Books

Self-Compassion by Kristin Neff, William Morrow, 2011
   The seminal book on self-compassion research and practices.
The Mindful Path to Self-Compassion by Christopher Germer,
   Guilford Press, 2009
   Practical guide with meditations and exercises.
Radical Compassion by Tara Brach, Anchor, 2021
   Blends self-compassion with mindfulness.
The Mindful Self-Compassion Workbook by Kristin Neff and
   Christopher Germer, Guilford Press, 2018
   Practical workbook based on the authors' eight-week
   mindful self-compassion programme.
*Fierce Self-Compassion: How Women Can Harness Kindness to
   Speak Up, Claim Their Power, and Thrive* by Kristin Neff,
   HarperOne, 2021
   Particularly useful to those who are compassionate to others
   but not to themselves.

Apps

Self-Compassion by Wylde One – iOS app with meditations, exercises, timer.
Headspace – Meditation app with loving-kindness and self-compassion sessions. www.headspace.com/meditation/self-compassion
The Self-Compassion App by Balanced Minds – Exercises and guided meditations for self-compassion and self-esteem. balancedminds.com

Websites

Self-Compassion.org – Website of Kristin Neff with resources, exercises, and workshop info. self-compassion.org
Greater Good Science Center – Research and articles on self-compassion. greatergood.berkeley.edu/topic/self_compassion
Chris Germer – Website of Center for Mindful Self-Compassion with resources, guided meditations, and courses. chrisgermer.com

Blog/journal articles

The Value of Self-Compassion – *Psychology Today*. www.psychologytoday.com/us/blog/living-forward/201912/the-value-self-compassion
Using Self-Compassion to Get Through Difficult Times – Verywell Mind. www.verywellmind.com/using-self-compassion-to-get-through-tough-times-3144787
Why Self-Compassion Makes a Practical Difference in Life – BBC. www.bbc.com/worklife/article/20210111-why-self-compassion-not-self-esteem-leads-to-success

The Power of Self-Compassion – Harvard
    Health. www.health.harvard.edu/healthbeat/
    the-power-of-self-compassion
What Does Self-Compassion Really Mean? –
    Harvard Business Review. hbr.org/2022/12/
    what-does-self-compassion-really-mean
Give Yourself a Break – The Power of Self-Compassion –
    Harvard Business Review. hbr.org/2018/09/
    give-yourself-a-break-the-power-of-self-compassion

Videos

Kristin Neff's TEDx Talk on Self-Compassion – The Space
    Between Self-Esteem and Self-Compassion.
Self-Compassion with Dr Kristin Neff – at Action for
    Happiness.
The Three Components of Self-Compassion by Kristin Neff.
The Science of Self-Compassion with Kristin Neff: Talks at
    Google.

Podcasts

The One You Feed – Episode on Self-compassion with Kristin
    Neff. www.oneyoufeed.net/kristin-neff
Happier with Gretchen Rubin – Episode on Better Money
    Habits Through Self-Compassion gretchenrubin.com/
    podcast-episode/231-better-money-habits-through-self-
    compassion
Can You Cultivate Self-Compassion? *Michelle McQuaid Podcast*
    with Kristin Neff. www.michellemcquaid.com/podcast
Tara Brach Podcast tarabrach.libsyn.com

CHAPTER 8

Meaning therapy

If cash talks, society's morals better back it up

Meaning therapy can be used to help people find meaning and purpose in life. This can improve your overall wellbeing, and that includes financial wellness too. Before we learn more about meaning therapy, please take this brief survey.

Money and meaning therapy questionnaire

The aim of this survey is to assist you in tracking and assessing your personal growth. For each of the ten statements, circle the number that corresponds with your level of agreement. Add the scores to obtain an initial sense of your sense of meaning around money. After studying the chapter and completing the suggested exercises, revisit the survey. Your answers remain confidential; it is simply a tool to gauge any shifts or advancements in your outlook.

1. **I have a clear sense of purpose and meaning in my life.**
   Strongly disagree – 1
   Disagree – 2
   Neutral – 3
   Agree – 4
   Strongly agree – 5

2. **My financial goals align with my core values.**
   Strongly disagree – 1
   Disagree – 2
   Neutral – 3
   Agree – 4
   Strongly agree – 5

3. **My spending and saving align with what is meaningful to me.**
   Strongly disagree – 1
   Disagree – 2
   Neutral – 3
   Agree – 4
   Strongly agree – 5

4. **I am able to find meaning during difficult financial circumstances.**
   Strongly disagree – 1
   Disagree – 2
   Neutral – 3
   Agree – 4
   Strongly agree – 5

5. **My life and identity are not overly tied to material wealth.**
   Strongly disagree – 1

Disagree – 2
Neutral – 3
Agree – 4
Strongly agree – 5

6. **My finances contribute to positive relationships.**
Strongly disagree – 1
Disagree – 2
Neutral – 3
Agree – 4
Strongly agree – 5

7. **Financial decisions that align with my values contribute to a sense of purpose and meaning in my life.**
Strongly disagree – 1
Disagree – 2
Neutral – 3
Agree – 4
Strongly agree – 5

8. **Connecting my work to a greater sense of purpose positively influences my financial wellbeing.**
Strongly disagree – 1
Disagree – 2
Neutral – 3
Agree – 4
Strongly agree – 5

9. **Mindful spending, where I consider the alignment with my values, is an important aspect of my financial decisions.**
Strongly disagree – 1
Disagree – 2

Neutral – 3
Agree – 4
Strongly agree – 5

10. **I actively seek financial goals that contribute to my legacy and long-term sense of purpose.**
Strongly disagree – 1
Disagree – 2
Neutral – 3
Agree – 4
Strongly agree – 5

My total score:

Introduction

Have you ever wondered how much money means to you? Or how much your income – or lack thereof – might be affecting your life? How much your lifestyle, your relationships with others or your sense of security is influenced by money? And how monetary wealth or the lack of it affects your overall sense of wellbeing? If so, meaning therapy might be of help to you.

Meaning therapy, pioneered by the Canadian psychologist Paul Wong, is a practical approach to finding and making meaning in life.[1] In this chapter, we'll examine how meaning therapy can help us think about money in more meaningful ways, and ultimately aid us in making more purposeful financial choices that better reflect the things we feel are most important to us.

However, before diving into the nitty-gritty of meaning therapy, it's first best to review what we actually know about money's meaning from psychological science.

The many meanings of money: What the research says

Money is a huge part of modern life, and psychologists have been exploring what it means to people for decades. The research has produced several different models and frameworks. Here are some of them.

Early research from Wernimont and Fitzpatrick showed that people associate largely negative or largely positive traits with money.[2] For instance, they said that money had connotations with power, control, romance, health, sadness, luck, doom and even freedom, and expressed the opinion that it 'represents conformity and achievement'. Yet the meanings were highly idiosyncratic, tailored to what was going on in each person's life.

Later, Tang created a measure called the money ethic scale (MES) to gauge attitudes to money.[3] This measure examines how people feel, think and act towards money. The MES highlights the layered psychology of money, indicating that people's experiences with money are multifaceted and built from an emotional, intellectual and value-oriented composite.

Mitchell and Mickel suggested that what money ultimately means to each of us is a reflection of the limits of our personality, values and life experience.[4] To put it another way, the meaning we assign to money is influenced by the values we hold in high esteem. So someone who values achievement might associate money with success, while someone who feels insecure might associate money with keeping people at a distance.

Furnham, Wilson and Telford described four types of attitudes towards money: security, power, love and freedom. Each type reflects a fundamentally unique way of thinking about and using money.

Nor is our attitude necessarily paired with pragmatic money metaphors. According to Belk and Wallendorf, money might also serve sacred meanings.[5] It is possible that money can serve as a container for the sacred, representing deeply held values and beliefs surrounding its use.

Many models have some common features, but they do reflect very different interpretations – and when in-depth analysis shows so many ways to try to understand the meaning of money, all of which appear to have merit, it indicates that the meaning is complex, varied and individual. And that has huge implications for the impact of money on our lives.

Understanding meaning therapy

So, what is meaning therapy? It is an approach that allows individuals to create a life narrative, or story of a meaningful life, that corresponds to their values and provides their life with meaning and purpose. Meaning therapy was originally conceptualised by Dr Paul Wong, and it is based on Viktor Frankl's logotherapy and humanistic psychology.

Meaning therapy is thus applicable to virtually any problem that someone may bring, by assisting them in finding meaning. It involves exploring how to grow and live in ways that feel more vital, authentic and alive.

In practice, meaning therapy can help someone determine what their life goals are and how those goals tie in with a larger purpose. By figuring this out, we can be enabled to flourish psychologically. And as we will see, this can be a useful roadmap for making financial decisions that align with our life goals.

Meaning therapy and the PERMA model: Two approaches to wellbeing

Two distinct yet complementary approaches, meaning therapy itself (developed by Paul Wong) and the PERMA model (developed by Martin Seligman), underscore the critical role of meaning in wellbeing and happiness.

Meaning therapy aims to help people develop meaningful goals, cultivate a sense of purpose and maintain resilience in the face of life's trials.[6] It borrows heavily from existential psychology, positive psychology and cognitive behavioural therapy in guiding people in discovering their values, strengths and hopes – strategies promoting a worthwhile life.[7]

Similarly, the PERMA model names meaning as one of five pillars of wellbeing, the others being positive emotion, engagement, relationships and accomplishment.[8] In this framework, meaning refers to the perception that your life has value and significance beyond mundane pursuits of pleasure or possessions.[9]

The two approaches are alike in recognising the role that a clear understanding of meaning and purpose plays in helping people to cope better with stress, make sense of challenges and adversity, and draw greater satisfaction and meaning from life in general.[10] While meaning therapy is a specific psychotherapy designed to enhance the subjective experience of meaning, the PERMA model offers a broader view of different areas of wellbeing.[11]

The link between meaning and money

Sheldon and Kasser's research suggests that the meaning and satisfaction we derive from spending money can either contribute to or detract from our sense of meaning in life.[12] In understanding this, we can more readily ensure that our choices about money are aligned with the priorities we want for the rest of our life. One thing is certain: the money-making aspect of our lives is inseparable from a host of psychological and emotional factors related to identity, security, status and more.[13]

Financial stress can compromise our wellbeing, yet spending money in ways that help others is associated with happiness.[14] Meaning therapy can help us consider how our financial behaviours and attitudes support or challenge our deeper meaning in life. For instance, spending too much on things we don't need might be a way of escaping the existential vacuum of our lives.

On the other hand, saving money in a thoughtful way might be a means of achieving goals that we are committed to.

Meaningful spending and saving

How do we put ourselves in a position to make these spending and savings choices in a way that is aligned with our life purpose and personal values? By practising mindful budgeting.[15] By clearly being intentional about our allocation of resources to what brings us closest to our meaningful purposes.

For example, one study by Dunn, Gilbert and Wilson includes some intriguing examples of how realistic, money-based meaning-making can change how we go about our financial lives.[16] Our everyday decision-making about spending provides plenty of opportunities to act in ways that reflect our values.[17] Someone who cares about the environment might purchase 'green' products. Someone who values generosity might make a charitable donation.

So, setting up savings targets for things that are likely to be meaningful – such as an education, annual family holidays, starting a business or even a rainy-day fund – may add a further layer of purpose to budgeting. An orientation towards meaning will allow us to re-evaluate our inclinations towards short-term temptations in light of longer-term, values-based objectives.

The role of work and career

For many of us, the majority of our waking hours are spent in work – and thus, it can be a major and meaningful form of life. Engaging in meaningful tasks at work is associated with job satisfaction, productivity, motivation and wellbeing.[18] Meaning therapy, then, tackles how people might make their working life more meaningful, either through service to others or through creative expression or 'doing good work' – that is, work that

MANAGE YOUR MONEY, MANAGE YOUR MIND

aligns with a person's values, talents and vocation. If we can do that, we'll probably thrive financially and psychologically.

Transcending materialism: Meaningful consumerism

Evidence further indicates that the tendency towards materialism is associated with reduced wellbeing and life satisfaction.[19] It's no coincidence that shopping sprees are commonly a misguided way to derive meaning from stuff. Meaning therapy can enable people to examine the belief that purchasing or possessing certain things will grant an enduring stream of positive feelings. Mindful consumption, distinguishing between needs and wants, and purchasing things that are in harmony with our personal values can all contribute to a more purposeful pattern of consumer behaviour. In concert with such practices, people can be helped to move beyond status-driven materialism and to cultivate meaningful forms of wealth.

Aligning financial goals with life purpose

Concrete financial goals can serve as bridges to our deeper meanings and our life vision, and can be explored or nurtured through meaning therapy exercises such as life review (reflecting on past experiences) and generativity conversations (discussing ways to create a positive impact for others).[20] For example, an entrepreneur might work towards building business equity to leave a legacy. A teacher might fund continuing education to fulfil their professional purpose. When we align our financial behaviours with a higher sense of meaning, it provides motivation and fulfilment.

Overcoming financial anxiety through meaning

Many of us live with anxiety about money. Meaning therapy can help people to face the existential anxieties that surface when they feel financially threatened. Logotherapy, for example, has been used to help reduce financial anxiety by grounding people in their life purpose. A technique called cognitive reframing helps people assign positive meaning to their financial situation. Values clarification can help people to understand their life goals and how to pursue them within their financial circumstances. The cognitive approach especially helps clients take 'constructive action'.[21]

Financial generosity and meaningful giving

Generous giving, and spending money on things that facilitate others, is associated with greater happiness and life satisfaction.[22] Donating money to charity can be a significant act of meaning-making, where we align our behaviour with our values (for instance, with compassion). Expending our labour or resources for the benefit of others can contribute to our sense of meaning and purpose, and enhance meaning in life. Acts of financial generosity might possess an inherent sense of meaning.

Money and interpersonal relationships

How we choose to spend our money can also affect our relationships with our spouses or partners, children, parents or relatives, and friends. Arguments about money are typically regarded as a major cause of stress in relationships. Shared meaning and purpose over financial decisions, such as planning a household budget, saving money or giving to charity, can promote intimacy with other people.[23] An example of the positive side of this is a couple growing closer to each other through volunteering together at a soup kitchen.

At the same time, differences in values can also create tension in a relationship. For instance, it might be important for one partner in a relationship to provide more for their children now while the other believes it is more important to save for their children's future. A similar situation can also arise when there are communication problems regarding meaning. For example, one person in a couple might keep money hidden from the other while the other says that financial candour is important. The more you share meanings and values with your partner, the easier and more joyful your journey together is likely to be.

Navigating financial setbacks with meaning

Financial setbacks such as job loss, recession or debt are often un-avoidable and can have a huge effect on our sense of meaning and purpose.[24] Meaning therapy can help individuals to rediscover meaning during times of financial hardship; this includes helping us to find alternate definitions of success, reframing situations, identifying lessons learned or finding growth opportunities.

Learning to be kinder to yourself in the face of financial distress is an important part of positive coping, too. Meaning-centred tools in meaning therapy seem well suited to helping people stay connected to a larger sense of meaning in the midst of financial catastrophe.

Conclusion

In summary, meaning therapy provides not only a vision of what financial planning could look like but also ideas for concrete applications, to help people orient their financial behaviours and habits within a larger framework of meaning, values and purpose. Integrating these ideas can help to improve financial literacy, and both financial planning and wellbeing.

Activity 8.1: Uncovering the meaning of money

Before starting this exercise, grab a pen and paper or open a blank document to jot down your thoughts. Set aside some quiet time to reflect and be honest with yourself – there are no right or wrong answers. This activity will help you uncover your deeper beliefs and emotions about money through simple reflection and brainstorming. Approach it with curiosity and an open mind, and try not to judge yourself as you go through each step.

1. **What comes to mind when you think about money?**
   Write down the first words or images that appear in your mind. Do not filter or organise your thoughts. Example: 'Bills, security, stress, freedom, greed.'

2. **How do these thoughts make you feel?**
   Reflect on the emotions that arise with your initial thoughts. Describe them as best as you can. Example: 'When I think of money, I feel anxious and stressed but also relieved when I think of security.'

3. **Follow each thought or word with the next thought that comes to mind.**
   Take each word from your initial thoughts and write down the next word or idea it brings to mind. Continue this chain of associations for at least five steps for each initial thought. Example:

   Bills → Responsibility → Overwhelmed → Work → Exhaustion
   Security → Safety → Family → Love → Happiness

4. **Reflect on each chain of associations.**
   What patterns or themes do you notice? How do

these chains relate to your experiences or beliefs about money? Example: 'Many of my associations lead to feelings of responsibility and stress, indicating that I see money as a burden rather than a tool for freedom.'

5. **Identify key themes or recurring ideas.**
Look over your associations and highlight any recurring themes or significant thoughts. Example: 'Responsibility, stress, family and safety appear frequently in my associations.'

Activity 8.2: Identify your core values

Step 1: Value identification

1. **List your core values related to money.**
Example: Security, generosity, independence, growth, simplicity.

2. **List your core values related to work.**
Example: Creativity, impact, collaboration, excellence, learning.

3. **List your core values related to life.**
Example: Family, health, adventure, integrity, spirituality.

Step 2: Reflection on alignment

1. **How do your financial goals align with your core values?**
Example: 'My value of security aligns with my goal to save for emergencies.'

2. Identify any discrepancies between your financial goals and your core values.
Example: 'I value simplicity, but my spending habits are often impulsive and cluttered.'

Step 3: Adjust financial decisions

1. What changes can you make to align your financial decisions with your values?
Example: 'I will create a minimalist budget to better reflect my value of simplicity.'

2. Set one or two specific actions you can take to adjust your financial decisions.
Example: 'Reduce unnecessary subscriptions and redirect that money to savings.'

Activity 8.3: Legacy planning

Consider what legacy you want to leave behind and connect your financial decisions to creating a meaningful legacy.

Step 1: Define your legacy

1. What kind of legacy do you want to leave behind?
Example: 'I want to leave a legacy of kindness and support for education.'

2. Identify who or what you want to impact with your legacy.
Example: 'My family, local schools, and charitable organisations.'

Step 2: Align financial decisions with legacy goals

1. **How do your current financial decisions support your legacy goals?**
   Example: 'My charitable donations support local schools.'

2. **Identify any areas where your financial decisions could better support your legacy goals.**
   Example: 'I haven't started a will or estate plan.'

Step 3: Action plan

1. **What specific steps can you take to align your finances with your legacy?**
   Example: 'Create a will and designate funds for charitable contributions.'

2. **Set one or two actions to start building your legacy.**
   Example: 'Meet with a financial planner to discuss estate planning.'

After completing all the activities, please go back to the start of the chapter and attempt the money and meaning therapy questionnaire again to check the difference in the result.

Resources

Explore these additional resources to broaden your understanding of meaning therapy and its role in improving wellbeing.

Books

Meaning Therapy: Assessments and Interventions by Paul Wong, Routledge, 2019

A comprehensive guide to assessments and interventions for fostering meaning in life.

The Human Quest for Meaning by Paul Wong, Routledge, 2010
Explores the quest for meaning as a fundamental human motivation.

The Art and Science of Meaning Therapy by Paul Wong, Routledge, 2021
Integrates art and science in therapeutic practices aimed at meaning-making.

Money and the Meaning of Life by Jacob Needleman, Harmony Books, 1991
Examines the relationship between money and the quest for a meaningful life.

Money Sanity Solutions by Kate Levinson, Greenleaf Book Group Press, 2015
Offers practical strategies for achieving emotional and financial wellbeing.

Money Harmony by Olivia Mellan, Atria Books, 2000
Explores the emotional aspects of money and how it impacts relationships.

Apps

iMeaning – Meaning-centered coaching app by Paul Wong

Websites

The International Network on Personal Meaning: www.meaning.ca

Meaning-Centered Counseling Institute: www.meaningtherapy.com

Money and Meaning: moneyandmeaning.com

Blog/journal articles

The Psychology of Meaning: An Introduction: www.jstor.org/stable/41603704

Meaning Therapy: Assessments and Interventions: www.researchgate.net/publication/326924745_Meaning_Therapy_Assessments_and_Interventions

Money, Meaning, and Eudaimonia: www.mdpi.com/2071-1050/10/4/1114

Money Beliefs and Financial Behaviors: Development of the Klontz Money Script Inventory: journaloffinancialtherapy.org/archives/vol-2-issue-1/money-beliefs-and-financial-behaviors-development-of-the-klontz-money-script-inventory

Videos

Paul Wong discusses meaning therapy
Finding Meaning and Purpose in Life
The Psychology of Money
The Meaning of Money

Podcasts

Meaning Matters – Interviews with experts on meaning: www.meaning.ca/meaning-matters-podcast

The Parents Under the Stairs – Episodes on meaning-centered living

Her Money with Jean Chatzky – Money and meaning episodes: www.hermoney.com/t/podcasts

Money Chronicles – Exploring money psychology: moneychronicles.buzzsprout.com

CHAPTER 9

The best possible self

Our best self isn't lost; just stuck in traffic

In need of some positive personal finance mojo? Try the 'best possible self' exercise from positive psychology. Researchers have found that imagining your ideal financial future – in detail – can increase your optimism and motivation, and inspire smart money habits. People who wrote about their best possible financial selves felt more satisfaction with how they got and spent money, saved more, and frittered away less cash on good-but-non-essential purchases. The scientists believed that picturing success stimulated preparedness in the brain for such change. So, set aside a few minutes to paint a happy financial picture of yourself, and watch out: you could be on your way to accelerating your wealth trajectory. Before you do, take the test below.

The best possible self: questionnaire

Here is a questionnaire to assess attitudes towards using the best possible self (BPS) intervention to improve financial wellbeing.

For each of the ten statements, circle the number that reflects your level of agreement. Add up the scores to gain an initial understanding of your financial wellbeing. After studying the chapter and completing the recommended exercises, revisit the survey. You needn't share your responses with anyone; it's merely a tool to assess any changes or improvements in your perspective.

1. **I can vividly imagine my financial life in the future.**
   Strongly disagree – 1
   Disagree – 2
   Neutral – 3
   Agree – 4
   Strongly agree – 5

2. **Imagining my future financial life motivates me to take actions to achieve my money goals.**
   Strongly disagree – 1
   Disagree – 2
   Neutral – 3
   Agree – 4
   Strongly agree – 5

3. **I have a clear picture of the financial life I want to have in the future.**
   Strongly disagree – 1
   Disagree – 2
   Neutral – 3
   Agree – 4
   Strongly agree – 5

4. **I feel a strong connection to the financial life I envision for my future self.**
   Strongly disagree – 1
   Disagree – 2

Neutral – 3
Agree – 4
Strongly agree – 5

5. **My current financial life is very close to my ideal.**
   Strongly disagree – 1
   Disagree – 2
   Neutral – 3
   Agree – 4
   Strongly agree – 5

6. **I energetically work towards my financial goals.**
   Strongly disagree – 1
   Disagree – 2
   Neutral – 3
   Agree – 4
   Strongly agree – 5

7. **I can think of many ways to achieve my financial goals.**
   Strongly disagree – 1
   Disagree – 2
   Neutral – 3
   Agree – 4
   Strongly agree – 5

8. **I feel satisfied with my current financial situation.**
   Strongly disagree – 1
   Disagree – 2
   Neutral – 3
   Agree – 4
   Strongly agree – 5

9. **I am optimistic about my ability to create the financial future I desire.**
   Strongly disagree – 1
   Disagree – 2
   Neutral – 3
   Agree – 4
   Strongly agree – 5

10. **When I imagine my ideal financial life, I feel hopeful and empowered.**
    Strongly disagree – 1
    Disagree – 2
    Neutral – 3
    Agree – 4
    Strongly agree – 5

My total score:

Introduction

Picture your life five, ten – perhaps even twenty years from now, in which everything has gone as well as it possibly could have . . . What comes to mind? This simple, yet powerful mental exercise – referred to as the best possible self (BPS) intervention – can be traced back to positive psychology. Introduced by its founder, Martin Seligman,[1] as a general strategy for increasing optimism and countering learned pessimism, BPS involves visualising and describing in writing your best possible self in the future. And it's seen to have beneficial effects on happiness, motivation and wellbeing.

How does the best possible self intervention work?

When you do the BPS exercise you are guided to envision your life in the future under the assumption that everything has worked out as well as it possibly could. You consider how things are going in various domains of your life – your work life, your social life, your romantic life, your life as a physical being, as a moral person, as a citizen. You get specific when you can and you reflect on what your ideal self and your ideal life might look like. In the process of doing this, you are tapping into the good feelings that can come with imagining success; this can serve as a confidence boost and motivate you to move towards your goals.[2]

The BPS intervention typically involves writing about your best possible self for 15–20 minutes a day for a week or two (there are variations, however, such as using mental imagery – picturing your best possible self in your mind's eye – or drawing or creating a vision board depicting your ideal future). The key is to think deeply about it.

Studies have found that the BPS intervention can lead to all sorts of benefits, like:

- feeling happier and more satisfied with life;
- feeling better about yourself and more driven to make positive changes;
- being better at setting goals and staying on track.[3]

What's more, these positive effects appear to occur more quickly with the BPS exercise when compared with other similar techniques: you don't have to practise for long before you start to see benefits.[4] Some research suggests that even a single session of BPS writing can result in an immediate increase in positive mood and optimism.[5]

Positive psychology and financial behaviours

Fair enough. But what's any of that got to do with money? Well, it turns out that positive psychology researchers have also found that building positive emotions, hope, meaning and self-efficacy leads to more constructive attitudes and behaviours in financial matters. For example: positive feelings increase cognitive diversity, expand behavioural options and make it easier for us to make better choices and decisions. By opening up our thinking and decision-making, positive emotions can lead us towards smarter financial options and increase our ability to pick the best actions for ourselves. As a concrete example, in the previously discussed study, when participants felt grateful, generous and liked, they were more likely to try new and quirky products that were outside of their comfort zone, but that were more suitable than existing choices.[6] Feeling hopeful and optimistic is connected to saving more and investing.[7] Gratitude and a sense of meaning can encourage us to spend more mindfully.[8] And positive psychology techniques have been shown to specifically boost financial knowledge and attitudes.[9]

Therefore, it makes sense that doing a positive psychology exercise such as BPS, tailored specifically towards visualising your optimal financial future self, might help to encourage desirable shifts in financial behaviour and outcomes. By mobilising optimism, self-efficacy and motivation in the financial domain, the BPS intervention can facilitate the ability of people to make better money decisions and to work towards their financial goals.

In short, having a hopeful, confident, resilient and wise 'money mindset' can translate into healthier money behaviours and greater satisfaction with our financial condition. The BPS exercise serves as one technique for achieving this goal.

Possible selves and goal setting

The intervention developed by the BPS is, in part, based on the idea of 'possible selves', as in the futures you envision for yourself.[10] A possible self is someone we actually are or imagine we could become in the future, and when we visualise our possible selves we connect to the hopes, fears and aspirations that drive our behaviour and shape our dreams.

Possible selves can be positive (such as your best possible financial self) or negative (such as your worst possible, debt-ridden self). Experiments actually demonstrate that, when your positive possible self is well crafted and vivid (for example, enthusiastic about turning your finances around), you'll be more motivated and goal-directed. A negative possible self (getting into more debt, and falling behind on your commitments to yourself) can spur avoidance, and even prevent you from wanting to try new things.[11]

Another important step is goal setting – approach-oriented goals (those that get us closer to what we want) that we set in line with our ideal possible selves are more likely to be attained compared with those which are avoidance-oriented, moving us away from what we don't want.[12] Therefore, implementing the BPS in your finances means putting an image and a picture to your hoped-for financial future self. What does your best possible financial life look like? How much would you choose to save and invest? How much would you choose to spend and on what? How would you plan to live your life and what values would shape your life and your financial choices? Thinking through your financial future in a positive way will help you see what your goals and hopes are, and the picture itself will make you feel motivated and hopeful about getting there and experiencing financial wellbeing.

Empirical studies and research findings

Increasing evidence also highlights that BPS intervention can promote positive material change in financial returns. Research has found that participants who complete BPS writing and visualisation exercises about finances report greater satisfaction with their current financial position, and are more motivated to greater saving and moderate spending compared with those who do not perform such exercises.[13]

Numbers corroborate this too. Having done a financial BPS visualisation, people score higher on questionnaires that measure financial self-efficacy (the belief in one's ability to manage one's finances). They also score higher on scales that measure self-regulation and goal setting.[14] When interviewed, participants say that they feel more hopeful and optimistic about their financial situation after having taken several minutes to imagine their best possible financial life and self.

Applied to low-income, financially unstable families, one study demonstrated that those following the BPS exercise borrowed money more carefully and accumulated more savings over six months, compared with a control group that didn't take the exercise. The researchers believe that the BPS technique enhances feelings of self-efficacy and hope, qualities that enable people to make good decisions about money, even when money is in very short supply.[15]

In another study, subjects did a BPS exercise about their financial future before making hypothetical spending decisions. Subjects in the BPS group decided to spend less money on short-term purchases than a general control group, saving more for the future. They were also more likely to contribute to a long-term investment scheme and allocated more of their finances to savings and investment than to immediate purchases.[16]

In sum, there is growing research that suggests that BPS is effective – that imagining and writing about your best possible financial life can increase your optimism, encourage pro-social spending and saving, and most importantly help to create financial goals, ultimately leading to better financial outcomes. Of course, more research is needed to find out if improved financial outcomes are maintained over time. The findings to date, however, have many positive implications. The field of positive psychology has demonstrated a great deal of promise in its impact on wellbeing, and that promise could be even greater for financial wellbeing.

Practical applications and case studies

Thankfully, we have several positive real-world examples of people using the BPS intervention, including financial advisers employing it with their clients. One financial planner says that, during the planning process, he asks clients to imagine their ideal retirement and future financial life. In the clients who have been through the BPS visualisation, he sees a unique shift where clients report feeling more motivated and clearer about their retirement goals.[17]

In a separate study, a woman with a tendency towards overspending reported that she yearned for luxury purchases less frequently after writing regularly about her best possible self.[18] Instead, she began to think more about what she was saving up for, and so was able to make better financial choices.

Financial counsellors, too, have found that teaching BPS techniques in workshops for people struggling with debt or overconsumption can lead to similar positive outcomes.[19] Imagining a life free of financial stress helped motivate people to reshape their habits. Some of the counsellors I spoke to described using guided BPS meditations or having clients construct vision boards of the future life they aspired to achieve one day.

There are also apps and online programmes that incorporate different aspects of the BPS intervention to assist with financial goal setting and bolster motivation. For example, the app Nav.it has a feature called 'My Future Self', in which the user is asked to envision a future in which they're ten or fifteen years older and have stayed true to their financial plan. According to the Nav.it website, doing this is meant to 'help you make smarter money choices in the present by invoking your future self'.

Integration with financial education and counselling

The research suggests that incorporating BPS within financial education programmes and counselling may be highly valuable; having students or clients consider and write about their BPS may motivate them, and bolster their sense of self-efficacy and their positive financial behaviours.[20]

Licensed counsellors can incorporate BPS visualisation and writing exercises into counselling sessions when clients are discussing debt, savings goals, estate planning or related subjects, including the accumulation of retirement savings. BPS-based interventions can also be a part of financial workshops with structured individual and group exercises geared towards picturing your own preferred financial sense of self.

Some specific ways to integrate BPS
- Have clients write a letter from their future financial self, describing their ideal financial situation and the steps they took to get there.
- Use guided imagery to have clients vividly picture a day in their ideal financial life.
- Assign BPS journalling as 'homework' between financial counselling sessions.
- Incorporate vision boards or other creative expressions of financial possible selves.
- Encourage financial education students to reflect on their best possible financial selves before learning about budgeting, investing, etc.

The key is to help people connect positive, hopeful visions of their financial future with concrete financial knowledge and behaviour. By getting in touch with their ideal financial selves, they may be more motivated to learn and take positive financial actions.

Conclusion

In summary, then, there is a growing evidence base that the BPS intervention from positive psychology has interesting applicability in the field of personal finance. When people create and contemplate in detail their BPS financial life, it seems that perceptions of optimism, self-efficacy, motivation, and prudent money management all increase. Done thoughtfully, the BPS exercise might prod some of us towards greater financial wisdom and wellbeing.

After all, visualising your richest future self is not a magic bullet. Like any tool, it should be used with supplementary financial literacy training, wise, fiscally prudent habits and professional help where needed. However, the available mental magic research seems to indicate that it's a potent tool – one that draws on the power of the mind, the human imagination and our capacity to author our own lives through narrative construction.

The more clearly we imagine an affirmative financial future, the more likely we are to picture ourselves living that reality, and the more inclined we are to take actions in the present that move us towards our future – a kind of north star for our finances. And, step by step, day by day, we can bridge the gap between the reality we're living in now, and the 'different me' we might be. The BPS intervention encourages us to engage with our imaginations, and use them to create that different self.

So take a moment, close your eyes, and visualise it: What does your best financial self look like? What does it do? What can you do now to start to bring it into being?

Activity 9.1: Written BPS narrative

Instructions:

- Write a story or journal entry describing your best possible financial life.
- Include specifics like your career, income, investments, the lifestyle you can afford, your philanthropic goals and values.
- Elaborate on your imagined ideal financial situation.

Details:

- **Career and income:** Describe your dream job and income.
- **Investments:** Outline your investment strategies and goals.
- **Lifestyle:** Detail your lifestyle, including housing, vacations and hobbies.
- **Philanthropy:** Explain your philanthropic goals and the causes you support.
- **Values:** Reflect on the values that guide your financial decisions.

Activity 9.2: Vision board

Instructions:

- Create a vision board or collage using images and words that represent your best possible financial future.
- Include pictures of homes, vacations, retirement activities and donation recipients that depict your aspirational wealth and lifestyle.

Details:

- **Images:** Cut and paste or draw images that represent your financial goals.
- **Words:** Add words or phrases that encapsulate your financial aspirations.
- **Themes:** Identify key emotional themes such as security, freedom or generosity.

Activity 9.3: Letter to your future financial self

Instructions:

- Write a letter to your future self detailing your financial aspirations, your goals, and the steps you plan to take to achieve them.
- Reflect on the positive changes you anticipate and express confidence in your ability to succeed.

Details:

- **Introduction:** Greet your future self and set the context.
- **Goals:** List your financial goals.
- **Steps:** Outline the steps you plan to take to achieve these goals.
- **Reflection:** Reflect on the positive changes you expect and express confidence in your future success.

Activity 9.4: Financial goal mind mapping

Instructions:

- Create a mind map of your financial goals.

- Use branches to represent different aspects of your financial life, such as savings, investments and debt reduction.
- Connect specific actions and strategies to each goal.

Details:

- **Central idea:** Write 'financial goals' in the centre of your mind map.
- **Branches:** Create branches for different aspects like savings, investments, debt reduction and expenses.
- **Sub-branches:** Add sub-branches for specific actions and strategies related to each main branch.
- **Connections:** Draw connections between actions, strategies and goals.

After completing all the activities, please go back to the start of the chapter and attempt the best possible self questionnaire again to check the difference in the result.

Resources

Below are some extra materials to enhance your comprehension of your best possible self and its influence on overall wellness.

Books

Flourish: A Visionary New Understanding of Happiness and Wellbeing by Martin Seligman, Free Press, 2011
 This book presents Seligman's theory of wellbeing, emphasising the importance of a fulfilling life through positive psychology.
The How of Happiness: A New Approach to Getting the Life You Want by Sonja Lyubomirsky, Penguin Press, 2007

Lyubomirsky offers scientifically backed strategies for increasing happiness and achieving a meaningful life.

Positivity by Barbara L. Fredrickson, Crown Publishing Group, 2009

A book exploring the power of positive emotions and how they can enhance our overall wellbeing and resilience.

Websites

Positive Psychology article on BPS intervention: positivepsychology.com/best-possible-self

Greater Good Magazine article explaining the BPS exercise: greatergood.berkeley.edu/article/item/try_this_the_best_possible_self

Psychology Today article on what is your best possible self: www.psychologytoday.com/us/blog/what-matters-most/201303/what-is-your-best-possible-self

Videos

TEDx Talk on using the BPS method

Sonja Lyubomirsky explaining the technique

Positive Psychology Intervention: Your Best Self (Ideal Self) | Science of Happiness

Apps

Woop – Has a feature for setting BPS goals: www.woopmylife.org

ThinkUp – Gratitude and positive psychology app with BPS exercises: www.thinkup.me

Blog/journal articles

'The Effects of a Best Possible Self Intervention on Positive Affect: A Randomized Controlled Trial' by Layous, L., Chancellor, J., et al. (2014), doi.org/10.1371/journal.pone.0094155
'Gratitude, Self-esteem, and the Science of Optimal Functioning: A Literature Review' by Wood, A. M., Joseph, S., et al. (2009), doi.org/10.1080/17439760902933690

Podcasts

The Happiness Lab podcast episode on optimising the best possible self: www.happinesslab.fm/season-1-episodes/the-optimized-best-self
Happier with Gretchen Rubin, podcast episode on imagining your best possible self: gretchenrubin.com/2012/01/transcript-21-imagining-your-best-possible-self
Happiness for Cynics podcast episode 98, how to be your best possible self: arieskelton.com/podcast-how-to-be-your-podcast-best-possible-self

Brain/psychology/ thoughts

This section explores how psychological insights and cognitive techniques can transform your relationship with money.

CHAPTER 10

Cognitive behavioural therapy

Stress is like a playlist – just hit
'next' on the bad thoughts

Before we explore how cognitive behavioural therapy (CBT) can assist in transforming unhelpful money beliefs, let's begin with a quick survey to assess your current comprehension of money and wellbeing.

CBT and money questionnaire

This questionnaire allows the identification of your money beliefs based on CBT theory about common cognitive distortions and unhelpful attitudes with regard to finances. The results can guide the focus of CBT interventions to challenge problematic thoughts and replace them with more adaptive money beliefs and behaviours.

Rate how much you agree with each statement below by circling the relevant number, and add up your score.

1. **I believe money is the key to happiness.**
   Strongly disagree – 1
   Disagree – 2
   Somewhat disagree – 3
   Neither agree nor disagree – 4
   Somewhat agree – 5
   Agree – 6
   Strongly agree – 7

2. **I feel I don't deserve to have a lot of money.**
   Strongly disagree – 1
   Disagree – 2
   Somewhat disagree – 3
   Neither agree nor disagree – 4
   Somewhat agree – 5
   Agree – 6
   Strongly agree – 7

3. **I think rich people are smarter than poor people.**
   Strongly disagree – 1
   Disagree – 2
   Somewhat disagree – 3
   Neither agree nor disagree – 4
   Somewhat agree – 5
   Agree – 6
   Strongly agree – 7

4. **I feel anxious when thinking about my finances.**
   Strongly disagree – 1
   Disagree – 2
   Somewhat disagree – 3
   Neither agree nor disagree – 4

Somewhat agree – 5
Agree – 6
Strongly agree – 7

5. **I feel I have little control over my financial situation.**
Strongly disagree – 1
Disagree – 2
Somewhat disagree – 3
Neither agree nor disagree – 4
Somewhat agree – 5
Agree – 6
Strongly agree – 7

6. **I deserve to buy myself things I want, even if I can't really afford them.**
Strongly disagree – 1
Disagree – 2
Somewhat disagree – 3
Neither agree nor disagree – 4
Somewhat agree – 5
Agree – 6
Strongly agree – 7

7. **Having the latest technology and clothes is important for showing I'm successful.**
Strongly disagree – 1
Disagree – 2
Somewhat disagree – 3
Neither agree nor disagree – 4
Somewhat agree – 5
Agree – 6
Strongly agree – 7

8. **I use shopping as a way to make myself feel better.**
   Strongly disagree – 1
   Disagree – 2
   Somewhat disagree – 3
   Neither agree nor disagree – 4
   Somewhat agree – 5
   Agree – 6
   Strongly agree – 7

9. **I avoid looking at my bank account because it causes too much stress.**
   Strongly disagree – 1
   Disagree – 2
   Somewhat disagree – 3
   Neither agree nor disagree – 4
   Somewhat agree – 5
   Agree – 6
   Strongly agree – 7

10. **I grew up believing money was scarce.**
    Strongly disagree – 1
    Disagree – 2
    Somewhat disagree – 3
    Neither agree nor disagree – 4
    Somewhat agree – 5
    Agree – 6
    Strongly agree – 7

My total score:

Let's now examine the research on utilising cognitive be-haviours therapy (CBT) to transform the detrimental financial behaviours that stem from irrational money mindsets.

Introduction

It's no fun to be stressed about money. It can make us into constant worriers, lead us to bicker with our partners, even feel ashamed. But there is good news: research shows that changing what we think can make a difference in how we spend, save or earn money. Cognitive behavioural therapy has been used to help people spot patterns in their thinking that lead them to make bad decisions. It can also teach them new, more helpful mental and emotional skills. In short, CBT has the potential to help people make much better decisions on a regular basis. In this chapter, we'll delve into some of the promising – and still-developing – CBT methods that researchers have recently studied to treat specific money blocks. We'll look at how CBT has been used to help ease anxiety for entrepreneurs and to stem shopping compulsions. Then we'll review how therapists can help patients peel back unhelpful money mindsets. It seems that it might be possible for well-tailored CBT to become part of the mental muscle system that brings more harmony to our financial lives. By shining a light onto the mental drivers hidden behind spending, saving or earning, CBT can help us write a healthier money story.[1]

The basic ideas behind using CBT for money problems

CBT intervenes in financial distress by making explicit relationships between our thoughts, feelings and habits that we might not otherwise notice. The starting point is that how we think about money, relationships, work and even our own self-worth are incredibly important factors in our subjective wellbeing.

However, our surface-level thinking about money often stems from deeper beliefs such as: 'I need to constantly hustle to make it happen'; 'I don't deserve to be wealthy'; 'using credit equals being free'. Therefore, money stress shows up when dysfunctional or inaccurate core beliefs are coupled with unhealthy automatic thoughts, intense feelings such as fear, anger or shame, and, ultimately, dysfunctional behaviours such as over-spending or compulsive hoarding of money, that undermine our own interests.

CBT theory suggests that paying attention to the mindsets that underpin repetitive thoughts and pointing out the illogical nature of those thoughts can generate awareness of what is driving money distress, as well as offering an opportunity to consider more useful thoughts by applying questions of logic and evidence checks. As awareness of these mental shifts sinks in, we become aware of our emotions and choices and can reframe them to produce different outcomes. Relief from money stress occurs when out-of-date and rigid ideas about finance and self-worth that no longer match our present-day life are adjusted.[2]

Our newfound mental flexibility and skill around working with discomfort, aids money behaviours such as budgeting, having difficult talks about shared money, staying in a job and finishing projects, or avoiding impulse purchases. CBT facilitates psychological insight, hope and useful tools to facilitate healthier money realities.

Common unhelpful money beliefs and thinking traps

Most money anxiety comes down to a handful of subtle but pervasive mental traps. Maybe you're plagued by perfectionism beliefs, such as that 'a budget is either perfect or it's a failure', which makes it hard to stick to when you make a mistake. Or you blame yourself with thoughts such as 'I spent some money on a dinner out, so I'm an irresponsible idiot who will never get my finances under control.'

Or you may have skewed perceptions of need – such as 'I need the latest iPhone if I'm going to fit in', if fitting in does not actually require a fancy phone – or unreasonable wants ('any frivolous spending is obviously wrong'). Both extremes stretch wellbeing in their own different ways.[3]

And it's all too easy to catastrophise – 'this unanticipated medical bill totally turns my world upside down!' Emotional reasoning is likewise rampant around money – 'I feel guilty about having bought this expensive gadget, so it must be profoundly wrong'.[4]

True, there are real money issues, but thinking traps make tense consumer situations even more stressed, adding character judgements or perfectionistic thinking to what might be a bump in the road or one of many learning curves. Indeed, one of the keys to challenging thoughts that are triggered automatically and reflexively in a situation is to recognise the pattern as it arises, so that it doesn't take over the way it did before.

How well does CBT work for money challenges?

Several studies have directly tested CBT with money issues. For example, group CBT workshops reduced financial anxiety and worry, and improved the confidence and skills associated with money management, in business owners and married couples.[5] Overcoming thought distortions about self-worth and teaching some basic budgeting skills appeared to drive these improvements. For compulsive shoppers, specific CBT aimed at identifying the emotions that trigger a need to buy, and following a series of steps that help to resist the rationalisations inhibiting healthy spending, produced meaningful reductions in buying urges.[6]

Training in awareness and reframing of financially related automatic thoughts helped debt-laden university students increase their monthly savings rates over six months.[7] When entrepreneurs suffering from rocky cash flow practised cognitive restructuring and visualisation techniques, they were helped to shift from their boom–bust mindsets to more consistent, process-oriented world views that were more focused on the steps and methods involved in achieving a goal and less shaken by intermittent successes and failures.[8]

More work is needed to test how CBT works in real-life contexts over longer periods of time. However, empirical studies do show that CBT is a promising road to building healthier financial attitudes and behaviours.[9] Initial findings on early intervention should also boost investment in new CBT approaches that are tailored to modern money disorders, and are accessible in formats such as apps or interactive workshops.

CBT for specific money-related challenges

Some researchers have adapted CBT techniques to target individuals' damaging money habits by means of 'psychological nudges' instead of autocratic budget controls. In one study that focused on America's biggest binge-shoppers – hoarders – eight weeks of CBT that put an emphasis on becoming aware of the emotional triggers that made them want to spend, not giving in to rationalisations of their spending, and being in the moment while shopping, decreased spending urges by an average of 83 per cent.[10] Journalling and visualising more meaningful ways to use the money went a long way to help those with maladaptive coping needs, while at the same time helping to boost their savings.

Another study was aimed at students in serious debt distress. Six virtual CBT lessons were delivered to change the automatic thinking that led them to blame themselves and to reinforce goal-setting skills that would allow them to repay debts responsibly, together with lessons in stress management techniques. Compared with an untrained healthy control group, the CBT group cut their debt approximately in half over six months and boosted their emotional wellbeing.[11] A third study used electronic delivery for a set of financial self-help training modules, combined with financial coaching. This produced positive effects on clients' self-reported quality of financial habits.[12]

The study found that a special group class was very helpful for people struggling with money issues.[13] The class combined two key elements:

- It retrained people's perfectionist mindsets about money.
- It reduced unhealthy comparisons to others.

After taking the class, participants saw a big improvement – over 30 per cent – in their confidence and ability to stand up for themselves when it came to money matters. This was much better than the results for people who were on a waiting list for the class.

The class also taught participants to be more flexible. This made it easier for them to let go of constant worries about money and instead focus on their true, authentic goals.

Group CBT v. individual CBT

Workshop and one-on-one CBT formats can both potentially shift unconscious problematic financial thinking. In groups, 'Aha!' moments of recognition and reassurance were gained from hearing fellow money-disordered individuals (such as compulsive gamblers) talk about their struggle.[14] However, some participants had issues of privacy around open discussion and mustering the courage to put one's personal 'dirt' on the table for others to observe. The accountability partners – individuals who support and motivate each other to achieve their goals – formed in the classes provide regular reminders to participants, which helps motivate them to practise the new skills between lessons. This reinforces the learning process and supports participants in applying what they've learned.

Studies of entrepreneurs report that group and individual CBT coaching were equally effective in increasing optimism and mental health – but it was noticed that the groups tended to create longer-lasting peer communities.[15] Cost-wise, individuals often can't afford the intimacy that one individual would provide. But specifically tailored guidance, once it homes in on your unique psychological pitfalls, hits the bullseye more precisely than a group model.

For those who need more intimacy but also want some of the accountability or camaraderie to be found in a group, hybrid options that involve using web-based individual lesson sequences with occasional group discussions or meetings might be a good compromise. In the end, whether in individual or group formats, CBT offers helpful frameworks that therapists can tailor into money stress solutions within a myriad of social formats, as long as these stay rooted in CBT's core principles of working on thinking traps by encouraging emotional awareness and critical thinking.

CBT and financial literacy education

Mixing evidence-based tools from CBT with typical money management lessons has proved more effective than straight-up dry lectures. When researchers combined techniques such as catching automatic negative thoughts about a budget or vis-ualising ideal future selves with standard lessons on numeracy, investing, insurance and so on, people who received CBT-enhanced financial literacy training were less overwhelmed and more motivated to apply what they learned than those who were taught plain literacy. For example, one study on low-income students combined eight weeks of CBT designed to shift money mindsets and games that taught critical financial concepts (such as interest rates or credit scores) to boost goal setting. Afterwards, 70 per cent of the CBT-boosted group repaid money into their savings accounts in the next six months compared with just 30 per cent of the group that received financial knowledge without psychological backup.[16]

Blending best practice in both cognitive behavioural interven-tions and personal finance education creates stronger engagement and more enduring behaviour change than financial literacy education programmes alone. Programmes that specifically educate about the problematic money beliefs and attitudes that underlie financial challenges can create huge value over and above simply providing functional money skills that too easily fall prey to poor follow-through.[17]

Boosting abundance-oriented money attitudes with positive psychology techniques

Complementing CBT's emphasis on neutralising negative thinking about money was evidence from researchers experimenting with positive psychology to promote more adaptive, constructive thinking and emotions, often by encouraging people to reflect on and consider how they'd ideally like to be in the world of work, money management and life.[18]

Visually imagining one's financial best self, along with every detail for each life domain, and clarifying which skills and strengths are required to bring that optimal future into reality, builds a stronger motivating force that draws people towards smarter choices.[19] One study of young adults found that prompting people to record their best possible financial self for fifteen minutes led to increased motivation and plans to earn, save and invest in the following month compared with a control group who wrote about a neutral topic.

An additional well-studied positive psychology intervention, recording daily gratitude, appears to serve an abundance mindset that resists the impulse to seek happiness through consumption as well as to spur patience that favours longer-run outcomes. Expressing gratitude for non-material sources of joy, such as relationships and experiences, appears to weaken the desire to buy oneself into contentment through goods. Daily reminders of appreciation spur the very patience that favours longer-run returns over short-term indulgences.[20]

We need more long-term data on the impact of these tentative positive psychology findings. Critics point out that, without concrete action, visualisations alone aren't enough but, according to meta-analyses, the interventions help to meaningfully boost optimism and positive affect.[21] It appears that these motivational and emotional changes, together with the more cognitive approach of CBT and improved financial education to give a basic knowledge, do form a powerful way of changing real financial behaviour. A range of tools, relying on the most persuasive techniques from both the CBT and positive psychology camps, seem to be a promising new frontier in helping us forge healthier financial habits.

Conclusion

In short, there are lots of studies demonstrating that CBT is effective in helping make you better at using money. Whether you're suffering from overspending, debt stress, or you've just never been any good with money, both individual and group CBT sessions really work in enabling you to identify when your money and spending thoughts might be a little skewed and provide tools to make more positive money moves. That said, more research still needs to be done around the effectiveness of CBT, but it looks so far as if CBT could be a good place to start making lasting positive changes with your money, particularly when allied to the positive psychology interventions detailed in other chapters.

Activity 10.1: Financial thought tracker

Over the next seven days, every time you experience an automatic negative thought or spiralling of thoughts about money, fill out the table on p. 188:

Description of table elements:

- **Day:** Record the specific day of the week to observe variations in your thought patterns over time.
- **Source of trigger:** Identify the specific event or context that prompted a negative thought, such as a financial decision, a conversation about money, or external stimuli like news articles or advertisements.
- **Duration of the trigger:** Note how long the trigger impacted your thoughts, indicating whether it was a fleeting moment of anxiety or a prolonged period of worry.
- **Automatic thought:** Write down the immediate thought that arose, capturing your instinctive reaction to the trigger (e.g. 'I can't afford this').
- **Cognitive distortion:** Label the specific type of cognitive distortion (e.g. all-or-nothing thinking or emotional reasoning) that characterises the automatic thought, helping to pinpoint flawed reasoning.[*]
- **Frequency:** Record how many times the thought occurred throughout the day in order to quantify its prevalence and understand its effect on your emotional state.
- **Intensity (1–10):** Rate the emotional intensity of the thought on a scale from 1 (minimal impact) to 10 (overwhelming), providing insight into the strength of your emotional response.

This table structure encourages you to record each element of an automatic thought every day through the space given for seven days. Recording the thought in a table format can help you recognise some unhelpful thinking habits around money that you can then address further by using other CBT techniques to help you change.

---

[*] The common distortion list is available in Appendix 1.

Day	Source of trigger	Duration of the trigger	Automatic thought	Cognitive distortion	Frequency	Intensity (1–10)
Day 1						
Day 2						
Day 3						
Day 4						
Day 5						
Day 6						
Day 7						

After you've done this activity for seven days, revisit the CBT and money questionnaire from the start of this chapter. Evaluate whether your responses have evolved or changed.

The common distortion list is available in Appendix 1.

Activity 10.2: A seven-day CBT programme for financial wellness

This seven-day programme is consistent with the techniques of CBT for altering a dysfunctional relationship with money, and adheres to the science of the brain (or cognitive processing) and of behavioural changes. If the goal is to change your relationship with money, the journey begins here.

Day 1: Self-reflection
On the first day, spend 15–20 minutes in self-reflection (by answering questions about your current money beliefs, such as thoughts, attitudes and feelings about money). Self-reflection can be viewed as the inspiration for change and is one of the metacognitive strategies to support changing how we think. It engages the prefrontal cortex which is important for self-awareness and cognitive changes.

Instructions:
- Spend 15–20 minutes in quiet contemplation.
- List your current money beliefs: what do you think, feel and believe about money?

Example: A common one is: 'I notice I worry a lot about checking my bank balance and experiencing guilt'.

Day 2: Automatic thoughts
The second day, think about your automatic negative thoughts

about money – the ones that come up all the time – and record them. Recognising and codifying these thoughts is the first stage of awareness when it comes to your money thinking. Here you engage brain regions that are connected to self-observation and emotion.

Instructions:
- Identify an automatic negative thought you often have about money.
- Write it down and record any associated emotions.

Example: You might identify an automatic thought such as: 'I'm terrible with money.' Then notice the feelings of self-criticism that follow that thought (such as hopelessness, worthlessness or helplessness).

Day 3: Cognitive distortions
Day 3 provides education about common 'cognitive distortions' that are associated with money beliefs.* These thinking errors can trigger unhelpful beliefs. Learning about them is an important component of recognising your thinking patterns and is consistent with cognitive restructuring.

Instructions:
- Study and understand common cognitive distortions related to money beliefs (e.g. catastrophising, all-or-nothing thinking).
- Identify and label which distortions apply to your money-related thoughts.

For example: 'If I mess up with money in any way my whole life will fall apart' (catastrophising).

---

* The common distortion list is available in Appendix 1.

Day 4: Challenging distortions

Identifying and addressing the irrational thought processes that underpin cognitive distortions is fundamental to cognitive restructuring, but it can be achieved by providing rational counterarguments or evidence, to promote cognitive flexibility.

Instructions:
- For each of the cognitive distortions you identified on Day 3, provide rational counterarguments or evidence.
- Begin the process of reframing these distorted beliefs into more balanced ones.

Example: If you have identified the distortion 'catastrophising', challenge it by reminding yourself of other financial setbacks you had in the past and managed to overcome.

Day 5: Reframing beliefs

Day 5 involves learning to reframe your problematic thoughts – in other words, to counter them with more adaptive or balanced beliefs. This engages the networks crucial for emotion regulation and cognitive control.

Instructions:
- Choose one of your negative thoughts about money to reframe as a more constructive or neutral one.
- Write down the new belief and consider how it differs from the original thought.

Example: 'I'm bad with money' becomes 'I'm getting better at managing my finances.'

Day 6: Positive affirmations

Day 6 looks at positive affirmations, which invoke the psychology of unhelpful cognitive patterns to ensure new beliefs are embedded.

Instructions:
- Create positive money affirmations based on the reframed belief from Day 5.
- Repeat these affirmations throughout the day to reinforce your new, healthier beliefs.

Example: If, instead, you needed to reframe your pattern to 'I'm getting better at managing my finances', your affirmation would be: 'I am money-savvy. I am getting smarter with money.'

Day 7: Commitment and action

Finally, on day 7, you focus on commitment and action. Write a commitment letter and develop an action plan so that your cognitive changes result in real material changes in your money management behaviours.

Instructions:
- Write a letter to yourself describing what you intend to do to support the healthier money thoughts in the left-hand column.
- Write an action plan, including the steps you will take to integrate your new beliefs into your financial activity.

Example: Your action plan could involve setting up a budget/seeking financial advice/following a savings plan.

You are welcome to use this programme with as many distorted thoughts as you'd like. I recommend starting with at least three thoughts for a comprehensive experience. After you've finished this activity for three distorted thoughts, revisit the CBT and money questionnaire at the start of this chapter. Evaluate whether your responses have evolved or changed.

Resources

Here are more resources to expand your understanding of CBT and how it contributes to wellbeing.

Books

Feeling Good: The New Mood Therapy by David D. Burns, HarperCollins, 1980
This groundbreaking book introduces cognitive therapy techniques to help individuals combat depression and improve their mood.

Mind Over Mood by Dennis Greenberger and Christine Padesky, Guilford Press, 1995
A practical guide to managing emotions through cognitive behavioural techniques, complete with worksheets and exercises for self-improvement.

The Cognitive Behavioral Workbook for Depression by William J. Knaus, New Harbinger Publications, 2004
A workbook providing structured activities and exercises to help individuals recognise and alter negative thinking patterns related to depression.

The Cognitive Behavioral Workbook for Anxiety by William J. Knaus, New Harbinger Publications, 2005
A comprehensive workbook designed to help individuals address anxiety through practical exercises based on cognitive behavioural principles.

When Panic Attacks by David D. Burns, The Crown Publishing Group, 2006
Burns offers effective techniques to combat panic attacks and anxiety, providing readers with strategies for reclaiming their lives.

Retrain Your Brain: Cognitive Behavioral Therapy in 7 Weeks by Seth Gillihan, New Harbinger Publications, 2016

This concise programme guides readers through CBT techniques over seven weeks to effectively change negative thinking patterns and improve mental health.

Cognitive Behavioral Therapy Made Simple by Seth Gillihan, Guilford Press, 2016

A straightforward introduction to cognitive behavioural therapy that provides readers with essential strategies to address various mental health issues.

Cognitive Behavioral Therapy for Dummies by Rob Willson and Rhena Branch, Wiley, 2007

An accessible guide that demystifies cognitive behavioural therapy and offers practical tools for managing emotions and behaviours.

The Cognitive Behavioral Therapy Workbook for Personality Disorders by Jeffrey Wood, New Harbinger Publications, 2015

This workbook provides strategies and exercises specifically tailored for managing symptoms related to personality disorders through cognitive behavioural therapy.

Mindfulness-Based Cognitive Therapy for Depression by Zindel Segal, Mark Williams and John Teasdale, Guilford Press, 2002

A unique approach that combines cognitive therapy with mindfulness practices to prevent the recurrence of depression and promote emotional resilience.

Apps

MoodTools
CBT Thought Record Diary
Cognitive Diary CBT Self-Help
nOCD
Woebot
Beat Panic
Think CBT

CBT Referee
CBT Thought Record
Cognitive Distortions

Websites

Academy of Cognitive Therapy: academyofct.org
Beck Institute: beckinstitute.org
Psychology Tools: www.psychologytools.com/
    cbt-techniques-worksheets
Centre for Clinical Interventions: www.cci.health.wa.gov.au/
    Resources/Looking-After-Yourself
Getselfhelp.co.uk: www.getselfhelp.co.uk/cbtstep1.htm
Psych Central CBT: psychcentral.com/lib/
    in-depth-cognitive-behavioral-therapy
GoodTherapy CBT: www.goodtherapy.org/
    learn-about-therapy/types/cognitive-behavioral-therapy
Verywell Mind CBT: www.verywellmind.com/cognitive-
    behavioral-therapy-for-better-mental-health-3145107
Healtherapy Inc CBT: healthengine.com.au/info/
    cognitive-behavioural-therapy-cbt
Teach CBT teachcbt.com

Blog/journal articles

Hofmann, S. G., Asnaani, A., Vonk, I. J. J., Sawyer, A. T. &
    Fang, A. (2012). 'A Meta-Analysis of Cognitive-Behavioral
    Therapy for Adult Anxiety Disorders'. *Clinical Psychology
    Review.* www.ncbi.nlm.nih.gov/pmc/articles/PMC2883180
Edinger, J. D., & Means, M. K. (2005). 'Efficacy of Cognitive-
    Behavioral Therapy for Persistent Insomnia'. *Sleep Medicine
    Clinics.* www.ncbi.nlm.nih.gov/pmc/articles/PMC446220
Hollon, S. D., Thase, M.E. & Markowitz, J. C. (2019).
    'Cognitive-Behavioral Therapy for Treatment-Resistant

Depression'. *Journal of Clinical Psychiatry.* www.ncbi.nlm.nih.
gov/pmc/articles/PMC6007702

Wampold, B. E., & Imel, Z. E. (2015). 'Evaluating Five
Decades of Psychotherapy Outcome Research'. *American
Psychologist.* psycnet.apa.org/record/2019-45337-001

Williams, A. C., de C. & Eccleston, C. (2015).
'Cognitive Behavioral Therapy for Chronic Pain'.
Pain Medicine. academic.oup.com/painmedicine/
article/16/9/1713/2452888

Fairburn, C. G. & Harrison, P. J. (2015). 'Cognitive Behaviour
Therapy for Eating Disorders'. *Behaviour Research and
Therapy.* www.sciencedirect.com/science/article/abs/pii/
S0005796715000406

Morin, C. M., Culbert, J. P. & Schwartz, S. M. (1999). 'A
Meta-Analysis of Cognitive-Behavioral Treatments
for Insomnia'. *Behavior Therapy.* pubmed.ncbi.nlm.nih.
gov/11783247

Scott, J., Colom, F. & Vieta, E. (2015). 'Cognitive Behavioral
Therapy for Bipolar Disorder'. *American Journal of Psychiatry.*
www.ncbi.nlm.nih.gov/pmc/articles/PMC4580802

Pollack, M. H. (2004). 'Combining CBT and Pharmacotherapy
in the Treatment of Anxiety Disorders'. *Psychiatric Times.*
www.psychiatrictimes.com/view/combining-cbt-and-
pharmacotherapy-treatment-anxiety-disorders

Kuipers, E., et al. (2014). 'Cognitive Behaviour Therapy
for Psychosis: Systematic review and meta-analysis'.
British Journal of Psychiatry. www.cambridge.org/
core/journals/the-british-journal-of-psychiatry/
article/cognitivebehaviour-therapy-for-the-
symptoms-of-schizophrenia-systematic-review-and-
metaanalysis-with-examination-of-potential-bias/
C25D4E6A37B3D31F35FD8AC01FCDF282

Videos

Cognitive Behavioral Therapy Explanation
Cognitive Behavioral Therapy Addressing Negative Thoughts
How CBT Works
The Future of CBT and Mood Gym (TED Talk)
3 Instantly Calming CBT Techniques For Anxiety
Improving Mental Health Through Food and Diet
A CBT Framework for Anxiety Recovery
Cognitive Behavioral Therapy: Retraining Your Brain
    (TED Talk)
Overcome Anxiety & Depression with CBT Mindfulness
Everything you know about Obesity is Wrong (TED Talk)

Podcasts

The CBT Podcast with Chris Williams: thecbtpodcast.libsyn.com
The Anxiety Podcast: theanxioustruth.com/category/podcast
The OCD Stories Podcast: theocdstories.com/podcast
The Depression Sessions: www.abc.net.au/radio/programs/
    the-depression-sessions
Therapy for Black Girls Podcast: therapyforblackgirls.com/podcast
The One You Feed Podcast: oneyoufeed.net/podcast
The Happiness Lab Podcast: www.pushkin.fm/show/
    the-happiness-lab-with-dr-laurie-santos
The Hilarious World of Depression Podcast: www.apmpodcasts.
    org/thwod
Mental Illness Happy Hour Podcast: mentalpod.com/shows/
    mental-illness-happy-hour

CHAPTER 11

Rational emotive behaviour therapy (REBT)

Drop the 'musts' – life isn't following your script anyway

Rational emotive behaviour therapy (REBT) helps people improve their financial wellbeing by targeting the irrational beliefs and emotions that drive poor money decisions. In this chapter you'll learn about REBT and do some practical activities, but before that try this small questionnaire about REBT.

REBT and money questionnaire

The purpose of this survey is to assist you in tracking and assessing your personal growth with the help of REBT intervention. For each of the ten statements provided, circle the number that corresponds with your level of agreement. Calculate the total score to obtain an initial sense of your financial wellbeing. Once you have completed the chapter and engaged in the suggested exercises, review the survey again. You are not required to disclose your answers; the survey is simply a tool to gauge any shifts or enhancements in your outlook.

1. **I can easily identify when my financial thoughts are influenced by irrational or unhelpful beliefs.**
   Strongly disagree – 1
   Disagree – 2
   Neutral – 3
   Agree – 4
   Strongly agree – 5

2. **I actively challenge and dispute irrational financial beliefs to promote healthier thinking.**
   Strongly disagree – 1
   Disagree – 2
   Neutral – 3
   Agree – 4
   Strongly agree – 5

3. **Engaging in open discussions about money is a comfortable and effective way for me to address financial issues.**
   Strongly disagree – 1
   Disagree – 2
   Neutral – 3
   Agree – 4
   Strongly agree – 5

4. **I am resilient in the face of financial setbacks, viewing them as opportunities for growth.**
   Strongly disagree – 1
   Disagree – 2
   Neutral – 3

Agree – 4
Strongly agree – 5

5. **I actively seek out new information and perspectives to enhance my financial knowledge.**
Strongly disagree – 1
Disagree – 2
Neutral – 3
Agree – 4
Strongly agree – 5

6. **I have more balanced, flexible preferences related to money rather than rigid demands.**
Strongly disagree – 1
Disagree – 2
Neutral – 3
Agree – 4
Strongly agree – 5

7. **I am aware of how my past experiences shape my current financial beliefs and behaviours.**
Strongly disagree – 1
Disagree – 2
Neutral – 3
Agree – 4
Strongly agree – 5

8. **I feel a sense of control over my financial decisions and actions.**
Strongly disagree – 1
Disagree – 2
Neutral – 3
Agree – 4
Strongly agree – 5

9. **I recognise the impact of my emotions on my financial decision-making.**
   Strongly disagree – 1
   Disagree – 2
   Neutral – 3
   Agree – 4
   Strongly agree – 5

10. **I consistently apply rational thinking when evaluating financial risks and opportunities.**
    Strongly disagree – 1
    Disagree – 2
    Neutral – 3
    Agree – 4
    Strongly agree – 5

My total score:

Now let's find out more about REBT and how it can be useful in developing financial wellbeing.

Introduction

Rational emotive behaviour therapy (REBT) is a brand of cognitive behavioural therapy developed by Albert Ellis in the 1950s. It's used to help people solve emotional and behavioural problems. To enhance your financial fitness, you need to think about the thoughts and feelings that affect your financial behaviours and attitudes, since all your financial choices involve both thought and feeling. As mentioned before, REBT offers a practical, effective approach to identifying and challenging your irrational money meanings and beliefs – ones that can lead to financial self-destruction. REBT achieves this by employing techniques that help you change how you think about your finances.

Foundations of REBT

According to REBT, irrational, extreme beliefs are the cause of unhealthy emotions and behaviours. The ABC model of REBT stands at the core of all the techniques taught in this therapy. It clearly displays the causes of certain emotional and behavioural responses. According to the ABC model, Activating events (As) trigger irrational Beliefs (Bs), which, ultimately, lead to unhealthy emotional and behavioural Consequences (Cs).[1]

For instance, maybe you finish school and can't get a well-paying job (A). So you tell yourself, 'I must get a high-paying job right away or I'll be a failure' (B). Now you start to feel anxious, ashamed and put off your job hunting (C). REBT helps you pinpoint, evaluate and question your rigid, irrational beliefs, allowing you to change your thinking – to replace irrational demands with more flexible and functional preferences. This in turn helps to reduce distress and improve behaviour.

The core types of irrational belief patterns in REBT are catastrophising about minor setbacks; overgeneralising failures as evidence of general worthlessness; taking negative events personally (e.g. 'If only I had said that' or 'If only I had had the courage to do that' or 'It is always my fault'); and rigid demands (from 'It would be better if . . . ' to 'I demand that this particular thing be changed'). Practices like logical analysis, rational discussion and testing of proposed generalisations, dichotomies and demands via hypothetical observations help REBT combat these irrationalities.

Financial behaviours and REBT

Research consistently finds that many financial behaviours are associated with money-related irrational beliefs.[2] General irrational money beliefs such as being overly materialistic or overly focused on collecting material goods, or fearing the loss of financial resources, are correlated with adverse financial outcomes. REBT interventions help to (1) identify these irrational money beliefs and (2) resolve (or at least mitigate) them – this helps to improve people's financial behaviours.[3] Research has identified numerous irrational money beliefs correlated with harmful financial behaviours and outcomes.[4]

For example:

- 'I must be able to afford anything I want' leads to overspending and too much debt.
- 'Investing in stocks is too risky, I'll definitely lose money' causes people to save too little and avoid investing.
- 'If I'm not rich, I'm a failure' results in working too much and taking risky get-rich-quick schemes.
- 'I can't stand owing money to anyone under any circumstances' stops people from using healthy credit.

Such extreme, unrealistic demands set people up for failure and for unhelpful financial behaviours when their demands aren't met, which – in the complicated, uncontrollable real world – is inevitable. In REBT, practitioners enable clients to reframe their irrational financial 'musts' and 'must nots' into rational preferences.

A classic example here is an unrealistic 'must' that an REBT therapist might help a client replace: 'I must be able to afford anything I want' (unrealistic demand) with 'I want to be able to afford some nice things and not have to do without, but I don't have to be able to buy just anything I want' (healthier preference and discomfort tolerance). This kind of reframing by a therapist can significantly reduce financial stress when your material desires outstrip your available means. Similarly, reasonable reframing of other irrational beliefs can translate into more responsible and adaptive financial decisions, and better overall financial wellbeing. Stunningly high rates of excessive financial risk-taking and underperformance are common among even trained financial professionals, whose poor financial decisions often stem from irrational beliefs they have about money.[5]

Using REBT for financial problems

A number of studies point to the utility of REBT for the treatment of other financial problems such as compulsive shopping,[6] problematic credit card use[7] or financial anxiety.[8] For example, an extreme shopaholic could hold irrational beliefs such as 'If I am sad, I absolutely need to go out and buy something'. In an REBT session, the shopaholic could be helped to identify and challenge this belief by finding exceptions to the belief, examining the evidence, hearing rebuttals and reframing rationally with thoughts such as 'I would probably rather prefer to cheer myself up in a more affordable way'. Irrational financial beliefs might include overgeneralisation of one's failure as incontrovertible proof of permanent financial incompetence. For instance, needing to dip into debt a few times in your life is not a reason to feel totally worthless.

REBT techniques for improving financial wellbeing

The REBT approach utilises cognitive restructuring, disputation and rational coping self-statements to help participants correct their irrational money beliefs and reach more balanced financial behaviours. At six months of follow-up financial and mental wellbeing assessments, there were statistically and clinically significant improvements in the participants' financial wellbeing.

- **Cognitive restructuring** – this is where we identify irrational beliefs and then evaluate their accuracy and appropriateness, before finding ways to reframe them into more rational statements, thus beginning to tell ourselves more helpful things. Individuals become increasingly attuned to absolute words such as 'must' or 'need' that flag up an irrational demand and begin to replace them with preferential words such as 'want' or 'prefer'.

- **Disputation** – In REBT disputation, individuals directly question the evidence for their irrational beliefs via methods such as logical analyses, hypothetical probing, perspective-taking exercises, and cost-benefit analysis, as well as evaluating the pros and cons of their irrational thoughts. For example, 'What evidence is there that this is 100 per cent absolutely true 100 per cent of the time?

- **Rational coping statements** – These are statements that people learn to create and internalise in opposition to their automatic irrational thoughts. For example: 'I'd rather have less debt, but I'm not a total failure just because I have some debt'.

- **Irrational belief questionnaires** – Used to probe common patterns in irrational beliefs, e.g. the irrational belief test. Ratings of strength allow irrational beliefs to be identified as more or less in need of disputation.

- **Roleplays** – With these, individuals can act out different financial scenarios, elicit irrational beliefs, and then practise disputation techniques. Here, roleplays provide applied practice where irrational beliefs can be elicited and then intervened on in a roleplay setting.

- **Homework using REBT in 'real life' activities** – Homework is needed to practise and further strengthen the new skills. Homework tasks include journalling about activating events, irrational and rational responses.

- **Visualisation** – Imagining responding to triggers for irrational financial beliefs with rational coping statements and behaviours. Imagining effective use of a technique improves self-efficacy.

These techniques help people become more aware of the irrational ways in which they commonly think, as well as strengthening their skills to dispute such irrational thoughts or beliefs more logically and based on evidence. Individuals are also encouraged to change the way they think about their relationship to money in order to achieve more profound, lasting changes in their financial behaviours.

Empirical evidence

Though further studies with greater rigour are needed, findings from preliminary REBT-based financial therapy studies have shown marked decreases in both financial anxiety and stress, as well as increases in both financial satisfaction and quality of life.[9] A systematic review of the literature from multiple studies from 2018 showed an increase in 'more adaptive financial behaviours' following REBT interventions, while noting that the quality of evidence so far leaves room for improvement. So, early data largely supports the efficacy of REBT.[10]

Practical applications

Professional financial counsellors and therapists have incorporated REBT into debt repayment workshops and programmes.[11] REBT has helped clients to identify irrational money beliefs, and to take back control of their finances. Sample financial counselling case studies illustrate the REBT process.[12] REBT has been applied to areas ranging from overspending and conspicuous consumption, dealing with financial emergencies,[13] to making more realistic assessments of financial risk.[14]

Integration with financial education

Teachers can include exercises to recognise and reframe the irrational financial thoughts that drive behaviours.[15] REBT can be used to assess and challenge automatic thoughts about money, and these techniques can be included in financial health evaluations and coaching. There is also potential to incorporate REBT into various financial literacy programmes.[16]

Conclusion

This chapter highlights the potential of REBT as an evidence-based tool for promoting financial wellbeing by targeting irrational beliefs or dysfunctional cognitive and emotional states around money. There are currently very few studies to back up these claims; nonetheless, REBT offers a helpful approach to financial counselling and education, aiming to improve financial wellbeing and behaviours related to managing money.

Now you've learned about REBT, let's try some exercises and challenge your irrational beliefs.

Activity 11.1: Identifying irrational beliefs

Objective:

To become a keen observer of situations where you experience visible stress or negative emotions connected to financial topics (such as spending or career), and identify any irrational beliefs associated with these instances. This exercise will assist you in identifying and debating negative thoughts, which will help you to positively affect your financial mindset.

Date and time	
1. Financial issue description:	Provide a detailed description of the financial issue or event that became stressful or resulted in negative feelings.
2. Emotions:	List the emotions you experienced during this financial situation.
3. Automatic thoughts:	What were your automatic thoughts during the experience? Note any other elements of your self-talk under 'self-talk about money'.
4. Irrational beliefs:	Examine your automatic thoughts. Which of them contain an irrational belief (extreme, rigid and/or unrealistic idea)? Write them down.

Instructions:

Use the worksheet on p. 208 to record your thoughts and emotions in financial situations: for example, cutting back on subscription services or limiting impulse shopping etc. Be honest and specific in describing your experiences to gain the most benefit from this exercise.

Activity 11.2: Financial behavioural experiments

You can design small financial experiments (such as putting off a non-essential purchase), and then watch what you do and how you feel, before writing down the financial outcome.

Keep an REBT focus by considering the three types of process – thoughts, emotions and behaviours. Show that adaptive financial choices can be made based on a clear and rational view.

Experiment details

1. *Experiment description:* Explain the financial experiment you will be conducting. For example: 'Despite being able to afford it, I will hold off on buying a non-essential item for at least two weeks.'
2. *Date and time of experiment:* Specify when you conducted the experiment.
3. *Pre-experiment thoughts:* Prior to the experiment, write down anything that comes to mind, be it a belief or an aspect of your beliefs that you view as irrational.

What was your state of mind before running the experiment? Describe your emotional/feeling state before you run your financial experiment.

Implementation of the experiment:

1. *Execution of the experiment:* How did you perform your financial experiment? What decisions did you make?
2. *Thoughts during the experiment:* Write down any thoughts or impressions you had while the experiment was going on.
3. *Emotional state during the experiment:* Reports of changes in self-state when reading the story.
4. *Behavioural responses:* Record your actual behaviour – did you actually carry out the financial decision you had planned to make?

Observations and reflections:

1. *Outcomes:* List the measurable financial consequences of the experiment – savings, lower expenses, etc.
2. *Post-experimental emotions:* Describe any changes in your emotions after completing the financial experiment.
3. *Reflection on initial thoughts and emotions:* Return to the thoughts and emotions that you recorded in Step 1 of this experiment. Have they changed? How do you feel about the financial choice you made?

Activity 11.3: Disputation roleplays

This activity looks at disputation. Use roleplay to actively practise disputing irrational financial beliefs in hypothetical scenarios. Use logic and provide evidence to foster more rational perspectives and reduce emotional intensity around financial situations. After the roleplay, participants reflect on their thoughts and emotional shifts, and then revisit the REBT and money questionnaire to assess progress.

Roleplay details

1. **Irrational belief to dispute:** What is the irrational belief you will be disputing during the roleplay? (e.g. 'Everyone is getting rich investing but me, I must be doing something wrong').
2. **Roleplay scenario:** Describe the context or situation in which the irrational belief is believed to be common. Set the scene.
3. **Your role:** State your role in the scene. How did you feel, think and act according to the unrealistic belief?
4. **Role of partner:** If you have a partner to roleplay with you, describe his or her role in terms of promoting or resisting your irrational belief.

Roleplay execution

5. **Actively dispute the irrational belief:** Roleplay the agreed-upon thought for 'active disputation'. Dispute the irrational belief with logic, evidence and hypothetical examples.
6. **Disputation styles:** Use specific disputing styles such as questioning evidence, implications or cognitive distortions.
7. **Cognitive shift:** Challenge yourself with more objective perspectives on the financial situation. Provide some alternative scenarios that make it unlikely that the irrational belief is truly correct.

Roleplay reflection

8. **Thoughts during disputation:** Take note of any changes in thinking as you actively argued against the irrational belief in the roleplay.

9. **Emotional responses:** Please describe how your emotional state shifted in the course of the roleplay. Did actively disputing the irrational belief alter your feelings?
10. **Main takeaways:** What were your key takeaways from the disputatious roleplay? What did you discover about yourself or perhaps about how to understand and approach disputes?

Partner feedback (if applicable):

11. **Partner's observations:** If you do the roleplay with a partner, have them make observations on your disputation techniques, and how effective they are.
12. **Collaborative insights:** Discuss any insights or alternative ways of looking at the situation that were collaboratively co-created during the roleplay.

After completing all the activities, please go back to the start of the chapter and attempt the REBT and money questionnaire again to check the difference in the result.

Resources

Check out these supplementary resources to better understand the connection between REBT and improved wellbeing.

Books

A Guide to Rational Living by Albert Ellis, Wilshire Book Company, 1961
This foundational text outlines the principles of Rational Emotive Behaviour Therapy (REBT) to help individuals develop a rational approach to their thoughts and emotions.

REBT Workbook by Windy Dryden, Routledge, 2012
   A practical workbook offering exercises and guidance
   on implementing Rational Emotive Behaviour Therapy
   techniques to enhance emotional wellbeing.
The Philosophy of Cognitive Behavioural Therapy by Donald
   Robertson, St. Augustine's Press, 2010
   This book explores the philosophical underpinnings
   of Cognitive Behavioural Therapy, integrating classic
   philosophical insights with modern psychological practices.
How to Stubbornly Refuse to Make Yourself Miserable by Albert
   Ellis, Robinson, 2019
   In this accessible book, Ellis provides practical strategies
   for overcoming self-imposed misery and achieving a more
   fulfilling life through rational thinking.
*The Myth of Self-esteem: How Rational Emotive Behavior Therapy
   Can Change Your Life Forever* by Albert Ellis, Prometheus
   Books, 2004
   This book challenges the conventional views on self-esteem
   and argues that it is more beneficial to focus on rational
   thinking to achieve personal happiness.

Apps

REBT Coach
CBT Thought Record Diary
nCBT
REBT Self-Help by Excel At Life
MoodKit: Mood Improvement Tools
Rational Emotive Behavior Therapy (REBT) by iTherapy

Websites

Albert Ellis Institute albertellis.org
REBT Network www.rational.org

Psychology Today REBT therapists www.psychologytoday.
com/us/therapy-types/rebt

PsychCentral – Rational Emotive Behavior Therapy (REBT)
psychcentral.com/lib/rational-emotive-behavior-therapy-rebt

Blog/journal articles

REBT Outline for Recovery from Addiction
REBToutlineforrecoveryfromaddiction_v1_
m56577569830563989.pdf

Using REBT with Children and Adolescents www.
inquiriesjournal.com/articles/1791/using-rational-emotive-
behavioral-therapy-rebt-with-children-and-adolescents-
application-effectiveness-and-techniques

REBT Case Formulation & Treatment
societyforpsychotherapy.org/
rebt-case-formulation-treatment

Rational Emotive Behavior Therapy: A Review by Windy Dryden

Effectiveness of Rational Emotive Behavior Therapy on
Anxiety and Psychological Well-being in Adolescents
by Asghar Dadkhah, et al www.researchgate.net/
publication/313848893_Effectiveness_of_Rational_
Emotive_Behavior_Therapy_on_Anxiety_and_
Psychological_Well-being_in_Adolescents

The ABCs of REBT (Rational Emotive Behavior Therapy)
by Mark Dombeck, Ph.D. www.mentalhelp.net/blogs/
the-abcs-of-rebt-rational-emotive-behavior-therapy

Videos

REBT Crash Course youtube/0M3U-4S7DUA

Roleplay Disputing Irrational Beliefs

How to Practice REBT youtube/eVnKE9nEE2Q

Albert Ellis – How to Stop Destroying Yourself (TEDx Talk)

Rational Emotive Behavior Therapy (REBT) – Full Session
  by Psychology Tools www.psychologytools.com/resource/
  rational-emotive-behavior-therapy-rebt-full-session
Introduction to Rational Emotive Behavior Therapy (REBT)
  by WyseTalk

Podcasts

Psychologist Off the Clock: REBT with Debbie Joffe Ellis
Thesis Whisperer: Irrational Beliefs in Academia
The OCD Stories: REBT for OCD
The REBT Advocate Podcast

CHAPTER 12

Acceptance and commitment therapy (ACT)

Co-authored with Kim Stephenson

You can't skip pain, but you can skip the drama

Involving work on psychological barriers, mindfulness, acceptance and value-driven action, acceptance and commitment therapy (ACT) shows promise as a robust psychological approach to improving financial wellbeing. As this approach is translated and tested, it can have the potential to transform our understanding of financial resilience and engagement with money. Let's first find out your current understanding about ACT. Attempt this questionnaire with an open mind and open heart.

ACT and money questionnaire

This survey aims to help you track and evaluate your understanding of ACT. Circle the number below each of the ten statements that aligns with your level of agreement. Calculate your total score for an initial sense of your progress. Once you've completed the chapter and the suggested exercises, retake the survey. Your answers remain confidential; it's simply a way to measure shifts or improvements in your outlook.

1. **I can accept my financial situation without judgement.**
   Strongly disagree – 1
   Disagree – 2
   Neutral – 3
   Agree – 4
   Strongly agree – 5

2. **I can handle financial setbacks with less emotional distress.**
   Strongly disagree – 1
   Disagree – 2
   Neutral – 3
   Agree – 4
   Strongly agree – 5

3. **I feel confident in setting financial goals that align with my values.**
   Strongly disagree – 1
   Disagree – 2
   Neutral – 3
   Agree – 4
   Strongly agree – 5

4. **I feel committed to taking steps towards my financial goals.**
   Strongly disagree – 1
   Disagree – 2
   Neutral – 3

Agree – 4
Strongly agree – 5

5. **I have started implementing actions towards better financial management.**
Strongly disagree – 1
Disagree – 2
Neutral – 3
Agree – 4
Strongly agree – 5

6. **I am able to recognise and challenge negative financial beliefs.**
Strongly disagree – 1
Disagree – 2
Neutral – 3
Agree – 4
Strongly agree – 5

7. **I have an understanding of how my identity is independent of my financial status.**
Strongly disagree – 1
Disagree – 2
Neutral – 3
Agree – 4
Strongly agree – 5

8. **I can view my financial challenges objectively.**
Strongly disagree – 1
Disagree – 2
Neutral – 3
Agree – 4
Strongly agree – 5

ACCEPTANCE AND COMMITMENT THERAPY

9. **I am reflective about my financial decisions.**
   Strongly disagree – 1
   Disagree – 2
   Neutral – 3
   Agree – 4
   Strongly agree – 5

10. **I am making steady progress towards my financial goals.**
    Strongly disagree – 1
    Disagree – 2
    Neutral – 3
    Agree – 4
    Strongly agree – 5

My total score:

Next, we need to discuss ACT theory to understand better how it really works and then apply the theory to you and whatever financial problems you are facing.

Introduction

Acceptance and commitment therapy, or ACT, is one of the most well-known 'third wave' cognitive therapies.[1] It has received much acclaim as a new approach because it focuses on the acceptance of emotions and the commitment to act on important values, as opposed to older cognitive and behavioural therapies that involved fighting against unpleasant feelings and emotions, and 'overcoming' them with logic and rational argument.[2] Tempering unrealistic wants with mindfulness and defusion, according to ACT, involves being in the present with difficult feelings, sitting with them and thus building awareness of their nature and origin. Then, through psychotherapy, happiness is achieved not by simply getting rid of pain and suffering (and thus fighting with unwanted feelings), but by accepting thoughts and feelings and engaging in action that promotes flourishing. ACT is a good fit for financial wellbeing, both with respect to bolstering healthy relationships with money, and to enabling flourishing and reducing destructive and unhealthy attitudes and behaviours.

At the centre of the ACT model we find psychological flexibility. This means adapting to a situation while taking action that is consistent with who you are (living your values).[3] There is evidence that psychological inflexibility and attempted avoidance of painful feelings are associated with lower household debt. This makes sense, as keeping a distance from our feelings might promote financial autonomy (keeping expenses low and building savings) when the behaviour actually performed matches what we value. Psychological flexibility, especially in terms of reconsidering goals but also flexibility in executing action, is associated with valued action and financial wellbeing in general.[4]

Foundations of ACT

ACT rests on six key domains: mindfulness, cognitive defusion, self-as-context, acceptance, values and committed action.[5]

They seem to work together in allowing people to put some distance between themselves and their thoughts and take step-by-step action to move towards what matters.[6] Examples of the principles of obtaining distance are defusion, the awareness that thoughts are thoughts ('I'm having the thought that I'll screw this up'), and mindfulness, which keeps you in the present moment, not flying off to some fantasy land of thoughts. In combination they seem to keep our thoughts from running the show, allowing us the freedom to react differently, to make choices based on reality rather than imagination, and to focus on what we want.

One of the key issues at the heart of ACT relates to

experiencing and avoiding, a behaviour known as experiential avoidance, which is correlated to many phobias – but also to experiences in life, including ones related to money. There's a desire to do something, whether it's getting on a plane or setting up a budget, but the closer you get to doing it, the more the feelings of fear and anxiety arise, and generate many negative emotions. Those unpleasant feelings, and the consequent discomfort in the body and mind about experiencing them, make the person back away from what they want to do, avoiding having the unpleasant experience but also missing out on what they wanted to do. With money, many people want to budget and gain more control of their finances. But 'my God, I've got to do a budget', and thinking about that creates fear and unease. Each time they think about the budget, while they know it's good for them, they feel the discomfort of those unpleasant feelings, and bingo, they put it off again. ACT is all about moving along, through that discomfort – being able to tolerate it and do what you really want to do, which is to get that budget made.[7]

Financial behaviours and ACT

Common issues with finance include absolute judgements. Among the examples are absolute core beliefs: 'I must ...', 'I shouldn't ...', and self-rated inadequacy: 'I can't ...', 'I don't know ...', and so forth.[8] Absolute beliefs make it difficult to think flexibly and to consider alternative options. Feelings of inadequacy typically serve to reinforce experiential avoidance, since trying to do something, even once, simply becomes way too painful. Through the development of ACT flexibility, changes occur in how the valence (the charged nature) of feelings permits or prevents certain behaviours to take place.[9]

Gaining insight that you are having a thought (one among forty thousand that you will have today) and that the thought is only a thought, not a fact, contributes to the flexibility of our thoughts and feelings. Many other ACT components serve to distance people from the way past events have previously determined their current and future behaviour. Understanding that even if certain situations and decisions in the past have turned out badly, they come to realise that the past is not destiny; they can develop different behaviours and different outcomes through the learning of different attitudes. And actions can flow towards their personally defined, valued future goals, rather than getting stuck at past problems.[10]

Using ACT for financial problems

We all worry about money, and the associated anxiety and doubt not only feel unpleasant, but also undermine our capacity to make good decisions about managing our finances. This can be fuelled by irrational concerns, rumination (the repetitive and passive focus on negative thoughts, emotions or past experiences) and the general existential dread of our financial futures. There is good evidence that ACT can help with this,[11] as well as with specific problems such as hoarding.[12] Such changes in emotion and behaviour have been shown to be possible in self-help situations, as well as in organised therapy. The same is true with depression, but here the evidence is even stronger.[13]

Through concepts such as defusion, acceptance and committed action, ACT helps people learn to cope with, rather than avoid, unwanted feelings and thoughts, and move forward on the foundation of their values. Below are six core principles of ACT, each offering practical strategies for cultivating psychological flexibility and resilience:

- **Defusion**: Recognising that a thought is just a thought; it comes and it goes. You could be in the company of a dictator within you, who pipes up with unhelpful thoughts of hating yourself or thinking negatively. You can notice it and, rather than fuse with it as absolute truth, step back from it.[14]

- **Self**: Every time you have a thought, remember that the thought itself is not who you really are. There is an 'I' inside you – a constant, observing presence – that is separate from the thoughts. This 'I' has always been there, even when you were young. It's the true, transcendent part of you that simply watches the thoughts come and go.[15]

- **Acceptance**: Experiential avoidance, trying to run and hide from painful feelings and giving up on the things that we really want to do as a result, is all too common; acceptance is a kind of active acceptance that it can be hard sometimes, that it's a gift to be given this struggle and to learn to move through it.[16]

- **Presence**: We have all had experiences of being aware that we have been reading, observing and listening, but have not taken anything in because our attention was elsewhere. Presence means being attentive – attending. When we can focus our attention, to see a tree, the wood, or both as we choose, we can see what is really going on, and we come to better decisions.[17]

- **Values**: What is important to you can be a powerful motivator. People can accomplish so-called 'miracles' if they care enough and if they're motivated enough. Learning what is important, not what's expected, or what we've always done, enables us to focus resources on areas that matter most; time and money are key resources here.[18]

- **Committed action**: Finally, it's doing that gets things done. Thinking is important, and motivation is important, but you need to 'do', not just 'think'. Moving the deckchairs, and making small amendments in an established set of activities, takes you along a bit.[19]

Self-applied strategies, including cognitive defusion and present moment mindfulness, can lead to lower levels of financial stress, greater clarity of goals and altered money orientations.[20]

Practical applications and case studies

A common problem with basic financial planning is the inability to budget. You might know that the way to make things happen in terms of prioritising your spending is to set a budget and stick to it, which means that having a purpose in life can be a reality and current spending can be kept in check. However, past history makes the process feel emotionally threatening and generates hopelessness. The fact that such hopelessness is based on previous bad experiences of 'never having done it well' (self), and the belief that 'I'm not able' (defusion), means it can be reassessed. Learning a more realistic way to address what has to be done, being aware of the true current circumstances (presence) and of unpleasant feelings (acceptance) brings greater clarity. Shifting focus to what is most important (values) helps with the motivation to take on board the lessons of past failure and assists with defusion and reality testing. That in turn helps with action (committed action) to ascertain the budget and stick to it. All the elements of ACT are working together to change both the emotional experience and what is done about it.[21]

Integration with financial education and counselling

ACT in financial education:
Solutions are well supported using ACT to many of the issues explored in financial wellbeing education: budgeting (see above: 'Practical applications and case studies'); control of credit; spending priorities; keeping long-term and short-term savings perspectives in balance; confronting the emotional content – the good feelings, the bad feelings and the fears – from overspending

or financial anxiety. ACT's embrace of whole-person acceptance is a good fit for financial education. The fact that ACT has been applied when participants did the training to teach themselves (rather than having ongoing therapy) suggests that training in the theory and methods would be effective here. ACT is being taught in the workplace.[22] Most, but not all, of these applications have been in the area of mental health but I see no obvious barrier to applying ACT education for financial issues.

Counselling and coaching:
A specific application of ACT to financial therapy (including a focus on the unique challenges related to women in finance) can be found in the work of Wada and Klontz.[23] More research is necessary in this area, but it holds promise – both in therapy contexts and in financial coaching and education.

Conclusion

In short, the research supports the idea that ACT is a very effective treatment for most psychological problems, including anxiety, depression and unrealistic, illogical beliefs about the world. Since most of these concerns relate in different ways to financial wellbeing, including financial anxiety and unrealistic, illogical beliefs about money, it's surely hard to top ACT when it comes to financial counselling, coaching and education. While we are very early in the use of ACT in those fields, it could be a particularly promising approach, in part because it combines many of the key areas into a single approach.

This chapter has highlighted the exciting promise of ACT as an effective way to bolster financial wellbeing and reduce general and financial anxiety through the development of psychological flexibility, ultimately empowering individuals to act in accordance with their most deeply held values. Using ACT in financial education, counselling and coaching provides a promising way to help consumers maximise financial wellness by addressing the emotional and behavioural barriers that often underlie financial struggles. Mindfulness, acceptance and committed action serve to enhance the effectiveness of financial education and coaching and position ACT to become essential components of these important programmes.

Activity 12.1: Defusion techniques for financial worries

This activity will help you separate yourself from your unhelpful thoughts about money.

Step 1: Understanding cognitive defusion

- Write a brief explanation of cognitive defusion in your own words (either in this book or in your own personal diary):

  _____

  _____

Step 2: Practising 'thanking your mind'

- Write down a common financial worry:

  _____

  _____

- Practise 'thanking your mind' by writing a response to the worry:
  'Thank you, mind, for this thought: _____

  _____,'

Step 3: Group practice

- Share and practise defusion techniques with a group.

- Reflect on how this practice affected your worry:

_____

_____

Step 4: Reflection

- How has your perception of your financial worry changed?

_____

_____

Activity 12.2: The mind train

Here you will observe your thoughts without getting caught up in them.

Background: Picture yourself on a railway bridge watching three trains on separate tracks: the train on the left (carrying your present feelings and sensations) and the train on the right (carrying your urges to act), with the train in the middle carrying the thoughts that pass through your mind. Pay attention to the tracks. For example, when you think of the money problem, close your eyes and watch the trains for five minutes. If you get distracted or become carried away into the content of a train car (for example, pain at having gone through a bankruptcy, or predictions of impending doom), note what pulled you away and bring yourself back up to the bridge. You're watching what's going on inside you – observing your processes, and then seeing your ability to bring yourself back to the present when your mind has been distracted.

Step 1: Understanding the mind train

- Write a brief explanation of the mind train metaphor in your own words:

_____

_____

Step 2: Guided visualisation

- Close your eyes and imagine yourself at a train station. Write down some thoughts (trains) you observed:

  _____

  _____

Step 3: Noting thoughts

- List any recurring or particularly strong thoughts you noticed:

  _____

  _____

Step 4: Reflection

- How did this exercise affect your perception of your financial thoughts?

  _____

  _____

Activity 12.3: Labelling thoughts

An exercise to increase your awareness and reduce the impact of unhelpful thoughts related to finances.

Experience these thoughts – perhaps plans, memories, reminders or judgements related to your beliefs, as well as thinking about your thoughts – for a few moments, and then say to yourself: 'I am having the thought/feeling/memory/bodily sensation/tendency that . . . '

For example: 'I'm anxious, feel so uncomfortable, feel so powerless, I'm anxious about these bills' rather than: 'I'm anxious about paying the bills'.

This is called defusion. It helps people realise that thoughts are just thoughts, not necessarily reflections of the world, or some uncomplicated truth.

Step 1: Learning to label thoughts

- Write down a few types of thoughts and label them (e.g. 'This is a worry thought'):

  _____

  _____

Step 2: Writing exercise

- Write down financial thoughts you observed and labelled during the exercise:

  _____

  _____

Step 3: Daily practice

- List times when you used labelling thoughts in daily life:

  _____

  _____

Step 4: Reflection

- How has labelling thoughts affected your emotional response and decision-making?

  _____

  _____

Activity 12.4: I am/I am not

Explore your self-identity and challenge unhelpful self-labels related to financial wellbeing. This exercise pushes against your self-conceptions and helps you see that they are not set in stone. We all have simplified fables about who we are, and we then act as though they are wholly real.

For example, you might tell yourself: 'I am always confident, always successful and always anxious'. Then ask yourself 'But is this absolutely true?', 'Is this always true in every situation?', and 'Is it true that I am confident or not/I am successful or not/I am anxious or not?' (the answer is usually 'no', as people are multi-faceted and their self-perceptions are not fixed).

The objective is to recognise that you have the capacity to view yourself as varying and changeable, and that you don't have to be dominated by a fixed, solid self-concept. This encourages fluidity and psychological wellbeing, as an abiding attachment to a specific self-perception isn't inherently helpful.

Step 1: List 'I am' statements

- Write down 'I am' statements related to your financial self-identity:

  _____

  _____

Step 2: Discuss their impact

- Reflect on how these statements affect your financial behaviours and emotions:

  _____

  _____

Step 3: Introduce 'I am not' statements

- Write down 'I am not' statements to challenge unhelpful self-labels:

  _____

  _____

Step 4: Develop a flexible self-identity

- Balance your 'I am' and 'I am not' statements:

  'I am: _____

  _____ ,

  'I am not: _____

  _____ ,

Reflection:

- How has this exercise helped you develop a more flexible self-identity?

  _____

  _____

By using these activities, you can apply ACT principles to improve your financial wellbeing, helping you to manage financial worries more effectively and achieve your financial goals.

After completing all these exercises don't forget to reattempt the ACT and money questionnaire and check how your perspective has changed.

Resources

These additional materials can provide deeper insight into how ACT affects your overall wellness.

Books

A Liberated Mind: How to Pivot Towards What Matters by Steven
Hayes, Avery, 2019
This book offers insights from acceptance and
commitment therapy (ACT) to help individuals overcome
psychological barriers and focus on what truly matters
in life.

*ACT Made Simple: An Easy-to-read Primer on Acceptance and
Commitment Therapy* by Russ Harris, New Harbinger
Publications, 2009
A user-friendly introduction to ACT that simplifies
its concepts and techniques for both practitioners and
individuals seeking personal growth.

*Get Out of Your Mind and Into Your Life: The New Acceptance and
Commitment Therapy* by Steven Hayes and Spencer Smith,
New Harbinger Publications, 2005
This guide presents ACT principles to help readers break
free from negative thoughts and live a more meaningful
and fulfilling life.

*ACTivate Your Life: An Acceptance and Commitment Therapy
Workbook for Building a Life that is Rich, Fulfilling and Fun* by
Joe Oliver, Jon Hill and Eric Morris, Robinson, 2024
A practical workbook designed to help individuals apply
ACT principles in everyday situations to enhance wellbeing
and enjoyment of life.

The Happiness Trap by Russ Harris, Robinson, 2022
This book challenges common myths about happiness and
provides tools based on ACT to create a more meaningful
and fulfilling life.

*ACT with Anxiety: An Acceptance and Commitment Therapy
Workbook to Get You Unstuck From Anxiety and Enrich Your
Life* by Richard Sears, New Harbinger Publications, 2014
A comprehensive workbook that combines ACT techniques

with practical exercises to help individuals manage anxiety and improve their quality of life.

The Reality Slap: How to survive and thrive when life hits hard by Russ Harris, Robinson, 2021
This book offers strategies based on ACT to help individuals cope with life's challenges and find peace and fulfilment amid adversity.

The Mindful & Effective Employee: An Acceptance & Commitment Training Manual for Improving Well-Being and Performance by Paul E. Flaxman, Frank W. Bond and Fredrik Livheim, Routledge, 2013
A training manual that combines ACT and mindfulness techniques to enhance employee wellbeing and productivity in the workplace.

The Confidence Gap: From Fear to Freedom by Russ Harris, Robinson, 2011
This book provides practical strategies based on ACT to help individuals overcome fear and self-doubt, building confidence and resilience in their lives.

Apps

ACT companion by Russ Harris: www.actcompanion.com

Websites

Steven Hayes: stevenchayes.com – resources include a course on ACT
Get self help: getselfhelp.co.uk/act-acceptance-commitment-therapy
Positive Psychology.com: positivepsychology.com/act-model
ACBS: contextualscience.org/acbs
Russ Harris: thehappinesstrap.com/free-resources

Blog/journal articles:

Harris, R., 'Acceptance and Commitment Therapy (ACT)', from *Psychology Today.* www.psychologytoday.com/us/ therapy-types/acceptance-and-commitment-therapy

Hayward, M. (2005). 'Introduction to Acceptance and Commitment Therapy'. *Advances in Psychiatric Treatment.* www.cambridge.org/core/journals/ advances-in-psychiatric-treatment/article/ introduction-to-acceptance-and-commitment-therapy/ D67B44FDED4147CA35C1AA8FA9D3DDA5

Videos

Series of short videos of Steven Hayes demonstrating ACT: www.psychotherapy.net/video/ acceptance-commitment-therapy

Ted Talk by Steven Hayes: bit.ly/StevesFirstTED

Ted Talk by Steven Hayes: bit.ly/StevesSecondTED

Short videos by Russ Harris: thehappinesstrap.com/free-resources and www.actmindfully.com.au/free-stuff/free-videos

Learning and applying ACT, Association of Contextual Behavioural Science: contextualscience.org/ free_videos_learning_about_and_applying_act

Podcasts

The Psychology podcast interview with Steven Hayes

ACT in Context: The Acceptance and Commitment Therapy Podcast: contextualscience.org/act_in_context_the_ acceptance_and_commitment_therapy_podcast

Association for Child and Adolescent Mental Health – In conversation series on ACT: www.acamh.org/podcasts/ acceptance-commitment-therapy-act/

Just ACT – series on the themes of Accept, Clarify, and
  Transform based on ACT
Become your own therapist with Steven Hayes
Psyche central podcast with Steven Hayes

CHAPTER 13

Expressive writing

*Writing: where you argue with
yourself until you win*

Expressive writing can provide a necessary outlet to process the emotional toll of financial stress. Given the pace of research, it's become increasingly evident that, in order for people to weather financial storms, we need to address both the psychological and the practical levels of the financial spiral. Integrating expressive writing into financial programmes can help people cultivate more resilience in the face of financial adversity and build healthier relationships with money. But before we learn more about expressive writing, give the following questionnaire a go.

Expressive writing and money questionnaire

This survey is designed to help you monitor and evaluate your personal development in financial wellbeing with the assistance of expressive writing intervention. Rate each of the ten statements by circling the number that aligns with your level of agreement. Total the scores to gain an initial understanding of your financial wellbeing. After studying the chapter and participating in the recommended exercises, revisit the survey. You need not share your responses with anyone; it serves as a tool to measure any changes or improvements in your perspective.

1. **Writing about my financial stressors would help me process my feelings about money issues.**
   Strongly disagree – 1
   Disagree – 2
   Neutral – 3
   Agree – 4
   Strongly agree – 5

2. **Expressive writing could help me gain insight into my financial struggles.**
   Strongly disagree – 1
   Disagree – 2
   Neutral – 3
   Agree – 4
   Strongly agree – 5

3. **Putting my financial concerns into words would reduce some stress and anxiety I feel.**
   Strongly disagree – 1
   Disagree – 2
   Neutral – 3
   Agree – 4
   Strongly agree – 5

4. **I feel writing openly about my financial situation could improve my money mindset and behaviours.**
   Strongly disagree – 1

Disagree – 2
Neutral – 3
Agree – 4
Strongly agree – 5

5. **I don't think expressing my feelings in writing would help me manage my finances better.**
Strongly disagree – 1
Disagree – 2
Neutral – 3
Agree – 4
Strongly agree – 5

6. **Writing about my financial goals and dreams would help motivate me to achieve them.**
Strongly disagree – 1
Disagree – 2
Neutral – 3
Agree – 4
Strongly agree – 5

7. **I would feel comfortable engaging in emotional expressive writing about financial issues.**
Strongly disagree – 1
Disagree – 2
Neutral – 3
Agree – 4
Strongly agree – 5

8. **Translating my financial fears and concerns into writing could provide a sense of relief.**
Strongly disagree – 1
Disagree – 2
Neutral – 3

Agree – 4
Strongly agree – 5

9. **Expressive writing seems like an effective tool for coping with financial stress.**
Strongly disagree – 1
Disagree – 2
Neutral – 3
Agree – 4
Strongly agree – 5

10. **I struggle to imagine how expressive writing could improve my financial wellbeing.**
Strongly disagree – 1
Disagree – 2
Neutral – 3
Agree – 4
Strongly agree – 5

My total score:

Well done for completing the questionnaire; now let's find out more about expressive writing.

Introduction

We've all experienced financial stress: it's the day-to-day burden of worrying about money and the impact it has on our wellbeing, relationships and behaviours.[1] Stressors such as personal debt, student debt, or the sudden loss of a salary or a home often feel like all-pervading claustrophobia, squeezing away at our capacity and space to breathe, feel, think and be. What if there was a simple intervention that could help us to process these feelings, paving the way to greater resilience in the face of financial adversity?

Enter expressive writing – the technique of writing about stressful experiences.

Research is clear that engaging in expressive writing can be transformative for mental and physical wellbeing, reducing stress and improving general mental health, and even promoting physical healing.[2] There is a growing interest in how writing can be used as a tool to address financial stress as well. Recent findings suggest that both reducing financial anxiety and improving financial behaviours can be achieved through expressive writing about money problems.[3]

Expressive writing: The basics

At its heart, expressive writing is a simple yet powerful intervention that involves turning our innermost thoughts and feelings into words. The hope is that by writing down our experiences, we will garner insight, process our emotions and, as a result, experience a reduction in psychological distress.

The roots of expressive writing can be directly traced to the pioneering work of the psychologist James Pennebaker, whose work in the late 1980s was among the first to suggest that writing about traumatic or stressful events could have powerful psychological and physical benefits.[4] In an early study, Pennebaker and his colleagues asked college students to write about either a traumatic event in their life or a neutral topic for fifteen minutes a day, for four consecutive days.[5] The results were remarkable: those asked to write about traumatic events showed dramatic increases in physical and mental health, compared with those asked to write their thoughts on a neutral matter.

Since then, many studies have been published that replicate and build upon these results, showing that expressive writing can have a range of positive effects on physical and mental health.[6] These effects emerge via two broad mechanisms: cognitive processing and emotional disclosure.[7]

Our thinking, in other words, is a form of cognitive processing – the rendering of what has been experienced, and giving it interpretive and explanatory shape. When we write our story about a difficult or traumatic experience, we are literally telling ourselves something about what happened, sifting through and identifying patterns, finding dots that can be connected, and this helps us see it in a new light.[8]

Emotional disclosure is the sense of relief we experience when we openly express our deepest feelings in the moment. In contrast, **emotional processing** involves acknowledging and sitting with emotions without labeling them as good or bad. Suppressing emotions can cause them to build up, leading to psychological distress. But if we judiciously give ourselves the space to allow those feelings out – in words – it can be a powerful form of release, which is why plotting on paper can be so helpful.[9] Writing offers a private, safe space to investigate emotions without external pressure.

Together, they form the basis for what many scientists believe is the magic behind the expressive writing method. Through cognitive processing and emotional disclosure, writing can untangle experience, releasing stored-up emotions, and in turn promote healing, resilience and personal growth.[10]

Financial stress and wellbeing

So where does financial stress fit into this picture? Well, it's no secret that a big cause of stress for many people is money worries, and in fact a recent study by the American Psychological Association revealed that 72 per cent of Americans reported that they felt at least occasionally stressed about money.[11]

From fretting about making next month's mortgage payment to trying to cope with the anxiety about saving enough for retirement years away; from financial distress over lost income or a mounting debt, all the way to general financial insecurity, the effects on our wellbeing can be substantial.

Study after study has found that financial stress is a significant predictor of both poor psychological and relational wellness.[12] When the money conversation consumes our thoughts, it's associated with all the hallmarks of anxiety: symptoms of depression, relationship tension, inexplicable physical ailments (think ulcers, headaches, heart conditions, etc.).[13]

One factor that appears to play a role in the link between financial stress and (lack of) wellbeing is emotional regulation (ER). Research indicates that emotional regulation represents the ability to inhibit, monitor and modify emotional responses within ourselves.[14]

When coping with stress due to financial worries, we might deliberately and consciously avoid facing those worries. This might involve financial avoidance behaviours such as making no attempt to deal with our financial obligations (e.g. paying bills) or avoiding making larger financial decisions (e.g. moving home, or spending on holidays).[15] In the long run, financial avoidance behaviours can exacerbate stress and worsen our financial situation.

On the other hand, when we're able to reliably soothe ourselves and our negative emotional responses to financial challenges, we're both more likely to make good financial decisions and feel more in control of our finances.[16]

This is where expressive writing may have a role to play: by giving us the means to manage the emotional turmoil associated with money, it might help us to break the cycle of financial avoidance and foster more adaptive financial behaviours.[17]

Using expressive writing for financial issues

In a study, by Zimbabwe, value-based writing prompts – such as 'Describe your most important financial value(s) and goals for the future' and 'Describe how your current financial behaviours line up (or don't) with your most important values and goals' – were used to examine how expressive writing influenced financial behaviours.[18]

Compared with the control group, participants who experienced the writing intervention reported that they were more motivated to undertake positive financial behaviours, such as saving money and paying off debt. Furthermore, they exhibited better financial health.

In my doctoral research, I explored the impact of expressive writing on financial wellbeing. Participants were asked to write about their thoughts and feelings related to money, responding to prompts such as 'What does money mean to you?', 'How does your current financial situation make you feel?', and 'What are your most prominent past memories about money?' Remarkably, after engaging in this exercise for just one day, many participants reported experiencing a cathartic release and a sense of liberation.

Implementing expressive writing for financial stress

If you are interested in practising expressive writing yourself to help deal with financial stress, here are several principles to keep in mind.

First, during an expressive writing session, an important element of its restorative mechanism is to allow yourself free-form, unbroken, continuous writing for 15–20 minutes on your innermost thoughts and feelings about a stressful experience. For financial stress, this might involve writing about your money worries and anxieties, exploring what emotions come up when you think about money and your finances, and how financial stress has affected your life in different ways.

You have to enter the process freely and without censure and judgement, without being constrained by the requirement of creating a finished piece of writing. It is not about writing, yet not about nothing. The point is to tell yourself what is on your mind and in your heart, but with a reach that starts internally. In this way, you begin to write, without worrying about spelling or grammar, and without pause; to achieve a free-flowing expression of your thoughts and feelings that allows this spontaneous process to foster creativity.

Many find it more helpful to practise expressive writing for a period of 3–5 days in a row, perhaps for 15–20 minutes per day, to build a sense of continuity over time. Some, however, experience emotional upheaval during a single session of writing – and even expressing yourself for a single session can be effective.[19]

In terms of the content of your writing, there are many different prompts and approaches you can use. Some common themes to explore might include:[20]

- your earliest memories and experiences related to money
- your current financial stressors and challenges
- your feelings about money (e.g. fear, shame, anger, etc.)
- how financial stress has impacted your relationships, work and overall quality of life
- your hopes and fears for your financial future.

Another way to help yourself is to use the writing process to develop a different way of looking at your finances. As you put your words on paper, make an effort to watch your thoughts and feelings from a distance, with curiosity and compassion. Do any patterns or insights emerge? Can you reframe your money problems from a more balanced or empowering perspective?[21]

After all, the process of writing can itself be a 'safe' vehicle for the emotional investigation of money. If you permit yourself to explore what you really feel about money, you might just find more clarity, power and resilience in your relationship with finances in all its many aspects.

Conclusion

Overall, expressive writing holds great promise, both as a way to harness the emotional energies caused by financial stressors, and as a crucial tool in helping people weather and survive those stressors. Looking ahead, as more research on this topic is published, we will continue to learn that to help and support people experiencing financial stress, we need to address not just practical financial education, advice, products and services, but also the psychological and emotional side-effects of financial stress.

Expressive writing can be one way of reconciling these two approaches, helping people develop a healthier and more harmonious connection with money. While its efficacy can depend on our individual, and potentially culturally specific, circumstances, expressive writing can play an important role within many different financial education and counselling programmes. Utilising this tool for financial wellness can set us on a path to improving our financial outcomes, and our overall wellness and life satisfaction.

Activity 13.1: Financial freedom through expressive writing: Healing past beliefs

This is an activity to improve financial wellbeing and overcome past beliefs and experiences about money.

Instructions:

1. **Set aside dedicated time and space:**
   - Choose a quiet, comfortable place where you won't be disturbed.
   - Choose a designated time of day to do your expressive writing, and stick with it.

2. **Gather your materials:**
   - Choose a medium that works best for you: a journal, notebook or digital document.
   - Make sure you have a comfortable pen, or a charged device if writing digitally.

3. **Select a prompt or topic:**
   - Pick a prompt from the list on p. 251, or choose a topic that feels right to you.
   - If you prefer, you can also free-write without a specific prompt.

4. **Set a time limit:**
   - Decide on a time limit for your writing session, typically 15–20 minutes.
   - Set a timer to keep yourself on track.

5. **Write continuously:**
   - Once you start writing, don't stop until the timer goes off.
   - Write without worrying about grammar, spelling or punctuation.
   - Write 'I don't know what to write' when you get stuck until something else comes to mind.

6. **Be honest and uncensored:**
   - Write about your deepest thoughts and feelings related to the topic or prompt.
   - Don't censor yourself or worry about what others might think.
   - Remember, this writing is for your eyes only.

7. **Explore emotions:**
   - Delve into the emotions that arise as you write.

- Describe how you feel and what these emotions mean to you.

8. **Reflect and analyse:**
   - After writing, take a few minutes to read what you've written.
   - Reflect on any insights, patterns or realisations that emerged during the writing process.

9. **Maintain privacy:**
   - Keep your writing private, unless you choose to share it with a trusted person.
   - Store your journal or digital document in a secure place.

10. **Repeat the process:**
    - Engage in expressive writing regularly, ideally daily.
    - Over time, you may notice patterns, insights and emotional shifts.

11. **Be patient and self-compassionate:**
    - Expressive writing can bring up difficult emotions. Be patient and kind to yourself.
    - If you feel overwhelmed, take a break and practise self-care.

12. **Seek support if needed:**
    - If you start to feel overwhelmed, please consult a therapist or counsellor.

Remember, expressive writing is a personal journey. Tailor these instructions to your needs and preferences, and most importantly, be honest and compassionate with yourself throughout the process.

Here's a list of prompts for an expressive writing activity focused on improving financial wellbeing and overcoming past beliefs and experiences about money:

1. How do you feel about money? Explore your inner thoughts and feelings with regard to money.
2. What is money to you? What does it mean to you?
3. With regard to your current finances: how do you feel? Write a description of your feelings.
4. When did you last experience joy or sadness on the subject of money? Write about it and what it taught you.
5. What are your strongest memories of money as a child and an impressionable teenager? How might these experiences have triggered your worldviews about money today?
6. What challenges in your life are related to money? How does it affect your life?
7. What does having money worries feel like in your body? Describe the sensations physically and as they affect you.
8. What would it mean financially for you to be successful? What is your optimal financial situation, and what does it feel like?
9. What was your first memory relating to money? And – if this is a fond memory – does it figure in your current money habits and outlook?
10. When was a time that you found yourself financially panicking? What were you doing? What kind of judgements were you making? How did the feelings make you feel? What was it like to go through those experiences? What steps did you take to handle the feelings?
11. In what ways did people around you, as a child – parents, grandparents, friends, teachers – shape your

attitudes about money? And in what ways did those attitudes translate into your own approach to money today?

12. Write an open letter to the cash in your wallet (or bank account), describing what you are feeling for it right now. Write your fears and your resentment and your aspirations.

13. Tell us about a time when you faced a major obstacle in solving a financial problem. How did you deal with it? What did you learn?

14. If you were already wealthy, what would your current life comprise in ten years?

15. What are some money-related ways you've been your own worst enemy in the past? What are any other limiting beliefs you have around money today? After you've identified these beliefs, identify an alternative, empowering perspective.

16. Is there one good money habit that you'd like to develop? What would this habit be and what small steps can you take this week that will help make that dream a reality?

17. Looking back, what were the key decisions, strategies or support systems that helped you stay on track and avoid getting lost or making mistakes in that situation?

18. Describe a situation in which you regret spending your money and explain why. If possible, suggest an alternative way you could have used the money. How can you avoid spending it in the same way in the future?

19. Develop an essay about your relationship with money. Does it make you happier? Stress you out? Both? Neither? Why?

20. What does financial freedom mean to you? How would you describe your daily life if you felt financially free?

21. What's your money attitude now? Look around at

your current circumstances. What are you grateful for and what changes would you make to get on firmer financial ground?

After completing the expressive writing activity, please go back to the start of the chapter and attempt the expressive writing and money questionnaire again in order to check the difference in the result.

Resources

These resources provide guidance on utilising expressive writing for healing, processing your emotions and improving your mental health and wellbeing.

Books

Writing to Heal: A Guided Journal for Recovering from Trauma & Emotional Upheaval by James W. Pennebaker, New Harbinger Publications, 1997
This guided journal provides exercises and prompts to help individuals process trauma and emotional upheaval through the therapeutic power of writing.

Opening Up by Writing It Down: How Expressive Writing Improves Health and Eases Emotional Pain by James W. Pennebaker and Joshua M. Smyth, Guilford Press, 2016
A book that explores the benefits of expressive writing for mental and physical health, offering practical techniques to ease emotional pain and promote healing.

Writing as a Way of Healing: How Telling Our Stories Transforms Our Lives by Louise DeSalvo, Beacon Press, 1999
DeSalvo discusses the transformative power of storytelling and writing as a means of healing emotional wounds and reclaiming one's life narrative.

Expressive Writing: Words that Heal by James F. Evans, Idyll
Arbor, 2010
A book highlighting the psychological benefits of expressive
writing, providing insights and exercises to help individuals
harness the healing potential of their words.

*The Writing Cure: How Expressive Writing Promotes Health
and Emotional Well-Being* by Susan J. Lepore, American
Psychological Association, 2002
Lepore examines the role of expressive writing in
enhancing health and emotional wellbeing, supported by
research and practical writing strategies.

Apps

Journey – a simple private journal app ideal for expressive
writing: journey.cloud

Penzu – a digital journal for capturing thoughts and feelings:
penzu.com

Moodnotes – A journalling app that incorporates CBT
techniques: www.thriveport.com/products/moodnotes

Day One – A journalling app that allows users to express their
thoughts and feelings: dayoneapp.com

Reflectly – A journalling app that utilises artificial intelligence
for personalised insights: reflectly.app

Websites

Pennebaker Writing Paradigm – Dr. James W. Pennebaker's
official website with information on expressive writing
research: liberalarts.utexas.edu/psychology/faculty/pennebaker

750 Words – A website that encourages daily expressive
writing with a goal of 750 words: 750words.com

Psych Central Expressive Writing Guide: psychcentral.com/lib/
the-health-benefits-of-journaling#1

Verywell Mind Expressive Writing Tips: www.verywellmind. com/how-to-use-expressive-writing-for-healing-4157642

Blog/journal articles

Pennebaker, J. W., & Chung, C. K. (2011). 'Expressive Writing and Its Links to Mental Health.' In H. S. Friedman (ed.), *The Oxford Handbook of Health Psychology*, pp. 417–37. DOI: 10.1093/oxfordhb/9780195342819.013.0015

Frattaroli, J. (2006). 'Experimental disclosure and its moderators: A meta-analysis.' *Psychological Bulletin*, 132(6), 823–865.

Expressive Writing Can Help You Heal: www.apa.org/ monitor/jun02/writing

Writing About Emotions May Ease Stress and Trauma: www. apa.org/news/press/releases/2016/09/writing-emotions

Videos

TedEx Benefits of Expressive Writing
Expressive Writing Exercise Demo

Podcasts

Therapy for Black Girls
The Psych Files

CHAPTER 14

Psychological emergency toolkit

Your brain's a Swiss Army knife - put it to work

A psychological emergency toolkit for financial crises is a lifeline for those navigating the stormy seas of economic hardship. It equips individuals with the tools to manage stress, regulate emotions and foster resilience in the face of financial adversity. By addressing the psychological dimensions of financial crises, this toolkit paves the way for effective problem-solving and long-term financial wellbeing. To understand more about this unique and new concept, first try this questionnaire.

Psychological emergency toolkit and money questionnaire

The objective of this survey is to aid you in tracking and assessing your personal growth. For each of the thirteen statements, circle the number that corresponds to your level of agreement. Add the scores to obtain an initial sense of your financial wellbeing. Once you have gone through the chapter and completed the suggested exercises, revisit the survey. Your answers remain confidential; it is simply a tool to gauge any shifts or advancements in your outlook.

Please indicate how frequently you imagine or worry about the following events, thoughts and feelings regarding money:

1. **Receiving unexpected bills that you can't pay immediately**
   Never – 1
   Rarely – 2
   Sometimes – 3
   Often – 4
   Almost all the time – 5

2. **Feeling that you are going backwards with your finances**
   Never – 1
   Rarely – 2
   Sometimes – 3
   Often – 4
   Almost all the time – 5

3. **The threat of redundancy or other income loss**
   Never – 1
   Rarely – 2
   Sometimes – 3
   Often – 4
   Almost all the time – 5

4. **Consequences of your illness or death, or that of your loved ones**
   Never – 1

Rarely – 2
Sometimes – 3
Often – 4
Almost all the time – 5

5. **Ongoing debt**
   Never – 1
   Rarely – 2
   Sometimes – 3
   Often – 4
   Almost all the time – 5

6. **Fear of bankruptcy or losing your home**
   Never – 1
   Rarely – 2
   Sometimes – 3
   Often – 4
   Almost all the time – 5

7. **Economic issues, like cost-of-living crises, hyperinflation or economic meltdowns**
   Never – 1
   Rarely – 2
   Sometimes – 3
   Often – 4
   Almost all the time – 5

Now, ask yourself how often you get these feelings when you worry about money:

8. **Stress, mind racing and needing relief**
   Never – 1
   Rarely – 2
   Sometimes – 3

Often – 4
Almost all the time – 5

9. **Depression, not being able to motivate yourself**
Never – 1
Rarely – 2
Sometimes – 3
Often – 4
Almost all the time – 5

10. **Helplessness and not being able to cope or figure any way out**
Never – 1
Rarely – 2
Sometimes – 3
Often – 4
Almost all the time – 5

11. **Anxiety, growing increasingly tense because you feel that something bad is happening**
Never – 1
Rarely – 2
Sometimes – 3
Often – 4
Almost all the time – 5

12. **Feelings of inadequacy, that you 'ought' to be able to cope, but can't**
Never – 1
Rarely – 2
Sometimes – 3
Often – 4
Almost all the time – 5

13. **Panic, feeling extreme fear, wanting to run away from your situation**
    Never – 1
    Rarely – 2
    Sometimes – 3
    Often – 4
    Almost all the time – 5

My total score:

Let's learn more about your psychological emergency toolkit and afterwards try some activities.

Introduction

Financial crises can result in stress, anxiety and helplessness, all of which can devastate our mental health.[1] A psychological emergency management toolkit consisting of resources and strategies to help manage these feelings is an essential resource.[2] Because the emotional cost of financial crises is so high, unresolved stress can keep financial difficulties intractable and make problem-solving difficult.

In this chapter, I'll describe a psychological emergency toolkit that can be used to support oneself when experiencing a financial crisis. I'll introduce the content of such toolkits and help you understand how this material supports the management of psychological consequences, builds resilience and strengthens overall financial wellbeing.

Understanding financial crises and their psychological impact

The sources of financial crises can be varied – job loss, bankruptcy, excessive debts, financial downturns[3] – and can certainly have a severe impact on our mental health, including heightened stress, anxiety, depression and feelings of helplessness.[4] Some of the common triggers and risk factors include standalone events such as accidental or sudden job loss, falling sick or experiencing a medical emergency, or divorce. Others may be longer-term, such as a simple lack of planning around finances.[5]

The consequences for our psychological wellbeing can be prolonged and profound, affecting our mental health, relationships, performance at work and quality of life.[6] The psychological impacts of financial crises can be among the most severe in our lives and it is therefore desirable to try to mitigate the impact or frequency of such problems where possible.[7]

Components of a psychological emergency toolkit for financial wellbeing

A psychological emergency toolkit needs a wide set of tools to address the different challenges connected to the financial crisis.[8] Here are some of the strategies to deal with crisis.

Cognitive behavioural strategies:[9]
- Techniques to challenge negative thoughts and irrational beliefs
- mindfulness techniques to focus on the present and reduce overthinking
- goal-setting and problem-solving skills to create action plans

Emotional regulation strategies:[10]
- relaxation techniques like deep breathing and progressive muscle relaxation
- practices to increase emotional awareness and acceptance
- gratitude practices to encourage a positive mindset

Social support and communication strategies:[11]

- building a supportive network of family, friends and professionals
- effective communication skills for discussing financial matters
- guidance on seeking professional help when needed

These components can help individuals manage stress, regulate emotions, develop coping mechanisms, and build resilience when facing financial hardship.[12]

Crisis intervention models and approaches for financial wellbeing

Many models and approaches, including psychosocial frameworks that address both psychological (mental health, emotions) and social (relationships, community) factors, have been developed to help deal with the psychological impact of financial crises. One example is the crisis intervention model for financial wellbeing (CIMFW). This integrates crisis intervention theory, cognitive behavioural therapy and financial therapy to address the emotional, cognitive and behavioural components of financial crisis, including the stages of assessment, crisis intervention, skill-building and follow-up support.[13]

Examples of evidence-based approaches to crisis intervention include financial counselling, debt management programmes and financial therapy. Financial counselling aims to provide clients with a knowledge base and skills to manage their money for better outcomes, including budgeting, debt reduction and remediation.[14] Debt management programmes are structured repayment plans involving counsellors and creditors, and are built around a budget and a debt reduction plan.[15] Financial therapy is embedded in the field of psychology and utilises therapeutic principles and techniques to offer interventions for the emotional and behavioural obstacles that arise in financial decision-making.[16]

In addition to anti-stigma initiatives and education about signs and symptoms of problems, mental health professionals, financial advisors and community organisations can provide crisis intervention services for the promotion of financial wellness.[17] These services include counselling and therapy for individuals experiencing psychological distress related to financial problems;[18] as well as financial advice for debt management, budgeting and long-term financial planning;[19] and resources, education and peer support provided by non-profit credit counselling agencies and support groups.[20]

Technology and digital tools for psychological emergency response in financial crises

Technology-based interventions and digital tools are emerging as assets for people in financial crisis – they provide easy and convenient means to deliver psychological emergency response and financial education.[21]

Mobile apps and online platforms that offer financial literacy, budgeting and expense tracking as well as mental health support abound. Mint and YNAB (You Need a Budget) are popular apps that help users create a budget and track their expenses. Talkspace and BetterHelp are examples of online counselling and therapy platforms.[22]

Providing remote psychological interventions (also termed 'teletherapy services') and counselling through video or phone calls can be vital in dealing with financial crises. Such services can be especially important for people who face barriers to accessing traditional mental health services, such as inadequate access to public transport or mobility issues.[23]

Technology-based interventions can be more convenient, accessible and cost-effective, but they also come with environmental and logistical limitations (for example, concerns about privacy and security and the potential for technology to create a less 'human' experience of the intervention).[24]

Training and education for financial crisis response

Effective responses to financial crises should prepare people for financial distress by teaching them specific skills and knowledge.[25] Financial literacy programmes teach the knowledge and skills needed for good money management, budgeting and wise financial decision-making. Presented in schools, at work and in the community, they can provide a foundation for financial resilience and wellbeing.[26]

Crisis intervention training for mental health professionals is essential, helping them understand and respond to these situations effectively. This includes learning to recognise the warning signs of financial crisis, using open and positive communication methods, and applying proven techniques to support financial wellbeing.[27]

Peer support networks and other community-based initiatives can be helpful in providing education and support for those who are experiencing financial shock.[28] They can help to provide community, shared experience and learning from others who have experienced financial stress.

Financial education and crisis preparedness can help to build resilience to financial shocks. This would involve giving people information to manage their finances. Regardless of how they are affected by financial shocks, providing people with knowledge about finance and safeguarding against the negative consequences of a financial crisis can help to mitigate the consequences of such events and increase the overall financial wellbeing of those concerned.[29]

Cultural considerations in financial crisis response

Even though financial crises may affect people from diverse cultural backgrounds, it is important to include cultural components when designing and implementing operational toolkits and crisis intervention. Cultural norms can shape how people experience, view and react to financial crises and affect their willingness to seek out and utilise support.[30]

Language barriers can impact our ability to communicate and provide financial education and mental health support, especially for families with limited English proficiency.[31] Multilingual resources and services, as well as the availability of culturally competent interpreters, can help break down these barriers and promote equal access to support.[32]

Cultural norms and values about money, indebtedness and financial decision-making can likewise influence attitudes and behaviours.[33] For instance, discussing money and finances may be considered taboo or shameful in some cultures. Respecting such norms and developing culturally sensitive approaches can bolster engagement with crisis intervention.[34]

Stigma related to experiencing mental health issues and their treatment remains a considerable barrier in some cultures.[35] Culturally tailored strategies that aim to ground treatments in culturally relevant idioms have been proposed to help overcome the stigma that may impede people in financial crisis from seeking the necessary support.

Collaboration with community leaders and cultural organisations, as well as members of specific cultural groups who are accepted as credible, might not only help with the design of culturally responsive interventions, but might also help these groups reach out and deliver those interventions to marginalised communities in a way that respects cultural differences.[36] Attending to cultural differences in financial crisis response is critical to ensuring equitable access to support services and to helping members of all communities cope both with the dire effects of financial distress and its accompanying suffering.[37]

Conclusion

The potential for psychological damage caused by financial crises illustrates the potential value of a psychological emergency toolkit that can properly identify and mitigate the mental health issues generated by such crises. Developing and implementing coordinated toolkits and crisis intervention protocols can improve people's resilience to financial burdens and buffer them against economic shocks. Attending to the psychological aspects of financial problems during a crisis can potentially help individuals to cope with stress, manage and adapt to coping mechanisms, and build resilience in order to solve complex problems effectively and improve financial wellbeing in the long run.

Activities

In this chapter the activities are divided into two groups: your short-term psychological toolkit and your middle- or long-term psychological toolkit.

Your short-term psychological toolkit

A short-term toolkit is developed to address acute psychological distress or crises, and the aim of the interventions in this toolkit is to provide rapid relief for a distressing situation. These interventions seek to help stabilise a person's mental state, often with the aim of providing a short-term reduction in distress and an improvement in wellbeing on a more immediate basis, so as to enhance the person's sense of safety or stability.

Your middle- or long-term psychological toolkit

In contrast, a middle- or long-term toolkit is there to help you deal with longer-lasting psychological issues. The preventive interventions within these toolkits, ranging from psychotherapy to lifestyle change measures, address the aspects of life that most impact psychological health in the long run and can thus help those with psychological difficulties return to a state of normal functioning while also enabling those without to reach lasting states of wellbeing. Both are valuable for different reasons and may be used together in providing a full package of psychological support.

Activity 14.1: Create your psychological emergency toolkit

Here are some examples to consider. Feel free to add other activities that come to mind for reducing stress and anxiety. These quick tips can help you manage stress more effectively and approach situations with greater clarity.

Here are some examples of short-term activities:

- listening to soothing or uplifting music;
- watching a motivational video;
- going for a walk, preferably in nature, maybe among trees or near water;
- talking to a close confidant (friend or family member);
- self-care – cooking fresh food or just taking a nice bath;
- breath counting – sitting up straight and counting each inhalation and exhalation to bring about mindfulness and concentration;
- creative expression – doing something creative such as drawing, painting or poetry writing, to express your feelings and experience self-expression;
- deep breathing: simple breathing exercises to alleviate stress and aid relaxation (including diaphragmatic breathing or 4-7-8 breathing, which involves 1. **Inhaling** through your nose for 4 seconds. 2. **Holding**

your breath for 7 seconds. 3. **Exhaling** through your mouth for 8 seconds.);

- grounding techniques: exercises to help focus on the here-and-now and reduce feelings of dissociation or overwhelm, such as 5-4-3-2-1 grounding (which involves 1. Acknowledging 5 things you can see around you. 2. Noticing 4 things you can touch. 3. Identifying 3 things you can hear. 4. Recognising 2 things you can smell. 5. Focusing on 1 thing you can taste);

- positive affirmations: for example, repeating positive statements such as 'I am good enough to succeed' or 'My situation is getting better' in order to counter negative self-narratives and bolster self-worth;

- progressive muscle relaxation (PMR): a systematic technique of tensing and relaxing the muscles in the body in order to let go of tension;

- aromatherapy: utilise your favourite essential oils, aromatherapy bracelet or bath salts scented with calming fragrances such as lavender, chamomile or bergamot. Inhaling soothing scents can be utilised during respiratory difficulties, when you may be unable to breathe in and out voluntarily;

- positive self-talk: counter negative 'thought catches' or negative self-talk with an encouraging word or calming reminder such as 'This is really hard, but I don't have to be perfect. I'm a really smart person. I can do hard things. I am capable. I can do this.' Remind yourself of your past successes and the traits that have helped carry you through the challenges so you can summon them to help see you through to the other side;

- mindful eating: practise eating mindfully, taking each bite slowly while noticing your food's tastes, textures and sensations. This can ensure you stay in the present and don't resort to stress eating;

- read a favourite book;
- watch a favourite film.

Here are some examples of middle- to long-term activities:

Stress management techniques

Deep breathing exercises:
- Practise slow, rhythmic breathing exercises to engage the relaxation response, which will help to turn off the stress response and the physiological manifestations of stress.
- Inhale deeply through the nose, hold for a few seconds, and exhale slowly through the mouth, noting the sensations of the breath.

Progressive muscle relaxation (PMR)
- Engage in progressive muscle relaxation to release tension and promote relaxation throughout the body.
- Tighten and relax each major muscle group one at a time, roughly in the order of: feet, calves, thighs, buttocks, solar plexus, hands and arms, shoulders and head.

Mindfulness meditation
- Use mindfulness meditation, which can improve our ability to live in the present moment and adopt a more non-judgemental stance towards money worries.
- Notice the feel of your breath, the sounds of your environment, and whenever the focus slides, just bring it back.

Guided imagery
- Imagery techniques: Use visualisation to see a peaceful,

calming image (for example, of a beautiful beach or a quiet forest) in your mind's eye.

- Imagine seeing yourself in some safe and comfortable setting. Notice how everything within the scene looks or feels. To help yourself relax, notice any feelings of relaxation or peace beginning to travel through your body.

Stress-busting physical activities

- Exercise regularly to lower stress hormones and buoy mood in the period after financial reversals.
- Pick activities that you love and that you can stick with – things you would do anyway, say, walking, jogging, yoga or dancing – and lodge in your calendar.

Time management and prioritisation

- Implement time management strategies to allocate time and energy effectively towards addressing financial challenges.
- Reserve time to think through your schedule, triage your tasks based on importance and urgency, and chunk them into smaller steps so as not to feel overwhelmed.

Coping skills training to deal with financial crisis:

Identify stressors and triggers

- Identify specific stressors and triggers as they relate to finances, such as debt, job loss, economic uncertainty, etc.
- Be self-aware and reflect on how these stressors impact thoughts, emotions and behaviours.

Cognitive restructuring

- Use cognitive restructuring techniques to challenge and reframe negative thoughts and beliefs about finances.

- Replace catastrophic thinking with more balanced, realistic attitudes and engage in problem-solving strategies.

Problem-solving skills
- Develop problem-solving skills to help cope with financial problems.
- Use a disciplined problem-solving phase model (definition, generation, evaluation, action plan).

Emotion regulation techniques
- Use emotion regulation skills to cope with strong feelings, such as anxiety, fear or frustration triggered by financial stress.
- Practise deep breathing, progressive muscle relaxation, mindfulness meditation or guided imagery to regain emotional equilibrium and resiliency.

Behavioural activation
- Engage in meaningful and pleasurable activities, even under financial constraints.
- Explore hobbies, interests and social activities that provide enjoyment and distraction from financial worries.

Financial planning and budgeting skills
- Develop financial planning and budgeting skills, so that you can take control of your finances and increase your confidence and capacity to make decisions.
- Use budgeting techniques, expense tracking, debt management strategies and ways to increase income or reduce expenses.

Communication and assertiveness skills

- Use social skills, assertiveness and advocacy skills to make interacting with brokers or tenants less daunting.
- Practise assertiveness training to set limits, raise concerns and negotiate with creditors, employers or family members.

Resilience preparation skills

- Create an album of favourite photos, upbeat or happy music, favourite films (the ones you feel good watching) and books (the ones you simply enjoy reading). Keep them handy for those occasions when you need a mood lift.
- Learn a new skill. Not only has it been shown that learning in general raises mood, but skills that are functional – for example, cooking – or that require manual coordination – such as Tai Chi, tango and ballroom dancing – improve physical capacity and mental function.

Resilience-building exercises to deal with financial crisis

Self-compassion and self-care

- Practise self-compassion by treating yourself with kindness and understanding during times of financial hardship.
- Use unconditional self-care activities such as exercise, relaxation techniques or hobbies that help you rejuvenate yourself.

Resilience-building visualisation

- Picture yourself coping successfully with the financial crisis, overcoming it and continuing to thrive with greater security and resilience.

- Imagine specific scenarios where you demonstrate resilience and adaptability in response to financial setbacks.

Reflective writing
- Keep a journal recording your thoughts and feelings about the financial crisis: what you are afraid of, why you are afraid, and your hopes and fears for the future.
- Reflect on past experiences of overcoming adversity and identify personal strengths and resources that can be leveraged during the current crisis.

Try as many of these activities as you want and then work through the psychological emergency toolkit and money questionnaire once more to record any changes.

Resources

Here are some further resources to enrich your knowledge of the psychological emergency toolkit and its impact on holistic wellbeing.

Books

The Little Book of Hygge: The Danish Way to Live Well by Meik Wiking, Penguin Life, 2016
This book explores the concept of *hygge*, a Danish philosophy centred on comfort, cosiness and wellbeing, offering practical tips for incorporating it into everyday life.
Shinrin-Yoku: The Art and Science of Forest Bathing by Dr Qing Li, Penguin Books, 2018
Dr Li introduces the practice of shinrin-yoku, or 'forest bathing', and its health benefits, emphasising the importance of nature in enhancing mental and physical wellbeing.

Coping Skills: Tools & Techniques for Every Stressful Situation by
   Faith G. Harper, Rebel Press, 2018
   This book provides a variety of coping strategies and tools
   to help individuals navigate stress and emotional challenges
   effectively.

Developing Resilience: A Cognitive-Behavioral Approach by Michael
   Neenan, Routledge, 2009
   Neenan offers a cognitive behavioural framework for building
   resilience, equipping readers with practical techniques to cope
   with adversity and enhance personal strength.

*Unwinding Anxiety: New Science Shows How to Break the Cycles
   of Worry and Fear to Heal Your Mind* by Judson Brewer,
   Avery, 2021
   Dr Brewer presents research-backed strategies to understand
   and manage anxiety, emphasising mindfulness practices to
   disrupt cycles of worry and fear.

*The Financial Anxiety Solution: A Step-by-Step Workbook to Stop
   Worrying about Money, Take Control of Your Finances, and Live
   a Happier Life* by Lindsay Bryan-Podvin, New Harbinger
   Publications, 2021
   This workbook provides actionable steps to help individuals
   overcome financial anxiety, regain control of their finances
   and cultivate a healthier relationship with money.

When Things Fall Apart: Heart Advice for Difficult Times by Pema
   Chödrön, Shambhala Publications, 2010
   Chödrön offers compassionate guidance for navigating life's
   challenges, encouraging readers to embrace uncertainty and
   cultivate resilience through mindfulness.

*Resilient: How to Grow an Unshakable Core of Calm, Strength,
   and Happiness* by Dr Rick Hanson with Forrest Hanson,
   Harmony Books, 2020
   A book combining neuroscience and practical exercises to
   help readers build resilience, fostering emotional strength
   and wellbeing in the face of life's difficulties.

Apps

You Need a Budget (YNAB): www.youneedabudget.com
Talkspace: www.talkspace.com
Breathwrk: www.breathwrk.com
MoneyHub: www.moneyhubapp.com
BetterHelp: www.betterhelp.com
What's Up?: www.thewhatsupapp.co.uk

Websites

Positive Psychology: positivepsychology.com/cope-with-stress
Cleveland Clinic: health.clevelandclinic.org/
    get-happy-exercise-can-lift-mood-infographic
Verywell Mind: www.verywellmind.com/
    tips-to-reduce-stress-3145195
Mind: www.mind.org.uk/information-support/
    types-of-mental-health-problems/depression/self-care
NHS (Every Mind Matters): www.nhs.uk/
    every-mind-matters/lifes-challenges/
    money-worries-mental-health
Healthline: www.healthline.com/health/anxiety/
    money-anxiety#causes
Happiful: happiful.com
Good Good Good: www.goodgoodgood.co/goodnews
Action for Happiness: actionforhappiness.org
    Happy Doggo: www.happydoggo.com

Blog/journal articles

Forest Bathing: www.npr.
    org/2023/08/22/1195337204/a-guide-to-forest-bathing
Tips to reduce stress: www.nhs.uk/mental-health/self-help/
    guides-tools-and-activities/tips-to-reduce-stress

How financial stress impacts your health (and 5 tips to deal): blog.calm.com/blog/financial-stress

Financial Stress: Symptoms, Effects, & How to Cope: www.choosingtherapy.com/financial-stress

Why are hobbies important for stress relief?: www.verywellmind.com/the-importance-of-hobbies-for-stress-relief-3144574

6 Ways to Reduce Financial Anxiety to Boost Mental Health: www.psychologytoday.com/us/blog/mental-wealth/202401/6-ways-to-reduce-financial-anxiety-to-boost-mental-health

Coping Skills for Depression: 10 Strategies & How to Use Them: www.choosingtherapy.com/coping-skills-for-depression

Depression and anxiety: Exercise eases symptoms: www.mayoclinic.org/diseases-conditions/depression/in-depth/depression-and-exercise/art-20046495

18 effective stress relief strategies: www.verywellmind.com/tips-to-reduce-stress-3145195

Move yourself happy! How to exercise to boost your mood – whatever your fitness level: www.theguardian.com/lifeandstyle/2022/jun/29/move-yourself-happy-how-to-exercise-boost-mood-fitness-level

100 Coping Skills You Can Practice Right Now: mind-bar.com/100-coping-skills

Self-care for depression: www.mind.org.uk/information-support/types-of-mental-health-problems/depression/self-care

33 Quick Ways to Cheer Yourself Up When You Feel Down: www.happierhuman.com/cheer-yourself-up

Videos

30 Minute Mood boost & anxiety release cardio workout
How To Stop Worrying About Money – A Proven Formula

When Debt Pushes You Over The Edge | Debt & Depression
Therapist Explains How Debt Affects your Mental Health
What is Financial Trauma? Managing Scarcity Mindset and
    Overspending
Resilience: planetpositivechange.com/
    the-10-best-resilience-videos

Podcasts

The Verywell Mind Podcast: www.verywellmind.com/
    the-verywell-mind-podcast-5187013
SilverCloud – Money Worries Program: www.silvercloudhealth.
    com/us/blog/money-worries-take-a-toll-on-mental-health
Financial Wellbeing Podcast: www.financialwell-being.co.uk
Money Worries and Financial Wellbeing Podcast:
    thefinancialwellbeingforum.org/podcast
Money Magpie: www.moneymagpie.com/podcast
The Happiness Lab: www.happinesslab.fm

SECTION 2, PART 3

Hand/financial behaviour/ action

In this section, you'll learn how to enhance financial wellbeing through interventions focused on actions, financial behaviours and practical habits.

CHAPTER 15

Money habits

Co-authored by Kim Stephenson

Habits are sneaky – by the time you notice them, they've moved in

Practising good financial habits is pivotal to fostering a stable and secure financial future. Such habits form the cornerstone of effective money management, influencing our ability to navigate economic challenges and achieve our long-term financial goals. By cultivating disciplined spending, saving and investment behaviours, individuals can lay the groundwork for financial wellbeing, ensuring resilience and prosperity in the face of an ever-changing financial landscape.

Money habits questionnaire

This survey aims to help you assess and track your personal development with regard to your money habits. Please rate how much you agree with each of the ten statements below by circling the corresponding number. Tally up your scores to get a baseline measurement of your current habits and mind-set. After working through the exercises in this chapter, take the survey again. Feel free to keep your responses private; this is simply a tool for you to measure any positive shifts or improvements.

1. **I know what products and services I spend most of my money on.**
   Strongly disagree – 1
   Disagree – 2
   Somewhat disagree – 3
   Neither agree nor disagree – 4
   Somewhat agree – 5
   Agree – 6
   Strongly agree – 7

2. **I know where I spend spontaneously (such as online, in sales, favourite stores).**
   Strongly disagree – 1
   Disagree – 2
   Somewhat disagree – 3
   Neither agree nor disagree – 4
   Somewhat agree – 5
   Agree – 6
   Strongly agree – 7

3. **I have organised records for my finances so I can find documents like insurance policies and payslips and pensions.**
   Strongly disagree – 1
   Disagree – 2
   Somewhat disagree – 3
   Neither agree nor disagree – 4
   Somewhat agree – 5

Agree – 6
Strongly agree – 7

4. **I have a system for dealing with new information, like credit card bills and bank statements.**
Strongly disagree – 1
Disagree – 2
Somewhat disagree – 3
Neither agree nor disagree – 4
Somewhat agree – 5
Agree – 6
Strongly agree – 7

5. **I have set up financial goals that I review regularly.**
Strongly disagree – 1
Disagree – 2
Somewhat disagree – 3
Neither agree nor disagree – 4
Somewhat agree – 5
Agree – 6
Strongly agree – 7

6. **I have set up prompts to remind me to check on my finances.**
Strongly disagree – 1
Disagree – 2
Somewhat disagree – 3
Neither agree nor disagree – 4
Somewhat agree – 5
Agree – 6
Strongly agree – 7

7. **I have deliberately set up a new financial habit in the past.**
Strongly disagree – 1
Disagree – 2
Somewhat disagree – 3
Neither agree nor disagree – 4
Somewhat agree – 5
Agree – 6
Strongly agree – 7

8. **I have previously managed to stop an unproductive financial habit.**
Strongly disagree – 1
Disagree – 2
Somewhat disagree – 3
Neither agree nor disagree – 4
Somewhat agree – 5
Agree – 6
Strongly agree – 7

9. **I have recognised at least one financial habit that I'd like to stop or change.**
Strongly disagree – 1
Disagree – 2
Somewhat disagree – 3
Neither agree nor disagree – 4
Somewhat agree – 5
Agree – 6
Strongly agree – 7

10. **I have at least one financial habit that I'd like to establish, to make life easier.**
Strongly disagree – 1
Disagree – 2

Somewhat disagree – 3
Neither agree nor disagree – 4
Somewhat agree – 5
Agree – 6
Strongly agree – 7

My total score:

Introduction

Habits are behaviours we perform automatically: we execute them unconsciously and effortlessly, a process helped along by our brain's ability to save time and energy by putting such activities on autopilot. Habits can certainly be useful in everyday life, when they automate behaviour that helps us. But if they are unhelpful, they can cause problems by keeping us behaving, unconsciously, in ways that we don't want. This is particularly true of financial habits. If they lead us to be prudent, to save, control our urges and spend wisely, that's great, but too often we have a legacy of poor financial habits that make it hard for us to do what we know would benefit us.[1]

The evidence strongly suggests that when our good intentions run up against poor money habits, the habitual routines win almost every time.[2] That's why positive new money habits – particularly those related to regularly and deliberately budgeting, saving and spending thoughtfully – are integral to making our financial lives more successful and sustainable.[3]

Trying to change habits

If we want to change our ingrained habits, what can be done? We might think the issue is to disseminate new knowledge or get people motivated. But in one of the largest health campaigns ever run, aimed at increasing the consumption of fruit and vegetables (crucially, mainly outside the home) in Great Britain, increasing people's awareness about the benefits of eating more fruit and vegetables had surprisingly little impact on what people actually ate.[4]

Likewise, in a highly publicised study, Zeedyk and colleagues reported that it wasn't enough to teach kids about healthy habits; for children to actually adopt those habits, their relationships would have to change. Knowledge and education alone aren't the keys to changing long-lasting habits.

A popular technique intended to alter our behaviours involves using planning or reminders to help individuals remember (and perhaps stick with) their intentions – for example, setting specific implementation intentions (such as planning exactly when and where you will do something) and prompts or cues (for example, setting your smartphone reminder). These strategies can be useful for short-term behaviour change, although there is little evidence that they have long-term effects on our habits. In fact, studies show that these techniques have only limited effects for habits that have developed over many years (i.e. deeply ingrained habits, such as eating badly, smoking, spending too much or not saving money).[5]

We often, through new situational or stress-driven conditions, fall back into our old stereotypical pathways, or force ourselves through a series of suboptimal decisions based on the tactical requirements of the moment, rather than focusing on strengthening our long-term goals. Furthermore, the gravitational pull of these habit zones (where we have learned to unwind) can create major challenges. Pavlov, the Russian physiologist who originally identified the principles of classical conditioning, commented in 1927 on his dog's response to the bell that it had become not only a reflex but, rather, a form of 'suggestion'. We can think of this as a more subtle and powerful version of a habit. It's perhaps this change in our environment and/or the cues that trigger our former habits that makes habit change so difficult. How do we deal with these challenges? We clearly need to pay attention to the situations in which we exist – to create spaces that encourage and support the habits we want to cultivate and extinguish the ones we don't want.

Habits and money

Several studies have investigated work related to savings behaviour, given its importance for the achievement of financial goals but also as a component of financial wellbeing.[6]

One illustrative study from Loibl and colleagues assessed whether membership in a savings programme altered the practice of regular savings and levels of financial stress. Those members of the twelve-month programme who developed a regular savings habit tended to report that their savings increased over the course of the programme and also that they experienced less financial stress when dealing with more difficult financial situations. Putting financial habits in place not only has financial benefits, it can also boost our emotional wellbeing and resilience.

But as we've already seen, telling people to save, or even amplifying their personal desire to save more, doesn't seem to be a sustained way to change behaviour. The difference may be in providing specific plans for action and ensuring that people make consistent actions to fulfil their intentions until they become habits.[7]

Other research has explored the role of habits in spending and borrowing. One study by Wood and Tam found that people spent based on 'cues of the location or environment in which they acquired their habits', the sorts of things they might accumulate around them – from credit card logos to the way a store was laid out.[8] Many of our habits are not up to us; they emerge from the context in which we make decisions.

Likewise, work exploring credit card debt has emphasised habit. A study showed that people who habitually used credit cards were more likely not only to underestimate how much they had spent but also to make impulse purchases.[9] Dissolving the dynamic forces of invisible money by using mindful spending habits, watching out for easily accessible credit cards that encourage overspending and impulse purchases, and signalling cues that could lure you into debt, could aid you to keep your financial bearings.

How habits work

In order to modify our habits, we might benefit from understanding more about the psychological underpinnings of habits at a very basic level. One easy way to think about it is that 'neurons that fire together, wire together', a maxim also known as Hebb's rule.[10] This means that the more we do something the way we've done it before, the more that neural pattern becomes cemented in our brains, so that the brain is able to execute the behaviour faster and more easily than before because of the neural pathways already established.[11]

Habits consist of a cue, something in our environment that triggers a craving; a behaviour, the action we perform that provides a reward; and the reward, fulfilling that craving. We initially have to think about each stage of the habit. But if we repeat the cycle enough times, a cue triggers the behaviour. And a behaviour leads to a reward automatically. This 'cue–behaviour–reward' pattern gets embedded in our brains so firmly that we end up performing habits unconsciously, and whether or not we still get the initial reward from the behaviour.[12]

We may consciously try to build habits to meet a goal (you might, say, decide to set a reminder to spend less money each month). At other times, habits take hold without our even trying; we are primed by the environment around us and by the feedback it provides us about how we behave.[13] When a habit is formed, it can stay put even if the reward no longer motivates us, or if the outcome of our behaviour becomes negative (think of keeping up a habit of spending money you don't have, even when it puts you in debt).[14]

Habit change is notoriously difficult to pin down, and some of the research can seem contradictory or confusing.[15] The big picture, however, is that when it comes to changing our habits, motivation alone is often not enough. This is because it can take a long time to adjust a habit or replace it with a new one, hence the need for repetition.[16]

Another crucial aspect is the extent to which immediate rewards facilitate the habit loop. Many of those immediate rewards, the buzz of buying something new, for example, are attractive and tend to create automatic habits because the reward is so easy to perceive. But they tend to be the habits we don't want. The valuable, longer-term rewards – saving for later life, for example – don't have so much immediate appeal as they are much harder to perceive. We think about immediate gratification, not how good we'll feel in twenty years' time. So many of our habits with money are formed because they give us very short-term rewards, and those tend to be the ones we want to change; the ones we want to develop are, almost by definition, rewarding only over the long term, and not so immediately appealing. So we often need to work out how to extinguish the existing ones, and to consciously build new, longer-term habits.[17]

Other recent research considers the issues around self-control and executive function and their role in habit change. For example, in a 2019 paper, it was reported that, when groups of people were followed over time, those who were better at self-control gained good habits (e.g. taking vitamins or saving money) and avoided bad habits (e.g. watching too much television) in greater numbers compared with those who were less able to rein in their impulses.[18] These observations suggest that improving our self-control by developing better capacities for regulating our actions and behaviours, as well as resisting temptations, could be an important part of habit-change success.

Conclusion

Research underscores the extent to which habits determine the details of how we go about making daily choices. They often 'happen' to us, meaning that we often carry out the action without much – if any – conscious thought.[19] Understanding the process of habit formation, as well as the means of habit maintenance and change, allows us to change unhelpful financial habits, replace them with more helpful ones and use new habits to achieve our long-term financial goals.[20]

Taking a habit-based approach to personal finance shifts our focus away from the fickleness of good intentions or the discipline of pure willpower towards developing consistent and repeatable behaviours that we can fit into our daily routines.[21] Establishing financial habits that better reflect the things we value in life can close the gap between knowing and doing when it comes to our money.[22]

None of these habits promise immediate results. It takes a while to develop good habits when it comes to money, and plenty of hard work. But the effect is profound: habits are the daily bridge that transforms vague intents into concrete actions. They connect today with faraway tomorrows so we can build ourselves a financial future that feels more solid and secure. Equipped with the power of habit, positive financial moves become slightly easier every time we have to make them until they make their way into an unconscious response. In other words, they start happening automatically, freeing up more of our mental energy for the things that are more important to us in life.[23]

To enhance the likelihood of transforming your financial habits and behaviours, having a clear goal is essential. Such a goal will extend beyond a mere monetary target, focusing instead on the person you aspire to be, your desired mindset and approach towards money, and the type of relationship you wish to cultivate with it. Gaining awareness of your current habits is pivotal in understanding their impact on your journey to self-improvement. The activities in this chapter serve as foundational tools to deepen this self-awareness.

Activity 15.1: What do you want to be?

Jot down your responses to the following query:

What are your aspirations regarding the person you aim to become in terms of financial matters? For instance, envision whether you:

- have confidence about money;
- aim to eliminate anxieties, stress and limiting beliefs;
- desire a sense of control;
- aspire to assist others with their financial concerns;
- help others with their money issues.

Activity 15.2: Self-reflection on money habits

Find out what exactly you aspire to be in the area of money. Record your answers to the following questions.

1. What negative (harmful) money habits do you have, that you would like to change? For example: Do you find that money mysteriously disappears? Do you avoid looking at your financial statements, your bills or other financial information because you are always worrying about where your money is going and if you are ever going to get back on top of things?
2. What kind of good, responsible money habit do you already have that you want to try to keep up? Maybe you always check your bank and credit card statements, or use an app for tracking your expenditure, or have direct debits for bill payments and savings deposits?

3. What healthy habits could you cultivate to improve your financial health? Things like automatic savings, setting up a personal system for managing your finances, or time-bound check-ins on goals with explicit plans would fit here.

4. How can you fortify or sustain the helpful financial habits you already possess?

5. Name one habit that is not helpful and that you wish to drop – e.g. impulse purchasing, putting off certain financial tasks.

6. Identify your assets – your tools – that will help you on this journey: financial apps proficiency, motivational dreams, willingness to learn, and more.

Activity 15.3: Establishing new habits

This activity is designed for situations where you aim to cultivate a new habit to align with your desired self. Follow these steps and examples for effective implementation:

1. *Think about aspirations:* Apply what you learned from Activity 15.1. Choose a place for a new habit.
   Example: Based on your reflections, you decide that a certain kind of financial security is important to you – and that you are the sort of person who wants to have the habit of systematic saving.

2. *Explore options:* Consider various methods to establish this new behaviour.
   Example: Search for a dedicated savings app, set up a standing order, or transfer the cash into a savings account yourself, weekly.

3. *Motivating and easy options:* Choose one or two options that sound positive to you, and that don't seem too

difficult. You might even dip your toe in the water and pick the easiest possibility. One item off the list might not seem like a lot, but it will add up.

Example: Choose to set up an automatic standing order, which automatically means your savings contribution should be hassle-free and consistent. This small step is both motivating and easy.

4. *Decide the frequency:* Decide how often this new habit will happen – daily, weekly, monthly. To save money, you might want to contribute to your savings account every month.

   Example: Decide that your saving level will be (for example) a month-to-month deposit scheduled around your payroll.

5. *Coordinate with ongoing activities:* What other regular activities do you accomplish at this time – e.g. property maintenance, tax returns, going to clubs?

   Example: Identify your routine activities, such as weekly property check-ins or monthly business returns.

6. *Link to an existing behaviour:* Pick an existing habitual behaviour that you intend to link to the new behaviour.

   Example: Once a month after I review my tax returns (cue/existing behaviour), I will transfer money to my savings account (new behaviour). This will make the behaviour easy/automatic and feel rewarding.

7. *Reward and build over time:* Realise the reward of improved health and financial control. Increase your frequency of extra actions or 'layers of complexity' incrementally over time, without having to fundamentally change your lifestyle.

Example: Celebrate every successful monthly transfer. Adding a check of the spending patterns or investigation of the investment possibilities would be beneficial only years later.

By following these steps and examples, you establish a structured approach to developing new habits, facilitating a gradual and rewarding transformation aligned with your aspirations.

Activity 15.4: Transforming habits

This activity is structured for individuals seeking to alter existing financial habits, promoting automatic positive behaviour.

1. *Examine habits* (output from Activity 15.2):
   Think about the financial habits you identified in Activity 2. Pick one that you wish to exchange and replace with a more helpful one that will help you better manage your finances.
   Example: Your reflection in Activity 15.2 reveals the habit of continuously overpaying for things you do not need to compromise your budget.

2. *Analyse cues:* If you're not sure about your habit-triggering cues, run an analysis, noting the habit that you want to break, and then identify potential cues, keeping in mind that conscious assessment is likely to reveal more than one factor.
   Example: Study what's causing your impulse buying. Is it stress? How about being with other people? Online shopping? Figure out exactly what your cues are.

3. *Select a significant cue:* Choose a key cue strongly linked to the habit. If, say, you just can't seem to avoid looking

at, or actually opening, financial statements even though they make you anxious, the receipt of a statement might be a great cue to target your habit.

Example: Make a key cue connected to overspending the focus of this trigger, such as feeling stressed. This feeling of stress is the cue that triggers my financial behaviour: I spend too much when I feel stressed.

4. *Define a small action:* Designate a subsequent action, tailored to your cue, that is relatively easy to implement.
Example: Tell yourself, 'I'll open and review the financial statements when I get them.' This intermediate step is easy to implement since it's a small piece of an emerging positive financial habit.
Stress response: For example, identify a tiny stress action, like meditating for ten minutes before buying any non-essential item, so that it will help you to address stress and impulsive spending.

5. *Initiate the habit:* Start performing the behaviour. In this case, open and review your financial statements weekly. This becomes your first habit. Why does it work this way? In the words of B. J. Fogg, the creator of the Tiny Habits method: 'The way to create new habits and behaviours is not to think big. It's to start small.'
Example: When buying something, make sure you do the ten-minute mindfulness exercise first. This is a 'routine' that is repeated and helps you to pause, think and make more thoughtful decisions.

6. *Progress and understanding:* Start by synthesising what you already know, and progress to a deeper level of sophistication (i.e. comparing the latest statement with preceding ones); and, if you are at a loss and feel

ill-equipped, either find a financial adviser or a friend with better financial literacy to translate the picture for you. This step constitutes an improvement in financial literacy.

Example: As you advance, compare your pre-practising mindfulness exercise versus your actual spending patterns. If you find difficulty in reading your financial statements or planning, enlist the help of financial resources or friends.

7. *Seek guidance if necessary:* If you have more complicated financial questions, consult an honest financial adviser, or a friend with more experience. Their opinions can give you a different viewpoint that will help you better grasp the issue and figure out what to do.

Example: If you realise you need help understanding how to read financial statements, once you start doing so regularly, ask a financial adviser or a finance-savvy friend to explain some of the basics to you, and to direct you to sound sources for improving your knowledge.

8. *Establish small, easy-to-implement habits:* Overall, the aim is to create small habits, easily woven into your days, which, even if they take several minutes, help you transform from your old habits of ignoring finances to becoming in charge, gaining the critical information you need to get ready to see new, healthy financial habits emerge.

Example: Add another simple practice, such as a weekly review of your budget tally, or exploring an educational website. These are small practices but, in the right sequence, they'll strengthen each other as you move from debt and overspending to a controlled, informed approach.

By following these steps, you create a structured approach to transform existing financial habits, fostering a positive shift in behaviour and financial wellbeing over time.

Engage in the provided activities and subsequently revisit the money habits questionnaire presented at the start of this chapter. Research indicates that the process of establishing new habits or eliminating old ones typically spans a duration ranging from 28 to 66 days.[24] This timeframe underscores the importance of consistent effort and commitment in reshaping financial behaviours.

Resources

Here are some further resources to enrich your knowledge of habits and its impact on holistic wellbeing.

Books

Changing to Thrive by James Prochaska and Janice Prochaska, Da Capo Lifelong Books, 2016
This book outlines a comprehensive approach to behavioural change, integrating the stages of change model to help readers cultivate lasting habits.

The Power of Habit by Charles Duhigg, Random House, 2012
Duhigg explores the science behind habits, explaining how they are formed and providing strategies to change them for personal and professional improvement.

Atomic Habits by James Clear, Avery, 2018
Clear offers a practical framework for building good habits and breaking bad ones, emphasising the importance of small, incremental changes for long-term success.

Goodbye, Things: The New Japanese Minimalism by Fumio Sasaki, W. W. Norton & Company, 2017
Sasaki shares his personal journey into minimalism,

advocating for the benefits of decluttering and simplifying life to enhance wellbeing and happiness.

The Willpower Instinct by Kelly McGonigal, Avery, 2011
McGonigal combines psychology and neuroscience to explain the science of willpower and offers strategies for harnessing it to achieve personal goals.

Nudge by Richard Thaler and Cass Sunstein, Penguin Press, 2008
This influential book discusses how subtle changes in the way choices are presented can significantly influence decisions and behaviours, promoting better outcomes.

Tiny Habits by B.J. Fogg, Houghton Mifflin Harcourt, 2019
Fogg introduces a simple method for creating lasting change through small, manageable habits, emphasising that tiny changes can lead to significant transformations.

Making Habits, Breaking Habits by Jeremy Dean, Da Capo Lifelong Books, 2016
This book provides an evidence-based approach to understanding how habits are formed and offers practical strategies for making and breaking habits.

Habit Stacking by S.J. Scott, CreateSpace Independent Publishing Platform, 2017
Scott presents a straightforward method for building new habits by stacking them onto existing ones, making it easier to integrate positive changes into daily life.

The Habit Blueprint by James Portland, Independently published, 2017
This guide offers a systematic approach to habit formation, providing tools and techniques to help readers develop sustainable habits for personal success.

How We Learn by Benedict Carey, Random House, 2014
Carey explores the latest research on learning, offering insights into how to optimise learning processes and retain information more effectively.

The Craving Mind by Judson Brewer, Yale University Press, 2017
   Brewer examines the nature of cravings and addiction,
   using mindfulness techniques to help individuals
   understand and overcome their compulsions.
Willpower by Roy Baumeister and John Tierney, Penguin
   Press, 2011
   This book delves into the science of self-control, explaining
   how willpower works and providing strategies to strengthen
   it for better decision-making and behaviour.

Apps

HabitBull: www.habitbull.com
Productive Habit Tracker
Streaks: streaksapp.com
Habitica: habitica.com
Streaks: streaksapp.com
Way of Life: wayoflifeapp.com
Done
Fabulous: thefabulous.co
TickTick: ticktick.com
Goalify: www.goalifyapp.com

Websites

Dr Jud Brewer: drjud.com
B J Fogg: www.bjfogg.com
James Clear: jamesclear.com
ZenHabits: zenhabits.net
DevelopGoodHabits: www.developgoodhabits.com
Lifehack: www.lifehack.org/articles/featured/good-habits.html
HabitNest: habitnest.com
TinyHabits: www.tinyhabits.com

Blog/journal articles

James Clear: jamesclear.com/articles?utm_source=feedspot
Develop Good Habits Blog: www.developgoodhabits.com/
good-habits-blog
Zen Habits Blog: zenhabits.net/blog
The Energy Project Blog: theenergyproject.com/category/
habits – Covers habits relating to energy, engagement and
productivity
Tiny Habits Blog: www.tinyhabits.com/blog – Introduces BJ
Fogg's Tiny Habits method for small habit change
Perfecting Discipline Blog: perfectingdiscipline.com/blog
Steve Pavlina Blog: www.stevepavlina.com/blog
The Startup Blog: medium.com/swlh/tagged/habits

Videos

The Power of Habit: Charles Duhigg (TED talk)
A simple way to break a bad habit. Jud Brewer (TED talk)
Forget Big Change – Start With A Tiny Habit by BJ Fogg
(TEDx talk)
Hacking Your Brain's 'Reward System' to Change Habits -
graphic. Jud Brewer
The power of believing that you can improve – Carol Dweck
(TED talk)
Shlomo Benartzi: Saving for tomorrow
How to Build Good Habits & Break Bad Ones – James Clear
How to Break Bad Habits – Jay Shetty
The Habit Power Scorecard & Daily Routine Builder
How I Broke Bad Habits + Formed GOOD HABITS –
Detailed Step-By-Step Process

Podcasts

The habit factor: podcast.thehabitfactor.com
Habits on purpose: habitsonpurpose.com/podcast
Changing habits changing lives: habitsonpurpose.com/podcast
James Clear on *Rich Roll* podcast
Kicking habits with Carol Urry

CHAPTER 16

Financial literacy

Co-authored by Kim Stephenson

Learn money smarts now, or stay broke later

Financial literacy is the way to a brighter tomorrow! If you want to be able to confidently pursue your dreams — maybe saving enough for that luxury vacation you've always envisioned, buying a first home, or ensuring that you don't experience a difficult, lean lifestyle during retirement, it pays to gain knowledge about budgeting, investing and managing debt. Financial literacy is not only empowering, it's the key to a brighter fiscal life. Tap into financial literacy today and watch your world become brighter. But first take this financial literacy test.

Financial literacy questionnaire

This survey will help you track and assess your personal growth. Circle the number corresponding to your agreement with each of the ten statements below, and add up your scores to get an initial sense of your development. After engaging in the chapter's exercises, revisit the survey. Your responses are private and serve as a tool to gauge any changes in your outlook.

1. **Creating and following a budget**
   Do not know about – 1
   Aware – 2
   Know some basics – 3
   Understand in principle – 4
   Understand and use – 5

2. **Understanding debit and loan terms like APR (Annual Percentage Rate) and EAR (Effective Annual Rate)**
   Do not know about – 1
   Aware – 2
   Know some basics – 3
   Understand in principle – 4
   Understand and use – 5

3. **Understanding compound interest**
   Do not know about – 1
   Aware – 2
   Know some basics – 3
   Understand in principle – 4
   Understand and use – 5

4. **Understanding the importance of short-term and emergency savings**
   Do not know about – 1
   Aware – 2
   Know some basics – 3
   Understand in principle – 4
   Understand and use – 5

5. **Understanding long-term savings strategies such as pensions**
   Do not know about – 1
   Aware – 2
   Know some basics – 3
   Understand in principle – 4
   Understand and use – 5

6. **Understanding different kinds of insurances like life insurance and property insurance (e.g. e.g. cars, houses, possessions)**
   Do not know about – 1
   Aware – 2
   Know some basics – 3
   Understand in principle – 4
   Understand and use – 5

7. **Understanding inflation and its impact**
   Do not know about – 1
   Aware – 2
   Know some basics – 3
   Understand in principle – 4
   Understand and use – 5

8. **Understanding the risk and reward of investments**
   Do not know about – 1
   Aware – 2
   Know some basics – 3
   Understand in principle – 4
   Understand and use – 5

9. **Understanding the differences between credit and debit cards**
   Do not know about – 1

Aware – 2
Know some basics – 3
Understand in principle – 4
Understand and use – 5

10. **Understanding different investment categories like mutual funds, stocks, bonds, etc.**
Do not know about – 1
Aware – 2
Know some basics – 3
Understand in principle – 4
Understand and use – 5

My total score:

Now, let's find out more about financial literacy and how it can help you in your life.

Introduction

Financial literacy is simply the ability to handle money in a way that ensures you feel financially healthy today and tomorrow.[1] It's a facet of financial wellbeing, and it involves knowing about different money concepts and making the right decisions about your personal finances.[2] Being financially literate means you meet your money needs, are secure about your future, and have nothing stealing your joy in life.

Understanding financial wellbeing

Financial security is important, but money is not freedom from financial worry.[3] There is more to financial wellbeing than money. Financial wellbeing means 'being in good financial health – feeling secure financially, having the freedom to choose to do what you want to do because you can afford it, and the financial mindset which enables you to enjoy life without paying constant attention to the dollars and cents'.[4] Financial security is being able to save for the unexpected; having choice also means that the decisions you make in your personal life are about what you want to do and not what you can afford; and enjoying life without money worry means having peace of mind about your money because you can do what is important to you without paying attention to it.

Key components of financial literacy

Budgeting

Budgeting means planning for how you're going to spend and save your money. Keeping track of how much money comes in and how much goes out ensures you are spending within your means. Budgeting is the cornerstone of financial literacy, as it helps you control your finances and helps you make wise decisions about your money.[5] Budgeting is essential, as it contributes to savings, financial stability, reduced stress, lower levels of debt, and greater independence.

Saving

You save by putting aside money for the future, to build up your emergency fund in case you have unexpected expenses, and to reach long-term money goals such as buying a home or saving up for retirement. You might use high-yield savings accounts and certificates of deposit to make your saved money work for you.[6]

Investing

To invest is to put your money in some other kind of financial product as a way to make a gain in the future. This would involve investment principles such as diversification (spreading out your money over numerous different types of investments so as to not make yourself vulnerable to a single market downturn) and holding on to your investments for as long as possible in order to avoid market volatility. Investing is one of the crucial activities in building a pathway to wealth and securing your financial legacy.[7]

Credit management

This means having a grasp of how credit works and how you can use it well. A good credit score can unlock lots of financial opportunities, such as buying a home by getting a mortgage offer or taking out a low-interest loan.[8] To have a good credit score, you can take actions such as paying your bills on time, keeping your credit card debt below its limit, and not applying for a lot of credit at the same time.[9]

Debt management

This involves the ability to appreciate the difference between good debt – borrowing money to buy things that have intrinsic value and might even increase in value over time (e.g. a house, an education) – and bad debt – borrowing money to buy things that have no intrinsic value and are more likely to lose value over time (e.g. most consumer goods).[10] Good strategies to manage debt include paying more than the minimum amount due; paying off debts with the highest interest rate first; and avoiding taking on new debt, where possible.[11]

Benefits of financial literacy

- **Better financial decisions**: Financial literacy means knowing all of the personal information you need to make decisions about how to spend, save and invest. It means you'll make better decisions. For example, you'll be more likely to consider the money decisions you're making in the long run.[12] You'll avoid impulsive money choices.[13]

- **Better management of debt**: If you know about how debt works, you can manage it better. For example, what interest is; which debts to pay off first; and how to learn to not take on too much debt. Better debt management means lower levels of distress and better financial wellbeing.

- **Greater financial security**: Financial literacy allows you to allocate money in case of emergencies and future expenses, which helps you to gain more financial security. Being aware of how much of your income to set aside towards your savings and in which account to keep your emergency funds, allows you to gain security and stability when funds are low.

- **Financial independence**: When you're financially literate, you have the tools and knowledge you need to live without relying on others for money. This means being able to support yourself, make your own financial decisions and enjoy more freedom of choice.

- **More money over time**: Being financially literate allows you to earn the most on your investment opportunities, for example by utilising compound interest effectively. By saving and investing early, in the right way to earn favourable returns, you naturally have more money over time.[14]

The impact of financial literacy on different life stages

Children and teens

When young people learn about money while they're young, they can build healthy attitudes and behaviours that last a lifetime. Teaching kids about how money works, how to save and spend, what it can and cannot do and other practical basics are linked with positive financial outcomes in adulthood. Adults can help children as young as six by having regular conversations at meals or during tasks about specific money-related issues that might be relevant to their young lives. Financial literacy and education programmes in schools are related to better money-handling skills and behaviours among students.

Young adults
Young adulthood – typically starting in a person's mid-twenties – can be a critical time to sharpen financial literacy as many people take on the responsibility of independently managing their money for the first time. This often includes student loan repayments, saving and investing for the future, and using credit. Being financially literate can help young adults avoid some of the common financial traps and put a foundation in place for a lifetime of economic independence.[15]

Midlife
In midlife, people often have to make big financial decisions – buying a home, saving for kids' college education, investing for their own retirement. To make it through these stages of your life with your finances intact, you need adequate financial literacy so you are on track to meet your long-term money goals.

Retirement
Retirement-age individuals have to make at least two financial decisions: how to convert their life savings into income, and how to manage their healthcare costs over the rest of their lives. Making sound financial decisions is key to securing your financial life after retirement. Financial literacy has the potential to increase access to financial services by helping retirees manage their savings so that they don't run out in retirement. This, in turn, can help retirees maintain a predetermined standard of living.

Financial literacy and mental wellbeing

- **Less stress about money:** Being financially literate can help you stress less about your money issues because you have the skills and knowhow to take care of your finances. When you're in the driver's seat financially, you have less financial stress and feel better as a result.
- **Greater faith in financial decisions:** Greater financial knowledge and confidence that you have all the facts, leads to feeling more confident and self-assured. For women, this confidence often translates to greater empowerment in other areas of life, which in turn leads to greater overall wellbeing.

Means of developing appropriate financial literacy skills

Given that financial skills and knowledge are fundamental to building financial wellbeing, and also that we are more likely to remember skills if they feel relevant to our current life situation, it makes sense to focus on those that have the most payoff. How you learn about money is up to you, but the list below can help you find the best way to learn that suits your needs and your learning style.

- **Budgeting workshops:** Find out about available budgeting workshops or webinars and sign up. Local banks and credit unions, community groups and many employers provide workshops, usually at little or no cost, to show you how to set up and manage a budget. There are also loads of budget spreadsheets, which are free or inexpensive, and budget-management templates that can be adapted to your use.
- **Online courses:** Enrol in online courses on personal finance. Many good online courses on personal finance

are available on Coursera, Udemy, Khan Academy and other learning websites. The Open University in the UK offers a free course on personal finance.

- **Personal finance books:** Read a personal finance book by an author you can trust. *The Total Money Makeover* by Dave Ramsey or *Your Money or Your Life* by Vicki Robin will help you take control of your money. *Pay It Down* by Jean Chatzky offers a simple, practical way to get on top of that pesky problem, debt.

- **Money apps:** You can use apps that give you budgeting tools, expense trackers and investing guidelines. Download Mint for Android and iOS, YNAB (You Need A Budget) for Android and iOS, Your Juno for iOS only, Plum and/or Chip for iOS only, and Personal Capital for Android and iOS.

- **Money seminars:** Attending money seminars or conferences related to finance literacy will help educate you on various aspects of personal finance. Many money experts and organisations have events around which you can gather various aspects of personal finance.

- **Money podcasts (education):** There are podcasters who speak on all kinds of money topics, from the fundamentals of personal money principles to the technical aspects of investing. For instance, *The Dave Ramsey Show, Bigger Pockets Money, The Wallet, Switch Your Money On, Money Clinic*, etc.

- **Financial literacy games:** Playing financial literacy games can be an entertaining way to learn about financial literacy. It can be helpful to 'try on' making money decisions prior to actually making such decisions. There are games and simulations online that have been developed for this purpose. Several of the websites mentioned on the resources page recommend certain money games or money challenges (e.g.

cashflow). These games provide space for you to practise making various money decisions without financial implications or risk.

- **Financial literacy programmes**: Attend the financial literacy programmes being offered by various community organisations, schools (even those for adults) or non-profit organisations, often featuring some basic information on money.
- **Interactive money quizzes and modules**: Use interactive quizzes and modules online. Numerous websites have quizzes you can take to learn and reinforce your money knowledge in a fun way.
- **A mentor and/or network**: Find a money-savvy mentor to teach you all they know about money – or join other financial literacy networks. Having a real-life person to learn from is helpful for many because they may have insights and help to offer that can aid your progress.
- **Investment simulations**: Try out investment simulations that are reminiscent of real market activity. Investment simulations allow you to develop various investment strategies risk-free, without having to put your own money on the line.

A Word of Caution: If you choose to use financial apps, tools or mentors etc., ensure they are trustworthy and align with your goals. Verify the credibility of the source, read reviews and be cautious of sharing sensitive information. Always prioritise security and seek professional advice when needed.

Conclusion

Personal finance literacy forms the cornerstone of overall financial wellness. It gives you the know-how to make smart money choices and build a financially secure future. It helps create freedom of choice throughout your life, from childhood through the teenage years, and endures well into retirement.

Indeed, it takes a continued commitment to learn and improve your financial literacy. There are so many tools and resources available, from books and online courses to apps and community resources, that you can finally take control of your financial future and achieve financial wellbeing.

Over time, then, if you want a sense of financial security and independence, enhancing financial literacy may be the key. You'll reduce money stress, bolster your self-confidence about money, and enjoy better overall wellbeing too. Let's manage our money wisely so that money doesn't manage us!

Activities

These activities are universal, and applicable to any financial situation and location. Many things won't apply to some people, and you should be aware there are local rules (taxes, state benefits, etc.) to be taken into account. They provide general principles, not specific financial advice.

Always seek professional financial advice. When you do, make sure your adviser is registered, carries professional indemnity insurance and acts as your fiduciary. Verify their guidelines and fees. Even if you understand the basics, you may still find using a professional worthwhile – but it should be much easier and hopefully cheaper.

Activity 16.1: Reality check: Gain clarity on your finances

Steps:

1. **Total income:**
   - Record all sources of income in a spreadsheet.
   - Include both regular and one-off payments, but avoid double-counting.
   - Record each source separately, net of tax or charges.
   - For self-employment income, record the amount received and list taxes under expenses.
   - Aim for an annual income estimate, adjusting for changes like new jobs.
   - Update the spreadsheet monthly for accuracy.

2. **Total spending:**
   - Gather your financial details (bank statements, bills, receipts) for at least three months, and ideally for a year.
   - Using the extensive list of possible expenses in Appendix 2 as a guide, create a personalised spreadsheet with relevant categories.
   - Start with broad categories and refine them over time for detailed tracking.
   - Avoid double-counting expenses (e.g. car insurance as both an insurance and motor expense).
   - Use actual figures over time to get a precise picture of your spending.
   - Download online bank statements to the spreadsheet and categorise spending accurately.
   - Track cash spending manually on the spreadsheet.
   - Aim to know your annual spending, considering different payment frequencies (weekly, monthly, yearly).

3. **Income v. expenses:**
   - Subtract your total annual expenses from your total annual income.
   - Determine whether your situation is sustainable (i.e. if income is greater than expenses).
   - Plan to use any surplus money or address deficits to avoid unsustainable spending.

4. **Ongoing monitoring:**
   - Regularly update your income and expenses in the spreadsheet.
   - Categorise your expenses to maintain an accurate financial snapshot.
   - Use this data to ensure you are moving towards your financial goals.

If you are unfamiliar with using spreadsheets, you can find a good existing spreadsheet that lets you record your income and expenses at www.moneysavingexpert.com/banking/budget-planning/#spreadsheet

Activity 16.2: Budgeting: Gain control of your money

Step 1: Where does the money go?

Activity 16.1 provided a yearly snapshot. To guide future actions, you need more precision:

1. Categorise your expenses into:
   - essential (e.g. rent, food)
   - important to you (e.g. car, internet)
   - non-essential (e.g. designer clothes, gym subscriptions)

2. Classify each expense accordingly.

Worksheet:

Expense category	Item description	Amount	Essential	Important	Non-essential
Rent	Monthly rent	£	Yes	No	No
Food	Groceries	£_	Yes	No	No
Car	Fuel	£	No	Yes	No
Clothing	Designer clothes	£	No	No	Yes
Gym	Membership	£	No	No	Yes

Step 2: Compare income and expenses

1. Identify and total your essential expenses.
2. Subtract your essential expenses from your total income.
3. Assess any remaining income against 'important to you' items.
4. Re-evaluate the importance of these items if necessary.
5. Refine categories for clearer tracking.
6. Establish a basic budget, ensuring essentials are covered and identifying areas where non-essentials can be cut back.
7. Adjust figures to match your lifestyle.

Worksheet:

Total income	£
Essential expenses	£
Remaining income	£

Important items	Amount	Re-evaluated amount
Car	£	£
Internet	£	£

Non-essential items	Amount	Re-evaluated amount
Designer clothes	£	£
Gym membership	£	£

Activity 16.3: Dealing with debt: eliminate bad debt and avoid excessive costs

Step 1: Distinguish debt types

- *Useful debt* (e.g. a low–interest mortgage) can increase your income/net worth.
- *Bad debt* (e.g. high–interest credit cards) reduces income and harms your finances.

Worksheet:

Debt type	Description	Amount	Interest rate	Useful debt	Bad debt
Mortgage	Home loan	£	%	Yes	No
Credit card	Monthly expenses	£	%	No	Yes
Car loan	Car purchase	£	%	No	Yes

Step 2: Prioritise debt reduction

1. Review the loan interest figures from Activity 16.1 and compare total expenses to income.
2. If expenses exceed income and you have bad debt, address this urgently.
3. Focus on reducing high-interest debts (e.g. e.g. credit cards).
4. Reconsider expenses and cut non-essentials.
5. Reduce debt by paying bills on time and clearing ongoing debts monthly.
6. Seek additional income or sell items to pay off debt.
7. Get reputable debt advice, verifying any fees payable.

Worksheet:

Total expenses	£
Total income	£
Remaining income	£

Action plan	Description	Deadline
Cut non-essential items	E.g. reduce dining out	
Pay bills on time	Avoid late fees	Ongoing
Seek additional income	Part-time job or freelance work	
Seek debt advice	Contact reputable debt advisory service	

Activity 16.4: Building resilience: Protect against misfortune and seize opportunities

Step 1: Build a savings buffer

- Set aside surplus funds after paying off urgent debt.
- Aim for three months of expenses in an accessible account for emergencies.

Worksheet:

Expense category	Monthly amount	3-Month amount
Essential (e.g. rent)	£	£
Important to you	£	£
Non-essential	£	£
Total savings target	£	£

Step 2: Save for short- to medium-term expenses

- Plan for expenses like home repairs or new appliances.
- Use higher interest accounts for savings not needed immediately.

Worksheet:

Planned expense	Amount needed	Savings account type
Home repairs	£	Fixed-term savings
New computer	£	High interest
Future bills	£	High interest

Step 3: Insurance and protection

- Consider insurance for income protection, personal accidents or medical needs.

Worksheet:

Insurance type	Coverage needed	Provider
Income protection	£	
Personal accident	£	
Medical insurance	£	

Step 4: Future savings

- Save to create future income beyond current needs.

Worksheet:

Savings goal	Amount needed	Timeframe
Retirement fund	£	20 years
Children's education	£	15 years
Investment fund	£	10 years

Step 5: Legal preparations

- Make a will and consider having a Power of Attorney (giving someone else legal authority to act financially on your behalf in the unforeseen event of illness, absence or other reasons).

Worksheet:

Legal document	Completed	Action needed
Will	Yes/No	
Power of Attorney	Yes/No	

Activity 16.5: Plan for life ahead: prepare for future experiences and later life

Step 1: Save for long-term goals

- Start saving regularly, even in small amounts, rather than waiting.

Worksheet:

Savings goal	Amount needed	Monthly contribution
Retirement fund	£	£
Children's education	£	£
Home purchase	£	£

Step 2: Utilise tax incentives

- Take advantage of tax benefits for pensions and long-term savings.

Worksheet:

Investment type	Tax benefit	Contribution
Pension plan	£	£
ISA (Individual Savings Account)	£	£

Step 3: Invest wisely

- Get professional advice or study investment options like shares, property and bonds.

Worksheet:

Investment option	Potential return	Risk level
Shares	£	High
Property	£	Medium
Bonds	£	Low

Step 4: Plan for later life

- Save efficiently for later life, health needs, and estate protection.

Worksheet:

Savings goal	Amount needed	Timeframe
Retirement fund	£	20 years
Health fund	£	10 years
Estate planning	£	5 years

General tips:
- Always seek appropriate professional financial advice in your jurisdiction.
- Check the guidelines and fees of financial advisers.
- Finance can be complex; professional advice can be valuable.
- Basic principles are learnable; understanding your situation can save money.

After completing all the above activities, give the financial literacy questionnaire another go and see if there are any changes in your score.

Resources

These resources will give you a greater perspective on the role financial literacy plays in boosting overall wellness.

Books

The Total Money Makeover: A Proven Plan for Financial Fitness by Dave Ramsey, Thomas Nelson, 2003
> This book provides a step-by-step plan for achieving financial health and eliminating debt.

Your Money or Your Life: 9 Steps to Transforming Your Relationship with Money and Achieving Financial Independence by Vicky Robin, Penguin Books, 1992
> A guide to help readers align their spending with their values and attain financial freedom.

Pay It Down!: From Debt to Wealth in 5 Steps by Jean Chatzky, Times Books, 2009
> This book offers practical strategies to eliminate debt and build wealth effectively.

Rich Dad Poor Dad: What the Rich Teach Their Kids About Money That the Poor and the Middle Class Do Not! by Robert Kiyosaki & Sharon Lechter, Warner Books, 1997
> A personal finance classic that contrasts the mindsets of the wealthy and the financially struggling.

The Little Book of Common Sense Investing: The Only Way to Guarantee Your Fair Share of Stock Market Returns by John C. Bogle, Wiley, 2007
> Bogle advocates for index fund investing as a straightforward strategy for building wealth over time.

The Long and the Short of It: Finance and Investment for Normally Intelligent People Who Aren't in the Industry by John Kay, PublicAffairs, 2011
A book that demystifies finance and investment, offering insights for those outside the industry.

The Intelligent Investor: The Definitive Book on Value Investing by Benjamin Graham, HarperBusiness, 2003 (Revised Edition)
A foundational text in value investing, emphasising long-term strategies and risk management.

The Richest Man in Babylon by George S. Clason, Penguin Books, 1926
This classic offers timeless financial wisdom through parables set in ancient Babylon.

The Millionaire Next Door: The Surprising Secrets of America's Wealthy by Thomas J. Stanley and William D. Danko, Taylor Trade Publishing, 1996
An exploration of the habits and traits of wealthy Americans, challenging common perceptions of wealth.

The Economic Socialisation of Young People by Adrian Furnham, Palgrave Macmillan, 2018
This book examines how young people learn about economics and financial behaviours from various influences.

Get Good with Money: Ten Simple Steps to Becoming Financially Whole by Tiffany Aliche, Hay House, 2021
A practical guide offering actionable steps to improve financial literacy and overall money management.

Personal Finance For Dummies by Eric Tyson, For Dummies, 2022 (Latest Edition)
A comprehensive guide to managing personal finances, covering budgeting, investing and retirement planning.

Apps

Moneyhub – Smart Money Manager: www.moneyhub.com/app

Emma – Budget Planner Tracker: emma-app.com

Snoop Finance – Budget Tracker: snoop.app

Fili: Financial Literacy: filiapp.treasury.gov.ph/Fili.html

Money skills – lessons and budget tools: www.moneyskillsapp.com/home

Starling Bank – mobile banking: www.starlingbank.com/download

Money Masters: Learn Finance: lessons/moneymasters.app

World of Money – lessons: www.worldofmoneyonline.org

MoneySavingExpert – budgeting and spending: www.moneysavingexpert.com/site/the-moneysavingexpert-app

CapitalDNA: Financial Literacy – lessons: www.capitaldna.finance

You need a budget (YNAB) – budget tools: www.ynab.com

Websites

Global Financial Literacy Excellence Centre – academic, with talks and videos: gflec.org

Investopedia – information, especially on investment: www.investopedia.com

The Motley Fool – investment: www.fool.com

Savings Champion – savings, UK based: savingschampion.co.uk

Money Helper – general information – useful Money Midlife MOT, UK based: www.moneyhelper.org.uk

Khan academy – online courses: www.khanacademy.org/college-careers-more/financial-literacy

Institute for Financial Literacy – Modules and talks, Singapore based: ifl.org.sg/modules/talks

Financial Literacy resources directory, US based: www.occ.
gov/topics/consumers-and-communities/community-
affairs/resource-directories/financial-literacy/
index-financial-literacy-resource-directory.html

Planning for Risk, Retirement and Investment – US
based course: www.edx.org/learn/risk-management/
indiana-university-planning-for-risk-and-retirement?

Blog/journal articles

Investopedia Ultimate guide to financial literacy: www.
investopedia.com/guide-to-financial-literacy-4800530

The difference between financial literacy and
personal finance: allthedifferences.com/
personal-finance-vs-financial-literacy

Financial Literacy: A Simple Beginner's Guide To Personal
Finance: bethebudget.com/financial-literacy

Why Financial Literacy Is Important And
How You Can Improve Yours: www.
forbes.com/sites/truetamplin/2023/09/21/
financial-literacy--meaning-components-benefits--strategies

What is financial literacy: www.fool.co.uk/personal-finance/
your-money/guides/what-is-financial-literacy

Videos

Financial literacy for Gen Z TedX – Sola Adesakin

Nelson Soh at TED – Financial Literacy & The Social Media
Generation

Financial literacy – UK curriculum materials from BBC, good
basic guide

Financial literacy for all – TEDx – Anil Lamba, India based

Personal finance: How to save, spend, and think rationally
about money – Big Think inc. Vicki Robin

An honest look at the personal finance crisis TEDx –
Elizabeth White

Building a Bridge to Financial Literacy TEDx – Brett Costello

Financial Literacy – A Beginner's Guide to Financial
Education – Charlee Wayne, Canada based

Financial Literacy 101 – The Finance Education For Beginners

Financial Literacy TEDx – Mellody Hobson

Podcasts

The Ramsey Show: www.ramseysolutions.com/shows/
the-ramsey-show

The Clark Howard Podcast: clark.com/podcasts

Women & Money: www.suzeorman.com/podcast

Investopedia: www.investopedia.com/podcasts-5225085

Moneybox: www.test.bbc.co.uk/programmes/b006qjnv/
episodes/downloads?page=1

So Money: podcast.farnoosh.tv

Optimal Finance Daily: tunein.com/podcasts/
Business--Economics-Podcasts/
Optimal-Finance-Daily-p860672

Bigger Pockets Money: www.biggerpockets.com/podcasts/money

Her Money: hermoney.com/t/podcasts

Money For the Rest of Us: moneyfortherestofus.com/episodes

Emilie Bellet: www.vestpod.com

The Meaningful Money: podcast meaningfulmoney.tv/
mmpodcast

CHAPTER 17

Journalling

*Got a pen? Congrats – you're
your own therapist*

If you want to transform the way you manage money, I can't recommend journalling enough. See if you find this method works for you, too: keep track of your spending, set your financial goals, and write your money mantra. Putting your money thoughts, intentions and expenditures down on paper can help you gain traction by boosting clarity, strengthening strategies and improving the financial narrative you're creating for yourself. Before you embark on this exciting journey, first take this journalling and money questionnaire.

Journalling and money questionnaire

The purpose of this survey is to assist you in tracking and assessing your personal growth. For each of the ten statements provided, indicate your level of agreement by circling the corresponding number. Add up the scores to gain an initial sense of your financial wellbeing. After completing the chapter and the suggested exercises, revisit the survey. Your answers are confidential; the survey is simply a tool to gauge any shifts or enhancements in your outlook.

1. **Journalling about my financial stressors would help me process my feelings about money issues.**
   Strongly disagree – 1
   Disagree – 2
   Neutral – 3
   Agree – 4
   Strongly agree – 5

2. **Regularly keeping a spending diary would assist me in identifying areas where I can save money.**
   Strongly disagree – 1
   Disagree – 2
   Neutral – 3
   Agree – 4
   Strongly agree – 5

3. **Maintaining a gratitude journal focused on financial matters would positively impact my mindset about money.**
   Strongly disagree – 1
   Disagree – 2
   Neutral – 3
   Agree – 4
   Strongly agree – 5

4. Setting and tracking financial goals through journalling would be beneficial for my financial wellbeing.
   Strongly disagree – 1
   Disagree – 2
   Neutral – 3
   Agree – 4
   Strongly agree – 5

5. Reflecting on my financial decisions in a journal would help me understand and manage my emotional reactions.
   Strongly disagree – 1
   Disagree – 2
   Neutral – 3
   Agree – 4
   Strongly agree – 5

6. Regularly reviewing and adjusting my budget in a journal would contribute to effective financial management.
   Strongly disagree – 1
   Disagree – 2
   Neutral – 3
   Agree – 4
   Strongly agree – 5

7. Documenting and celebrating milestones in reducing debt through journalling would be motivating.
   Strongly disagree – 1
   Disagree – 2
   Neutral – 3
   Agree – 4
   Strongly agree – 5

8. **Tracking investment decisions and outcomes in a journal would enhance my awareness of financial strategies.**
Strongly disagree – 1
Disagree – 2
Neutral – 3
Agree – 4
Strongly agree – 5

9. **Visualising financial goals through a financial vision board in a journal would inspire and focus my objectives.**
Strongly disagree – 1
Disagree – 2
Neutral – 3
Agree – 4
Strongly agree – 5

10. **Practising money mindfulness through journalling would improve my awareness of financial decisions.**
Strongly disagree – 1
Disagree – 2
Neutral – 3
Agree – 4
Strongly agree – 5

My total score:

Introduction

Over the past decade, financial journalling has emerged as a mechanism to boost financial wellbeing. With increasing numbers of financially vulnerable people across the globe, it is becoming imperative to seek ways to improve financial health.[1]

Journalling is a method you can apply to a wide range of contexts to foster self, affective and behavioural change around money via self-reflection and emotion processing. In this chapter I'll discuss (1) the relationship between journalling and financial outcomes; (2) the potential psychological mechanisms that may facilitate the experience of financial wellbeing; and (3) the different journalling styles that may lead to better financial outcomes.

Journalling as a therapeutic tool

As we saw in Chapter 13, the notion of expressive writing took off with Pennebaker and his colleague James Beall's finding that people who wrote about their difficult emotions found it improved their physical and mental health.[2] Journalling can be seen as a type of expressive writing that involves recording events, thoughts and feelings with the aim of evaluating and reflecting on yourself.[3] While the practices of both journalling and expressive writing serve the purpose of cognitive processing (making sense of things), journalling as a practice leans towards self-reflection and insight.

Several meta-analyses confirm the therapeutic effects of expressive writing and journalling.[4] For instance, journalling contributes to improving patients' ability to cope and recover in healthcare.[5] Throughout learning, reflective writing strengthens students' learning, motivation and metacognition (the process of thinking about one's thinking and learning).[6] In psychology, guided journalling helps clinical clients improve their self-awareness and adaptive coping skills.[7] The research evidence supports the use of journalling as a therapeutic tool in a host of different ways.

Financial stress and wellbeing

There are many ways that financial stress could affect mental and physical health.[8] In particular, long-term financial difficulties might raise the risk of mood disorders or substance abuse, and contribute to sleep disruption, high blood pressure and inflammatory disease. Financial stress can make it harder to make good decisions, by impairing executive function.[9] Financial concerns might decrease resources for decision-making, and a 'scarcity mindset' changes attention, outlook and the way we understand the world.[10] This kind of depletion can make it harder to escape financial insecurity: enough is never quite enough.

Practising emotional resilience and building coping skills can help to mitigate the negative health effects of financial stress.[11] For instance, optimism and social support were found to moderate stress responses, and reframing stressors in positive ways can also provide a buffer.[12] Engaging in problem-solving skills and information seeking, as well as avoiding other forms of impulsive coping that are maladaptive, such as substance use, were also protective.[13] One possible avenue for developing financial resilience is journalling, because the act of reflective writing helped reduce stress reactivity.[14] This could help people develop their own means of coping with financial stress, as writing about a financial concern could help them make sense of what is happening.

Benefits of journalling for financial wellbeing

More recent research demonstrates the benefits of journalling for financial performance. Andel *et al.* demonstrated that short journalling prompts increased financial self-efficacy and decreased self-reported spending.[15] Gratitude journalling was associated with reduced materialism, allowing individuals to become more appreciative of life experiences rather than material possessions.[16] Other analyses suggest that money journalling increases adherence to budgeting by boosting our self-awareness of consumption,[17] and that writing about our aspirations leads to enhanced achievement of financial goals.[18]

There are other monetary dividends: value-affirming journalling can lead to a reduction in impulsive spending;[19] and motivational journalling can increase our adherence to our stated goals.[20] Participants report that journalling has helped them gain financial insights;[21] reduce money-related anxiety; and increase their financial literacy, e.g. by revealing the underlying emotional drivers behind poor behaviour or buying patterns (e.g. triggering traps, shopping when sad). To sum up, the evidence so far suggests that journalling could be a low-cost, sustainable, potentially useful and, in many ways, a promising tool for improving financial wellbeing.

Mechanisms of change

Psychological mechanisms, such as cognitive processing and emotional disclosure, reduce financial pressure through expressive writing.[22] Individuals who write to reduce their physiological responses to upsetting events can find it helps them gain 'psychological distancing' from the emotional aspects of financial stressors – they perceive their finances as less threatening and uncontrollable, and as less central to their identity.[23] As well as enabling psychological distancing, writing can elicit reductions in distress via cognitive restructuring, i.e. the modification of mental models. For instance, when individuals share their inner thoughts and feelings by writing, the exploration of more helpful thought patterns can lead to new perceptions about stressful events, such as credit card debt.[24] Journalling can also help alleviate catastrophic or exaggerated thinking about debt by allowing it to be realistically reappraised.

Thinking about money values and goals can help us clarify our intrinsic financial motivation and decision-making, while journalling can help us synthesise and codify the belief that our stated values reflect who we are and how we wish to behave.[25] Here, the act of journalling can also heighten awareness of value discrepancies, potentially promoting more adaptive behaviour.[26] This greater financial self-awareness or 'metacognition' will likely foster further positive financial behaviours. Finally, writing about consumption habits can also help people to experience emotional catharsis and stabilisation.[27] When they journal about their financial stressors, people feel more able to release pent-up worries. Perhaps worries felt less manageable when presented as simply a string of inner conflict, but when a person starts assigning meaning to the stressor and finding solutions, they become more manageable. In sum, the combination of the cognitive and emotional benefits of these journalling exercises seems to help people adaptively respond to the challenge of financial stress.

Types of financial journalling

Various journalling approaches enable people to target different aspects of financial wellbeing:

- **Gratitude journals**: Focusing on abundance and financial security cultivates patience and contentment.[28]
- **Spending diaries**: Tracking our expenditure increases mindfulness of our consumption habits, allowing us to improve our budgeting.[29]
- **Goal journals**: Articulating financial goals and values boosts motivation and long-term achievement.[30]
- **Reflection journals**: Processing feelings, thoughts and behaviours around money reduces financial stress.[31]

When the journey of journalling is tailored to how someone struggles with money, it maximises benefit. The impulsive spender might track their expenditure, while the budgeter might articulate the values at play. Finally, using more than one technique together can deepen our financial knowledge and understanding.

Implementation

There is evidence of the most effective ways to initiate and practise financial journalling. Journalling several times a week for brief daily sessions maximises the benefit.[32] Connecting journalling with financial education, and undergoing counselling along with journalling, also increases its impact by supplementing self-reflection with external guidance.[33] Timing journalling sessions to coincide with major financial events or transitions also facilitates critical reflection. The powerful effects of this practice can help people experience lasting change if they keep a financial journal for a long period of time.[34]

Empirical evidence

Qualitative and quantitative studies suggest that financial journalling can be useful in specific situations. Survey results show that financial journalling interventions are associated with heightened financial literacy, greater budget adherence, and less impulsive spending.[35] Interviews reveal that the participants in such programmes themselves find that journals assist them in creating awareness about and motivating them to take control of their financial lives.[36] These empirical findings can help us to develop a science-influenced financial journalling model.

Practical applications and case studies

Evidence for the helpfulness of journalling comes from the early case studies, which showed that it was feasible to successfully integrate journalling into financial programming. Local credit unions have begun to offer journal clubs to help people set financial goals and think more strategically about money. University financial counselling programmes include 'home-work' journals that encourage better reflection on what money means to university students, and allow them to practise financial skills and management. In individual counselling, client reports demonstrate that keeping a spending diary can be instrumental in effecting significant changes in financial behaviour – and, through the use of gratitude journals, that keeping track of everyday blessings can lead to changes in how we treat ourselves and others.[37] These stories from the real world illustrate the many ways journalling can be applied in practice.

Integration with financial education

Journalling best practice can also be used to enhance financial literacy programmes. Reflective prompts and diaries can be used to stimulate discussion during financial workshops. Gratitude and goal-setting journals reinforce lessons about our values, motivation and mindset, and spending trackers reinforce the budgeting behaviours promoted within such programmes. Using journalling throughout financial programmes helps participants to sustain and build on the important financial lessons over time.[38]

Conclusion

This chapter has explored how writing can help people improve their financial lives by increasing their self-awareness, helping them process their emotions, and encouraging mindful financial behaviour. Journalling can help individuals with whatever financial difficulty they face, and can enhance the impact of financial education. Although further research is needed to fully understand the application of reflective writing to financial wellbeing, this chapter offers some preliminary evidence for its promise.

Activity 17.1: Spending diary worksheet

This worksheet will help you to track your daily expenses and analyse your spending patterns. Record every purchase and categorise your expenses to identify areas for potential savings.

Date: _____

Item	Category	Amount	Notes

Weekly summary:

1. Total spent: _____

_____

_____

2. Categories with highest spending:

_____

_____

3. Areas for potential savings:

_____

_____

Reflection:

- What spending habits surprised you this week?
- Where can you make adjustments to save more?

Activity 17.2: Gratitude journal worksheet

The aim of this worksheet is to help you foster a positive mindset towards finances. Write down financial aspects you are grateful for, cultivating a sense of abundance and satisfaction.

Date: _____

Financial gratitude entries:

1. Today, I am grateful for:

_____

_____

2. One thing that brings financial joy to my life is:

_____

_____

3. I appreciate my ability to:

_____

_____

4. Reflect on a recent financial decision you are proud of:

_____

_____

Reflection:

- How does focusing on gratitude affect your perspective on money?
- In what ways does this practice change your financial behaviour?

Activity 17.3: Reflection journal worksheet

This worksheet is for exploring emotions and thoughts related to money. Reflect on financial decisions, identify emotional triggers and explore ways to manage reactions.

Date: _____

Reflective questions:

1. Describe a recent financial decision and how you felt about it:
2. Identify any emotions that frequently come up when you think about money:
3. What financial situations trigger stress or anxiety for you?
4. How can you manage these emotional triggers better?

Reflection:

- How does reflecting on your financial emotions help you understand your behaviour?
- What steps can you take to create a healthier relationship with money?

Activity 17.4: Financial freedom journal worksheet

Here you will explore the concept of financial freedom. Define what financial freedom means to you, set milestones, and outline steps to achieve financial independence.

Date: _____

Defining financial freedom:

1. What does financial freedom mean to you?

   _____

   _____

   _____

2. List your top three financial freedom goals:

   _____

   _____

   _____

3. Milestones to achieve these goals:

   _____

   _____

   _____

Action plan:

1. Steps to take this month:

   _____

   _____

   _____

2. Resources or skills needed:

   _____

   _____

   _____

3. Potential challenges and solutions:

   _____

   _____

   _____

Reflection:

- How close do you feel to achieving financial freedom?
- What progress have you made, and what do you need to focus on next?

Activity 17.5: Money mindfulness journal worksheet

Use this worksheet to cultivate mindfulness in financial decisions. Practise being present in financial activities, such as making purchases, to enhance awareness and conscious spending.

Date: _____

Mindful spending entries:

1. Today, I made a mindful purchase by:

   _____

   _____

2. Describe your thoughts and feelings during this purchase:

_____

_____

3. How did this mindful approach affect your decision?

_____

_____

4. What did you learn about your spending habits today?

_____

_____

Reflection:

- How does practising mindfulness in financial decisions benefit you?
- In what other areas can you apply mindfulness to improve your financial wellbeing?

After completing these activities, please go back to the start of the chapter and re-attempt the journalling and money questionnaire to check the difference in the result.

Resources

For a deeper understanding of how journalling can improve wellbeing, here are some additional resources to explore.

Books

The Artist's Way: A Spiritual Path to Higher Creativity by Julia Cameron, TarcherPerigee, 1992
This book provides a twelve-week programme to recover creativity and unleash artistic potential.
Write It Down, Make It Happen: Knowing What You Want and

Getting It by Henriette Anne Klauser, HarperCollins, 1990
Klauser explores the power of writing to clarify goals and manifest desires in life.

The Four Agreements Companion Book: Using The Four Agreements to Master the Dream of Your Life by Don Miguel Ruiz, Amber-Allen Publishing, 1999
This companion guide deepens the understanding of the four agreements and their application in daily life.

Journal to the Self: Twenty-Two Paths to Personal Growth by Kathleen Adams, Penguin Books, 1990
This book offers techniques for self-discovery and personal growth through the practice of journalling.

The Miracle Morning Journal: Transform Your Life Before 8AM by Hal Elrod, Hal Elrod International, 2015
A guided journal designed to complement the miracle morning routine, promoting personal development and goal-setting.

Apps

Day One: dayoneapp.com
Journey: journey.cloud
Penzu: penzu.com
Reflectly: reflectly.app
Daylio: daylio.webflow.io

Websites

Journaling.com: www.journaling.com
Bullet Journal: bulletjournal.com
The Center for Journal Therapy: journaltherapy.com
750 Words: 750words.com
Gratefulness.org: gratefulness.org

Blog/journal articles

Psychology Today – 'The Health Benefits of Journaling': www.
    psychologytoday.com/us/blog/words-matter/201907/
    the-health-benefits-journaling
Harvard Health Blog – 'Writing About Emotions May Ease
    Stress and Trauma': www.health.harvard.edu/blog/writing-
    about-emotions-may-ease-stress-and-trauma-2018102415100
The New York Times – 'Writing Your Way to Happiness': www.
    nytimes.com/2015/01/19/opinion/sunday/writing-your-
    way-to-happiness.html
PositivePsychology.com – '83 Benefits of Journaling for
    Depression, Anxiety, and Stress': positivepsychology.com/
    benefits-of-journaling
Verywell Mind – 'How to Start Journaling for
    Better Mental Health': www.verywellmind.com/
    the-benefits-of-journaling-for-stress-management-3144611

Videos

TED-Ed – How to Journal Effectively
Ryder Carroll – The Bullet Journal Method
Lavendaire – How to Start Journaling for Beginners
Boho Berry – My Top 5 Journaling Tips for Mental Health
The Messy Heads – Journaling as a Form of Self-Care

Podcasts

The Lavendaire Lifestyle – Episode on Journaling for Self-
    Discovery: www.lavendaire.com/lifestyle
The Pen Addict – Explores various aspects of analogue writing,
    including journalling: www.relay.fm/penaddict
Journal Theory – A podcast dedicated to exploring the benefits
    of journalling: www.katiedalebout.com/the-podcast

The Mindful Kind – Features episodes on mindfulness and
    journalling: www.rachaelkable.com/podcast
The Art of Charm – *Journaling Your Way to Success*:
    theartofcharm.com/podcast-episodes/aoa-217-journaling

CHAPTER 18

Goal setting

Dream big, but slap a due date on it

Staying on track with your financial goals feels like giving your money a mission! Think about what you want to achieve financially, whether it's saving up for a vacation, paying off debt or working towards a nest egg. When you set your money goals, they'll keep you motivated. You'll be better able to make wise spending decisions, and you'll take satisfaction in your accomplishments. Start setting your money goals and take your financial fitness to a whole new level! In order to do it, first take the goal setting and money questionnaire.

Goal setting and money questionnaire

This survey is intended to help you monitor and evaluate your personal development. For each of the ten statements, circle the number that best represents your level of agreement. Total the scores to gain an initial understanding of your financial well-being. Once you have gone through the chapter and engaged in the recommended exercises, revisit the survey. You need not share your responses; it is merely a tool to measure any changes or improvements in your perspective.

1. **I believe setting financial goals can help me achieve better money management.**
   Strongly disagree – 1
   Disagree – 2
   Neutral – 3
   Agree – 4
   Strongly agree – 5

2. **I believe that goal setting can increase my accountability and self-discipline with money.**
   Strongly disagree – 1
   Disagree – 2
   Neutral – 3
   Agree – 4
   Strongly agree – 5

3. **My financial goals are achievable given my current income and expenses.**
   Strongly disagree – 1
   Disagree – 2
   Neutral – 3
   Agree – 4
   Strongly agree – 5

4. **I consider my financial goals to be relevant to my overall financial wellbeing.**
   Strongly disagree – 1
   Disagree – 2
   Neutral – 3
   Agree – 4
   Strongly agree – 5

5. **I have set deadlines or timeframes for achieving my financial goals.**
   Strongly disagree – 1
   Disagree – 2
   Neutral – 3
   Agree – 4
   Strongly agree – 5

6. **I regularly review my progress towards my financial goals and make adjustments as needed.**
   Strongly disagree – 1
   Disagree – 2
   Neutral – 3
   Agree – 4
   Strongly agree – 5

7. **I have a clear plan of action for each of my financial goals.**
   Strongly disagree – 1
   Disagree – 2
   Neutral – 3
   Agree – 4
   Strongly agree – 5

8. **I seek support and guidance when needed to help me achieve my financial goals.**
   Strongly disagree – 1
   Disagree – 2
   Neutral – 3
   Agree – 4
   Strongly agree – 5

9. **I believe that goal setting can help me identify and overcome potential financial obstacles.**
   Strongly disagree – 1
   Disagree – 2
   Neutral – 3
   Agree – 4
   Strongly agree – 5

10. **I am willing to invest time and effort into setting and pursuing financial goals.**
   Strongly disagree – 1
   Disagree – 2
   Neutral – 3
   Agree – 4
   Strongly agree – 5

My total score:

Now let's take a deep dive into the available literature about goal setting and learn some practical methods for setting your financial goals.

Introduction

Goal setting is important on the road to financial wellness. It means identifying what you want, or what you want to do with your money, and how you're going to get there.[1] Financial wellness is being comfortable and satisfied with your finances – your savings, your debts and other aspects of your financial resilience.[2] Having clear financial goals can make it easier to know what's important to you, or help you prioritise your money uses, and also chart your steps towards financial security.[3] When you set specific monetary goals, you can react purposefully towards those objectives. That's an empowering feeling.

Key theories behind goal setting

Goal-setting theory

Set your goal to be SMART: Specific, Measurable, Achievable, Relevant and Time-bound.[4] The harder the goal, the better the performance – but only up to a certain point, after which easy goals actually work better.[5] You need to be personally committed to your goals, and that is influenced by, among other things, how important the goal is to you, how much you believe you can complete it, and what rewards you might get from the outside world.[6] You need frequent feedback on your progress, and you ought to constantly adjust your goal as you move along.[7]

Self-regulation and self-control theories

Self-regulation is the process of monitoring your behaviour, thoughts and feelings in order to attain your goals.[8] Self-control is the ability to refrain from impulses or behaviours that would otherwise interfere with your ability to achieve your goals.[9] The strength model of self-control is that your capacity for self-control is like a muscle. Your ability to control your impulses is used up in self-control activity, but you can also build up your capacity for self-control. Self-regulation refers to the specific strategies you can use to reach your goals better.[10] Some helpful self-regulation strategies are goal-setting, goal-monitoring and self-reinforcement.[11]

Motivational theories

Intrinsic motivation (doing something because you enjoy it) and autonomous regulation (goal pursuit that is in alignment with your personal interests and values) are associated with more persistent goal pursuit and wellbeing.[12] Extrinsic motivation (doing something for external rewards or to avoid punishment) can be helpful but may not be ideal for pursuing longer-term goals.[13] Goals that satisfy our basic psychological needs for autonomy, competence and relatedness are more likely to be internalised and pursued with greater persistence.[14]

Psychological theories

Mental accounting is the cognitive process by which we categorise, evaluate and track the flow of money, which can influence financial goal setting and goal-pursuit behaviours.[15]

Prospect theory

This highlights the cognitive biases that can lead people to preferentially frame gains and losses differently, which influences risk preferences when it comes to money.[16] The way that people treat money and think differently about it than other resources can be attributed to cognitive biases and mental shortcuts.[17]

With such knowledge in hand, we become better able to design more successful financial plans that are in keeping with our personal values, motivations and underlying psychological processes.

Goal setting and financial behaviours

Goal setting has been widely applied to various financial areas, influencing key financial behaviours:

- **Budgeting and saving**: For instance, if you set a specific savings goal, it helps you keep a budget, promote saving habits and achieve the goals. You are motivated by clear goals to save, rather than incurring unnecessary expenditures.[18]
- **Debt management**: Goals to control your debt can help you work on a budget for your finances, and give you some grounding in taking care of debt.[19] Concrete goals can provide you with a pathway to eliminate debt. You might become a more financially healthy person as a result.

- **Investment and wealth accumulation**: Investment goals can help determine your asset-allocation decisions, and keep you on track with regular contributions towards long-term wealth accumulation.[20]
- **Planning for retirement**: Having a goal for how much you want to have saved in retirement makes your future challenges more real, and makes you think about planning and investing for financial security during your post-work life sooner.[21] Specific goals may motivate you to change your current financial behaviour to achieve the goal.

Goal setting can help provide direction for and shape financial behaviours in many domains, leading to better financial behaviours and goals.

Types of financial goals

Financial goals can be categorised based on their time horizon, scope and purpose:

- **Short-term goals**: What would you like to accomplish in the next year – maybe to build an emergency fund, pay off a credit card or save for that next emergency purchase?
- **Long-term goals**: These are goals for the far future, between several years and several decades away – for example, saving for retirement, children's education or buying a home.
- **Savings goals**: Goals of preservation, for setting aside money for the future such as an emergency fund or the down payment on a house, or retirement.
- **Investment goals**: These are the type of goals that are sought through prudent investment decisions – for

example, compounding wealth, accumulating a target portfolio, or building recurring passive income streams.

Studies show that having a specific and difficult financial goal encourages greater persistence than a vague or easy goal. Goals can be supported by anchoring them to your values and intrinsic motivations.

Mechanisms and moderators

Several factors influence how effective goal setting is in improving financial wellbeing:

- **Characteristics of goals**: Whether your goals are specified and challenging, and the degree to which you're committed to them, can make them more or less effective.
- **Goal framing and mental accounting**: How you frame your financial goals can impact your decision processes. Mental accounting, or the categorisation and labelling of financial resources, can influence your allocation of funds towards your goals.
- **Implementation intentions and action plans**: The creation of specific action plans and implementation intentions (e.g. specifying when, where and how you are going to do it) will close the intention/action gap and will therefore increase the likelihood that you successfully reach your goals.
- **Periodic self-monitoring and feedback**: Frequent self-monitoring and receiving feedback on your progress in pursuit of a goal increases self-regulatory processes and might help in the pursuit of the goal. Regularly tracking your progress and making necessary adjustments increases the likelihood of achieving your goal.

- **Moderators:** Personality and situational attributes might enhance the efficacy of goal setting: for example, demographic factors (e.g. age, income level), personality factors (e.g. conscientiousness) and financial literacy.

Learning about these factors can help you develop and implement an effective, tailored approach to setting goals for yourself.

Creating financial goals: A step-by-step guide

Financial goal statement is the motto behind this whole process as it sets you to solve your financial future problems. Here is a breakdown of how you can write your own financial goals:

1. **Assess your current financial position:** How much do you earn each year? How much do you spend each year? How much are your debts? How much do you have in the bank? For example, 'I earn £42,000 each year. I spend £3,000. I have £10,000 debt on my credit card. I have £5,000 in the bank'.
2. **State your financial goals:** First define exactly what you want to achieve financially, both in the short term and in the long term. For example, your short-term goals might include paying off £5,000 of credit card debt in the next twelve months, while one of your longer-term goals might be saving £50,000 in five years for the down payment on a house.
3. **Make goals specific and measurable:** Every financial goal needs to be expressed in terms of a specific outcome: not just 'save money', but exactly how much, for what purpose, and when you want to reach your objective. For example: 'Save £500 per month for six months as an emergency fund'.

4. **Keep goals in order:** If you have multiple financial goals, prioritise them and list what you want to spend or save for and when, starting with the most urgent or most important goal. For instance, if you have debt on which you're being charged high interest, pay that off before moving on to other goals.

5. **Divide big goals into smaller, actionable steps:** If you're looking to save £10,000 to go on vacation, break it up and save £1,000 a month, ten months in a row. Set some measurable milestones and have clearer deadlines for each step in order to keep up the momentum.

6. **Set realistic targets:** Test the achievability of your financial goals by checking if you can accomplish them within your current financial capacity. If you make £4,000 a month, you might not be able to reach a £3,000 savings target. Try instead, to reach a realistic target such as saving £500 a month.

7. **Set a budget:** Have a budget that supports your financial goals. Use your available money to reach your goals while allowing yourself to cover your expenses. For instance, if your financial goal is to spend £500 per month, allocate your budget accordingly so that you spend less on unnecessary expenses.

8. **Automate savings and payments:** Make use of automation tools to make your financial life easier. Automate transfers between your current and savings or investment accounts. You might like to automate a £500 transfer into your savings account each month.

9. **Monitor and adjust:** Check in on your progress towards your financial goals frequently. For example, check your budget at least monthly to ensure that you are on track to reach your savings target and, if you are not, make adjustments to your spending habits.

10. **Seek professional advice**: Please note that the above is provided for informational purposes only and should not be taken as a substitute for professional advice. Please seek advice from your financial adviser or other financial professional before implementing any financial decisions.

When you adhere to these steps and provide detailed and actionable examples, you'll find that you have created clear, attainable financial goals that put you on the path to financial stability and security going forward. Do yourself a favour: stick to your financial goals.

Goal setting interventions and empirical evidence

A number of interventions have been developed, evaluated and implemented to help people set goals and improve their financial wellbeing:

- **Financial education programmes and workshops:** These interventions aim at providing basic financial knowledge, goal setting or money strategies, and encouraging practical coping mechanisms for remaining financially afloat.
- **Online and mobile goal setting tools:** Numerous goal setting digital platforms and apps have been developed to help users to set and track their goals, send reminders and monitor progress.
- **Coaching and counselling approaches:** Financially empowering counsellors and coaches can help individuals set goals, develop action plans, and provide encouragement and accountability for clients throughout the goal-setting journey.

Fortunately, empirical evidence shows that goal setting interventions can indeed have a positive impact on people's financial behaviours and outcomes. Numerous quantitative studies have shown that goal setting is positively associated with increased savings rates, debt repayment and overall financial wellbeing. Other researchers have identified behavioural markers of financial goal setting and explored what types of goals individuals create and why. Qualitative studies showing how consumers experience goal setting and what makes it easier or harder for them have provided important insights.

Challenges and limitations

Goal setting is often recommended as a strategy to improve financial wellness, but implementation comes with challenges:

1. Because the positive results published by researchers tend to outnumber the negative, it's hard to tell if goal setting is just lip service.
2. It depends on the context; goal setting might not work for those who are impoverished and struggling with small steps, and probably not in meritocratic or incentivised climates.
3. Goal setting could face limitations and might be effective only for some areas of wellness.

- **Goal conflicts and trade-offs**: An individual might have competing financial goals or priorities so that achieving one expense or goal might come at the cost of not being able to meet another priority or goal.
- **Obstacles to attaining the goal**: Experiencing financial goal failure can be caused by numerous psychological, social and environmental barriers to attaining the goal, including personal self-control issues, lack of support from family or friends, or life events.

- **Situational and contextual factors**: Goal setting can be influenced by situational and contextual factors such as country-level economic conditions, cultural norms and beliefs, and the availability of financial services and products.
- **Maintenance of long-term goal pursuit**: While the initial setting of goals can be effective, maintaining wider motivation and commitment for the longer term (e.g. financial or career-based targets) should be considered process.

Thoughtful interventions, supportive systems and ongoing monitoring can help to mitigate these challenges and limitations in ways that advance the goal of building economically resilient and sustainable notions of financial wellbeing.

Conclusion

Financial goal setting is one of the most powerful tools for financial wellbeing that we have, backed by both theory and data. By setting specific, challenging and personally meaningful financial goals, you can shape your financial behaviours, build self-regulation, and improve your financial security and satisfaction. By advancing our understanding of goal setting in the context of financial wellbeing, we can better equip ourselves for financial security during our wealth accumulation years and later.

Now you have learned about the theory of goal setting, it's time to use that knowledge and put it into practice.

Activity 18.1: Financial goal: Build an emergency fund

Try putting together an emergency fund using the SMART criteria:

- Specific: Save an amount per month towards building an emergency fund.
- Measurable: Track your progress monthly by recording the amount saved in a budgeting spreadsheet.
- Achievable: Determine feasibility based on current income and expenses, and adjust spending habits accordingly.
- Relevant: Saving for an emergency fund is relevant to financial wellbeing because it makes the goal more likely to succeed.
- Time-bound: Save the same amount each month for the next twelve months, e.g., between 1 January and 31 December.

Breakdown of goal into smaller steps:

- **January**
- **February**
- **March**
- **April**
- **May**
- **June**
- **July**
- **August**
- **September**
- **October**
- **November**
- **December**

Action plan

- *Assessment:* Look at where your money is going at the moment. Is it possible to save £500 per month based on your income and expenses?
- *Budgeting:* Set up a monthly budget that saves a certain amount and specifies where it might be possible to save more.
- *Automatic savings:* Use automatic transfers from current to savings account every month.
- *Monitor progress:* Regularly review the budget and savings account to track progress towards the goal.
- *Adjust spend:* Adjust your spending as necessary in line with the monthly goal of saving the amount you have determined.

Example SMART goal:
- Specific per month towards building an emergency fund.
- Measurable: Each month, look at the bank statement and record the amount transferred in the spreadsheet.
- Realistic: Existing income and expenditure allow saving £500 per month as long as Monica adjusts spending habits and puts saving first.
- Relevant: Creating an emergency fund is pertinent to financial wellbeing; it provides a backup so you don't have to go to a payday loan when you accidentally run over your neighbour's cat.
- Time-bound: Payable by the 1st of the month for twelve consecutive months, from January to December.

Completing this activity will give you a clear and actionable plan for setting and achieving your financial goal using the SMART criteria.

Activity 18.2: Reverse goal setting

In this activity, start with your long-term financial goals and work backwards to identify the short-term and medium-term goals needed to achieve the long-term ones. Break down these goals into specific, measurable and time-bound steps.

Step 1: Identify long-term financial goals

- List your long-term financial goals (e.g. retirement, children's education, dream home):

  1. _____
  2. _____
  3. _____

Step 2: Identify medium-term goals

- For each long-term goal, list the medium-term goals needed to achieve it:

  Long-term goal 1:
  Medium-term goal 1: _____

  _____

  Medium-term goal 2: _____

  _____

  Long-term Goal 2:
  Medium-term goal 1: _____

  _____

  Medium-term goal 2: _____

  _____

Long-term goal 3:
Medium-term goal 1: _____

_____

Medium-term goal 2: _____

_____

Step 3: Identify short-term goals

- For each medium-term goal, list the short-term goals
  needed to achieve it:

Medium-term goal 1:
Short-term goal 1: _____

_____

Short-term goal 2: _____

_____

Medium-term goal 2:
Short-term goal 1: _____

_____

Short-term goal 2: _____

_____

Step 4: Break down goals into specific, measurable, time-bound steps

- For each short-term goal, list specific actions with
  deadlines:

Short-term goal 1:
Action 1: _____

_____

Deadline: _____

Action 2: _____

_____

Deadline: _____

Short-term goal 2:
Action 1: _____

_____

Deadline: _____

Action 2: _____

_____

Deadline: _____

Activity 18.3: Money bucket list

Make a list of financial experiences or achievements you want to accomplish in your lifetime. Prioritise the items on the list and set goals to work towards them.

Step 1: List financial experiences or achievements

- Financial bucket list items:

  1. _____
  2. _____
  3. _____
  4. _____
  5. _____

Step 2: Prioritise the items

- Rank the items based on importance or urgency:

  1. _____
  2. _____
  3. _____
  4. _____
  5. _____

Step 3: Set goals for each item

- For each item, set specific, measurable and time-bound goals:

  Item 1:
  Goal: _____
  _____

  Action steps:
  Step 1: _____
  _____

  Step 2: _____
  _____

  Deadline: _____

  Item 2:
  Goal: _____
  _____

  Action steps:
  Step 1: _____
  _____

  Step 2: _____
  _____

  Deadline: _____

Activity 18.4: Income optimisation

Here, you will identify ways to increase your income, set goals for developing additional income streams or negotiating a pay increase, and calculate how additional income can accelerate your financial goals.

Step 1: Identify ways to increase income

- Potential income sources:

  1. _____
  2. _____
  3. _____

Step 2: Set goals for additional income streams or negotiating a pay rise

- For each potential income source, set specific goals:

  Income Source 1:
  Goal: _____

  _____

  Action steps:
  Step 1: _____

  _____

  Step 2: _____

  _____

  Deadline: _____

  Income Source 2:
  Goal: _____

  _____

Action steps:

Step 1: _____

_____

Step 2: _____

_____

Deadline: _____

Income Source 3:

Goal: _____

_____

Action steps:

Step 1: _____

_____

Step 2: _____

_____

Deadline: _____

Step 3: Calculate impact on financial goals

- Additional monthly income: £_____
- How this income will be allocated:
  Towards savings: £_____
  Towards debt repayment: £_____
  Towards investments: £_____

- Revised timeline for financial goals:
  Goal 1: _____

  _____

  New timeline: _____

  Goal 2: _____

  _____

  New timeline: _____

Don't forget to take the goal setting and money questionnaire again after completing all the activities. If you want to learn more about goal setting, please refer to the resources.

Resources

Here are more materials that can help improve your comprehension of goal setting's effects on your overall wellbeing.

Books

The Millionaire Next Door by Thomas J. Stanley and William D. Danko, Pocket Books, 1996
    An insightful exploration of the habits and characteristics of financially successful individuals who build wealth steadily over time.
The Richest Man in Babylon by George S. Clason, Penguin, 2002 (originally published in 1926)
    A timeless collection of parables that impart practical financial wisdom and principles for building and preserving wealth.
Your Money or Your Life: 9 Steps to Transforming Your Relationship with Money and Achieving Financial Independence by Vicki Robin and Joe Dominguez, Penguin, 2018 (updated edition)
    An updated version of the personal finance classic, offering a step-by-step guide to achieving financial freedom.
The Total Money Makeover: A Proven Plan for Financial Fitness by Dave Ramsey, Thomas Nelson, 2013
    A straightforward, no-nonsense approach to getting out of debt and building lasting financial security.
Rich Dad Poor Dad: What the Rich Teach Their Kids About Money That the Poor and Middle Class Do Not! by Robert T. Kiyosaki, Plata Publishing, 2017 (20th anniversary edition)

A personal finance classic that challenges conventional wisdom and encourages readers to adopt the mindset of the wealthy.

Apps

Mint: www.mint.com
PocketGuard: www.pocketguard.com
Wally: wally.me
Qapital: www.qapital.com
Stash: www.stashinvest.com
YNAB (You Need A Budget): www.youneedabudget.com
Acorns: www.acorns.com
Personal Capital: www.personalcapital.com
Robinhood: www.robinhood.com

Websites

MyMoney.gov: www.mymoney.gov
NerdWallet: www.nerdwallet.com
Bankrate: www.bankrate.com
The Simple Dollar: www.thesimpledollar.com
Money Under 30: www.moneyunder30.com
Investopedia: www.investopedia.com
The Balance: www.thebalance.com

Blog/journal articles

'The Science of Setting and Achieving Goals' (*Psychology Today*): www.psychologytoday.com/ us/blog/the-science-behind-behavior/201811/ the-science-setting-and-achieving-goals
'The Power of Setting Goals' (*Harvard Business Review*): hbr. org/2018/11/the-power-of-setting-goals

'The Psychology of Goal Setting: How to Set Better
    Goals' (Verywell Mind): www.verywellmind.com/
    the-psychology-of-goal-setting-2795983
'The Science Behind Goal Setting and How to Do It'
    (Entrepreneur): www.entrepreneur.com/article/339973

Videos

'How to Design Your Life (My Process For Achieving Goals)'
    (YouTube – Matt D'Avella)
'Goal Setting: The Secret to Achieving Your Financial Goals'
    (YouTube – Debt Free Millennials)
'How to Set Financial Goals' (YouTube – The Dave
    Ramsey Show)
TED Talks: Money: www.ted.com/topics/money
The Dave Ramsey Show: www.youtube.com/user/
    DaveRamseyShow
Graham Stephan: www.youtube.com/c/GrahamStephan

Podcasts

Money Girl: www.quickanddirtytips.com/
    money-girl-audio-finances
HerMoney with Jean Chatzky: www.hermoneymedia.com/
    podcast
The Mindful Millionaire: mindful-millionaire.com/podcast
Stacking Benjamins: www.stackingbenjamins.com
The Dave Ramsey Show: www.daveramsey.com/shows/
    the-dave-ramsey-show
The Financial Diet: www.thefinancialdiet.com/podcast
ChooseFI: www.choosefi.com

CHAPTER 19

Charitable giving

*Generosity never sent anyone
to the poorhouse*

Ever thought about how giving can develop your own financial wellbeing? When we give, research has shown that we are more likely to experience increased happiness and a greater sense of meaning and purpose in our lives, and our overall financial decision-making is likely to improve. The next time you're looking to make a charitable gift or considering spending in a way that benefits others, remind yourself that you are not only giving to the world but to your own personal financial wellbeing. If you want to learn more about how giving others can help you, try the following test first and check how you currently feel about giving.

Charitable giving questionnaire

This questionnaire is designed to help you monitor and evaluate your personal development journey of financial wellbeing. For each of the ten statements, circle the number that best reflects your level of agreement. Calculate the total score to gain an initial understanding of your financial wellbeing. After studying the chapter and engaging in the exercises, revisit the survey. You are not required to disclose your responses; it is merely a tool to assess any changes or improvements in your perspective.

1. **Engaging in charitable giving/prosocial spending activities fills me with joy.**
   Strongly disagree – 1
   Disagree – 2
   Neither agree nor disagree – 3
   Agree – 4
   Strongly agree – 5

2. **Donating my time/money gives me a sense of pride.**
   Strongly disagree – 1
   Disagree – 2
   Neither agree nor disagree – 3
   Agree – 4
   Strongly agree – 5

3. **Doing good for others aligns with how I view myself.**
   Strongly disagree – 1
   Disagree – 2
   Neither agree nor disagree – 3
   Agree – 4
   Strongly agree – 5

4. **I regularly contribute to charitable causes.**
   Strongly disagree – 1
   Disagree – 2
   Neither agree nor disagree – 3
   Agree – 4
   Strongly agree – 5

5. **I allocate a specific portion of my budget for charitable giving.**
   Strongly disagree – 1
   Disagree – 2
   Neither agree nor disagree – 3
   Agree – 4
   Strongly agree – 5

6. **I actively seek information about charitable organisations before making donations.**
   Strongly disagree – 1
   Disagree – 2
   Neither agree nor disagree – 3
   Agree – 4
   Strongly agree – 5

7. **I participate in local community initiatives or volunteer work.**
   Strongly disagree – 1
   Disagree – 2
   Neither agree nor disagree – 3
   Agree – 4
   Strongly agree – 5

8. **I tend to support charitable causes that have a personal significance to me.**
   Strongly disagree – 1
   Disagree – 2
   Neither agree nor disagree – 3
   Agree – 4
   Strongly agree – 5

9. **I feel satisfied with my contributions to charitable causes.**
Strongly disagree – 1
Disagree – 2
Neither agree nor disagree – 3
Agree – 4
Strongly agree – 5

10. **I regularly assess the impact of my charitable contributions on the causes I support.**
Strongly disagree – 1
Disagree – 2
Neither agree nor disagree – 3
Agree – 4
Strongly agree – 5

My total score:

Introduction

Charitable giving and prosocial spending – spending that benefits others – represent the voluntary sharing of our material resources (e.g. money, time and skills) with other people and with society at large. This type of behaviour reflects the desire to make a positive impact on the world by supporting causes important to us.[1] Understanding the link between altruistic behaviour and our financial wellbeing has practical implications for how these two factors might mutually influence each other. Specifically, if we look at how charitable giving and prosocial spending influence our financial attitudes and behaviours, we can identify how to make our financial world a better place.

Charitable giving and prosocial spending: theoretical foundations

How can we explain our willingness to give to prosocial causes or engage in prosocial spending? The answer, using insight from psychological and sociological theory, is multi-faceted. Shalom Schwartz's functional theory of human values, for instance, maintains that we are motivated to act in ways that are both reflected in and affirm our values.[2] For instance, if you value benevolence and/or universalism then you are more likely to give to charities involved in such goals (e.g. providing social services or environmental protection).

Research from the field of self-determination theory also comes into play here. According to this model, intrinsic motivation, autonomy and having our psychological needs met generally lead to increased psychological wellbeing.[3] Charitable giving and prosocial spending might help us feel related and competent, which in turn can boost our life satisfaction.[4]

Sociological theories, such as social identity theory and social exchange theory,[5] also explain why we give and spend on others. You might do these things to cement social bonds, gain social approval or pay things forward.

According to identity-based motivation theory, we behave in ways that affirm our preferred identities[6] – so, for example, if we would like to see ourselves as generous and altruistic, then we might be more motivated to give to charity, and to spend money on other people, and as a result our financial behaviour might be guided by this concern.

Materialistic values models, like the material values scale, suggest that if we prioritise material possessions and wealth over everything else, it can actually reduce our wellbeing.[7] Engaging in charitable giving and prosocial spending can help counter-act these materialistic tendencies and promote more intrinsic motivations.

Psychological benefits of charitable giving

Research shows that acts of charitable giving and prosocial spending can have many psychological benefits, such as increasing positive emotions such as joy, gratitude and pride, all of which can enhance wellbeing.[8] They can also remind us of a deeper sense of meaning and purpose in our lives, by contributing to causes that are important to us.[9]

Charitable giving, and other forms of prosocial spending, promote social connections that can also foster our wellbeing, by fortifying our relationships and creating a sense of community.[10] Such behaviours are in line with self-transcendent values. According to religion scholar William James, this aspect of the self is characterised by a moral step, a turn 'towards every neighbour's gate'.[11]

Some scholars have found a correlation between charitable giving and satisfaction with life,[12] although it could be a two-way relationship: put simply, life satisfaction could predispose individuals to engage in prosocial behaviours, and these behaviours, in turn, could increase satisfaction with life.[13]

Financial benefits of charitable giving

Giving to charity and engaging in prosocial spending can actually be good for both your mental wellbeing and your finances. Research shows that these actions can give you a sense of purpose and meaning,[14] reduce materialistic attitudes, and encourage you to be more thoughtful and intentional about how you manage your money. In other words, being generous and focused on helping others, rather than just on acquiring more for yourself, can have a positive ripple effect on your financial mindset and behaviours. This, in turn, can lead to healthier financial habits over time.

When people make prosocial donations, they are likely to put more weight on their intrinsic goals – those identifiable with relationships, self-respect and community involvement – than on their extrinsic ones – which are identifiable with prestige and social status.[15] By reinforcing the importance of intrinsic goals, we can exercise better behavioural control. By putting our money towards the things that 'accomplish purpose and goals', we can learn better ways of budgeting and spend less on material excesses.

Charitable giving and prosocial spending can lead us to become more financially literate and aware. This increase in our financial literacy can in turn cement prosocial spending as our go-to habit because we'll have taken a moment to think about our finances and how we want to spend our money.[16]

Mechanisms of change

What actually drives the relationship between charitable giving, prosocial spending and broader financial behaviours? There are multiple psychological mechanisms that could explain this.

Self-perceptual theory posits behaviour as a key source of inference about attitudes and beliefs. That is, prosocial behaviour (such as charitable giving or prosocial spending) can promote inferences about ourselves as generous and altruistic, which may have a subsequent influence on our broader financial priorities and decision-making.[17]

Cognitive dissonance theory also comes into play. Changes in attitudes or behaviours that follow charitable giving or prosocial spending can occur because we experience dissonance (psychological tension) when our behaviours contradict our beliefs or values.[18] We could re-adapt our behaviour to create congruence with our giving to reduce the dissonance. That is, someone who donates money to a cause may subsequently adopt more frugal financial habits to reinforce their identity as a generous person.[19]

Charitable giving and prosocial spending can also lead to spending shifts, as we tend to channel more of our spending towards purpose-based, rather than material, purchases.[20] Such a shift can contribute to enhanced life satisfaction, too, as we find greater satisfaction in non-material pursuits.[21]

If the relationship between charitable giving and financial health depends on financial socialisation – the process of learning about money through experiences and exposure to money values and actions – then perhaps it's the experience of being around generous adults and learning altruistic values and behaviours when children, that transfers to positive financial behaviours as adults.[22]

Moderators and mediators

But there are many factors that could moderate or mediate that relationship, and could influence giving behaviours based on our income level, personality traits and other individual differences, including personal beliefs.[23]

The context of charitable behaviour matters, too – whether giving money, time or skill – and this can, in turn, affect our own financial attitudes and behaviours.[24] So can the context in which the act occurs: spontaneous acts of kindness may not have the same effect as a planned initiative.

However, the relative influence of charitable giving and prosocial spending on financial wellbeing can be significantly moderated by the way these acts are communicated and framed – for instance, highlighting the happy personal side-effects of charitable giving, such as the increased good feeling or improved social ties, can amplify its positive effects.[25]

Social norms, traditions and economic factors can also moderate the connection between charitable giving, prosocial spending and financial wellbeing.[26] In some cultures, charitable giving may be an integral part of belonging to a religious community, which in turn shapes financial attitudes and behaviours.

Empirical evidence

There has been a substantial body of empirical work on the link between charitable giving, prosocial spending and financial wellbeing. Quantitative work shows that there is a correlation between charitable giving and perceived life satisfaction,[27] as well as a negative correlation between materialism and wellbeing.[28]

Several experimental studies have also shown the causal effects of prosocial spending on happiness: for instance, Dunn *et al.* found that those who spent money on others reported greater happiness than those who had spent money on themselves.[29]

Qualitative research has shed new light on lived experiences and motivations for charitable giving and prosocial spending, for example by scrutinising the narratives of prosocial action that are offered up by donors and volunteers to explain their engagement to researchers. Wiepking and Maas explained how donors derived meaning from charitable behaviour by identifying and exploring themes such as intrinsic values, interpersonal relationships and social capital.[30]

Practical applications and case studies

Real-world stories and case studies can also provide recognisable details about the applications of charitable giving and prosocial spending in genuine financial settings. For example, some financial institutions have created corporate social responsibility (CSR) programmes in which employees are eligible to take part in charity initiatives or volunteering programmes.

There are real-life examples of how people, families and organisations include charitable giving as part of their budgeting and spending.[31] Sharing the details of how they do this, and the benefits they experience, could inspire others to try it too.

Integration with financial education

The principles of charitable giving and prosocial spending have a place in financial education programmes aimed at fostering positive and healthy financial behaviour over the course of our lives. When educators are better able to describe the psychological and financial advantages of these practices, learners can be encouraged to marry their financial practices to their personal values and goals.

Financial literacy programmes can also focus on the potential overlaps between charitable donations, prosocial spending and financial responsibility: budgeting skills and other forms of money management can be taught in conjunction with techniques for allocating resources towards good causes.

Conclusion

In this chapter, we have examined the relationships between charitable giving and prosocial spending, and their impact on financial wellbeing. Empirical and theoretical evidence supports the intriguing idea that giving to others results in wellbeing benefits for the giver. Examples of such benefits include improved life satisfaction and self-esteem, as well as increased overall wellbeing. As such, wellbeing benefits can in turn shape other financial attitudes and prosocial behaviours, such as increased conscientiousness with respect to finances and budgeting, as well as a deep-rooted anti-materialistic mindset. There are also other psychological benefits to giving, such as the empowerment of the giver through the decision-making process, as well as an increased sense of meaning to their life. In brief, charity and prosocial spending stand as valuable tools in creating feelings of wellbeing, which in turn becomes a mechanism for creating more responsible finance attitudes and prosocial behaviours. To conclude, we can proactively foster our own financial wellbeing, while also improving the overall wellbeing of society.

Activity 19.1: Budgeting for generosity

Create a monthly budget and dedicate an allotted amount of your money to charitable giving and prosocial spending. Your first step should be to write down your total income, then to record your expenses under four categories: fixed expenses (rent, utility bills) and variable expenses (grocery, entertainment); then record your projected savings, and finally your projected contributions to charitable giving or prosocial spending. Organise your categories accordingly in a table like the one below, indicating the budget and actual amounts under each category.

- List at least three causes or organisations you want to support.
- Briefly describe why you chose each one.

Cause/organisation	Reason for selection
1.	
2.	
3.	

End-of-month reflection

Reflect on your experience of intentionally budgeting for generosity. Use the prompts below to guide your reflection.

Reflection prompts:
- How did it feel to allocate part of your budget to charitable donations?
- What challenges did you face in sticking to your budget?
- How did the act of giving impact your overall financial attitude and wellbeing?

Activity 19.2: Volunteering

Start by volunteering your time and skills to a nonprofit organisation or community initiative. Choose an organisation that aligns with your interests and values. Describe the organisation and your specific role as a volunteer.

Reflection on volunteering experience

Reflect on the experience of contributing non-monetary resources. Use the prompts below to guide your reflection.

Reflection prompts:
- What did you learn from volunteering?
- How did volunteering influence your sense of personal growth?
- What benefits did you observe in terms of financial literacy and career development?

Discussion

Discuss the benefits of volunteering with peers or in a group setting. Summarise the key takeaways from the discussion.

Activity 19.3: Peer storytelling

Instructions:

1. **Share personal stories:**
   Share your personal stories and experiences related to charitable giving, prosocial spending or receiving acts of kindness. Use the table below to capture the key points from each story shared.

Storyteller	Story summary	Emotional impact	Social impact	Financial impact

2. **Discussion:**
   Explore the emotional, social and financial implications of these experiences. Identify common themes and insights from the shared narratives.

Discussion prompts:
- What common themes emerged from the stories shared?
- How did these stories affect your perception of generosity and financial wellbeing?
- What insights can you apply to your own financial practices?

Activity 19.4: Act of kindness or giving money

Select an amount of money that you consider neither too much nor too little and donate or give it away. Pay attention to your feelings during the process of giving. Afterwards, reflect on your experience of charitable giving.

Reflection prompts:
- How did giving away money make you feel?
- What thoughts or emotions did you experience before, during and after the act of giving?
- How did this experience influence your view on charitable giving and personal finances?

After completing all the activities, don't forget to retake the charitable giving questionnaire to check the difference in your score.

Resources

To better grasp the benefits of charitable giving for your wellbeing, consider exploring these additional resources.

Books

The Paradox of Generosity by Christian Smith and Hilary
    Davidson, Oxford University Press, 2014
    An academic study exploring how the act of giving can lead
    to greater personal fulfilment and wellbeing.
The Life You Can Save by Peter Singer, Random House, 2010
    A philosophical work that makes a compelling case for
    why and how individuals should donate to highly effective
    charities to alleviate global poverty.
The Power of Giving by Azim Jamal and Harvey McKinnon,
    Tarcher, 2007
    A practical guide that demonstrates how the act of giving
    can transform both the giver and the recipient, leading to
    greater personal and societal benefits.
The Giving Way to Happiness by Jenny Santi, Penguin, 2015
    Explores the psychological and emotional rewards that
    come from practising generosity and philanthropic giving.
Giving 2.0 by Laura Arrillaga-Andreessen, Jossey-Bass, 2011
    An in-depth exploration of how technology and social
    media are transforming the landscape of charitable giving
    and volunteer work.

Apps

Charity Miles: charitymiles.org
Donated: www.donated.app
Share the Meal: sharethemeal.org/en/app.html
Coin Up: coinupapp.com

Websites

CharityNavigator.org: www.charitynavigator.org
GlobalGiving.org: www.globalgiving.org

JustGiving.com: www.justgiving.com
GreatNonprofits.org: greatnonprofits.org
Fidelity.com/Charitable: www.fidelitycharitable.org

Blog/journal articles

'The Brilliant Psychology of Charitable Giving': www.
    psychologytoday.com/us/blog/the-awake-mind/202012/
    the-brilliant-psychology-charitable-giving
'The Science Behind Why Giving Is So Gratifying': www.
    wsj.com/articles/the-science-behind-why-giving-is-so-
    gratifying-1481834706
'How Giving Makes You Happier': www.health.harvard.edu/
    mind-and-mood/how-giving-makes-you-happier
'The Relationship Between Charitable Giving and Financial
    Well-Being': jpm.pm-research.com/content/45/6/41
'Exploring the Positive Byproducts of Prosocial Behavior' by
    Pradnya Surana and Tim Lomas: www.frontiersin.org/
    articles/10.3389/fpsyg.2014.01539/full

Videos

'The Paradox of Generosity': www.ted.com/talks/
    christian_smith_the_paradox_of_generosity
'The Power of Giving': www.thersa.org/video/2012/06/
    the-power-of-giving
'Why Giving Matters': www.fidelitycharitable.org/why-
    giving-matters.shtml
'The Science of Generosity'

Podcasts

'The Science of Happiness': ggsc.berkeley.edu/podcasts/story/
    the_science_of_generosity

'The Life You Can Save': www.thelifeyoucansave.org/podcast
'Giving Thought': www.philanthropyroundtable.org/series/
    giving-thought-podcast/
'The Nonprofit Exchange': unitedwaymiami.org/
    nonprofit-exchange-podcast

CHAPTER 20

Financial hygiene
and maintenance

Want to stay well? Wash and rinse, repeat

The saying above underlines the significant role that maintaining good hygiene plays in overall health and wellbeing. It suggests that cleanliness and hygiene are crucial components of staying healthy, making up a major part of what it means to live healthily. Similarly, having a good financial hygiene and maintenance routine can significantly improve financial wellbeing. Before we understand this new and unique concept, take this quick test and find out about your current understanding of the topic.

Financial hygiene and maintenance questionnaire

This survey helps you assess your personal growth. Circle the number that aligns with your agreement for each of the ten statements, and total your scores for an initial assessment. Once you've completed the chapter and exercises, retake the survey.

Your answers remain private, serving as a tool to gauge any shifts or improvements in your outlook.

1. **I regularly monitor my income and expenses to ensure they align with my financial goals.**
   Strongly disagree – 1
   Disagree – 2
   Somewhat disagree – 3
   Neither agree nor disagree – 4
   Somewhat agree – 5
   Agree – 6
   Strongly agree – 7

2. **I prioritise saving a portion of my income for future needs and emergencies.**
   Strongly disagree – 1
   Disagree – 2
   Somewhat disagree – 3
   Neither agree nor disagree – 4
   Somewhat agree – 5
   Agree – 6
   Strongly agree – 7

3. **I actively seek out financial education resources to improve my understanding of personal finance.**
   Strongly disagree – 1
   Disagree – 2
   Somewhat disagree – 3
   Neither agree nor disagree – 4
   Somewhat agree – 5
   Agree – 6
   Strongly agree – 7

4. **I have a clear understanding of my financial situation, including my debts, savings, and investments.**
Strongly disagree – 1
Disagree – 2
Somewhat disagree – 3
Neither agree nor disagree – 4
Somewhat agree – 5
Agree – 6
Strongly agree – 7

5. **I have an optimistic outlook on my financial future, believing that I can achieve my financial goals.**
Strongly disagree – 1
Disagree – 2
Somewhat disagree – 3
Neither agree nor disagree – 4
Somewhat agree – 5
Agree – 6
Strongly agree – 7

6. **I regularly review my financial goals and adjust them as needed to adapt to changing circumstances.**
Strongly disagree – 1
Disagree – 2
Somewhat disagree – 3
Neither agree nor disagree – 4
Somewhat agree – 5
Agree – 6
Strongly agree – 7

7. **I avoid unnecessary or impulsive spending habits.**
Strongly disagree – 1

Disagree – 2
Somewhat disagree – 3
Neither agree nor disagree – 4
Somewhat agree – 5
Agree – 6
Strongly agree – 7

8. **I have a plan in place to pay off any outstanding debts or loans.**
Strongly disagree – 1
Disagree – 2
Somewhat disagree – 3
Neither agree nor disagree – 4
Somewhat agree – 5
Agree – 6
Strongly agree – 7

9. **I don't feel stressed or anxious about my financial situation.**
Strongly disagree – 1
Disagree – 2
Somewhat disagree – 3
Neither agree nor disagree – 4
Somewhat agree – 5
Agree – 6
Strongly agree – 7

10. **I believe that managing my finances well is within my control and achievable.**
Strongly disagree – 1
Disagree – 2
Somewhat disagree – 3
Neither agree nor disagree – 4
Somewhat agree – 5

Agree – 6
Strongly agree – 7

My total score:

Introduction

Just as brushing your teeth and taking showers play a vital role in your physical wellbeing, practising financial hygiene is important for your money health. If you pay no attention to personal hygiene, you can get sick. The same holds true for your financial wellbeing.

Financial self-care – budgeting, saving, getting your debts under control – will avoid bigger problems later on, just as the precautions you take for your body will keep you out of emergency rooms. In the same way that flossing after every meal, eating healthily and checking on your blood pressure regularly may not be essential, nor are tracking your spending weekly, saving some of your income consistently, and running a credit report on yourself every year. But both are sets of simple, regular and low-cost activities to save potentially huge, expensive and life- or lifestyle-threatening problems later on.

Like having regular check-ups and self-exams to catch health problems early, you need to periodically review your financial statements, credit scores and net worth to catch financial problems at an early stage. Like seeing specialist doctors and dentists for specialised care, financial problems may demand the help of advisers, accountants and planners for particular issues. And like healthy living, which entails regular exercise and a balanced diet to suit your general health and circumstances, maintaining your finances over the course of your life involves tweaking of strategies and rebalancing of investments to match your financial circumstances.

Think of financial hygiene as a broad approach to your overall finances: you take in what you need in the short term and, in the long term, you manage risk and you build financial resilience. It's like how 'health' is far broader than lab values or blood pressure readings. It covers physical, mental and emotional wellbeing. To be proactive about your finances is empowering – it can prevent poor outcomes (e.g. avoiding costly penalties or even bankruptcy), just as regular health checks can prevent costly illnesses later in life.

Repossession and debt consolidation are examples of an 'unhealthy' financial lifestyle that can drain your resources and affect your quality of life. Becoming financially healthy today is akin to practising good hygiene when you're young. The beneficial aspects of good money habits continue into the distant future – it's good to start when you're young but it's not too late to start later in life, just like how exercise and healthy eating can boost your health at any age.[1]

What is financial hygiene?

What we mean by financial hygiene is keeping your finances healthy through active money control: budgeting, saving, balancing debt with your income, investing your money, and being prudent by regularly assessing your assets and liabilities.

Financial hygiene is being financially aware and responsible. It's ultimately not about getting rich or achieving certain money goals – it's about creating and adopting a mindset and a set of behaviours that puts financial health and stability first.

Financial hygiene is a lifelong practice, not a product to be purchased or a pill to be swallowed. It requires discipline, consistency and staying nimble. There is no set of rules to follow, no one-size-fits-all strategy. Your financial habits derive from your particular circumstances, objectives and risk tolerance.

Financial hygiene is much more about avoiding spills than it is about earning high returns or other investment machismo. While investing can and should be part of any effective financial hygiene plan, it's also about risk management and diversification, not to mention a healthy dose of long-term thinking.

The point of financial hygiene isn't to make more money either: a steady, adequate income is a plus, but financial hygiene is about managing your money responsibly – wisely, in the best sense of the word – no matter how much you have or don't have. It's about you taking charge of your money to manage your life instead of the money being in charge and it dictating your life. That means deciding carefully where you spend, making the most of your money whether you have a little or a lot.

Financial hygiene isn't just for the wealthy or those with complicated finances. It's a mindset and habits that can help everyone, regardless of how much money is involved. It makes a difference whether or not you're newly started, or managing hundreds of thousands of pounds in a 401(k) retirement savings plan or pension pot. In any case, you'll always benefit from these financial hygiene concepts.

In other words, financial hygiene is about proactively managing your financial life in a big-picture way: cultivating financial competency and nurturing responsible money habits and a long-term vision of financial wellness. Prioritising financial hygiene reduces money stress and the risks of expensive money mistakes. Doing so also sets the stage for achieving your financial dreams.[2]

Theoretical foundations

In his book *Flourish*, Martin Seligman has argued that wellbeing involves more than happiness or life satisfaction; it involves flourishing, which he describes in terms of five key elements: positive emotions, engagement, relationships, meaning and accomplishment (PERMA). This has huge implications for the identity and role of financial wellbeing as a component of flourishing.

- Positive emotions: When you are financially secure, you are less stressed and worried about money. You may feel more peaceful in general when you know that you are on track for your money goals and have a solid financial standing.
- Engagement: Good financial hygiene, such as budgeting, saving and investing, creates a feeling of being more engaged with shaping your future as opposed to being influenced by whim or circumstance. Being in control of your money creates the sensation of being in control of your life, creating a sense of purpose and accomplishment, which boosts wellbeing.
- Relationships: Financial problems are a major cause of stress – and arguments – in relationships, both personal and family. Implementing financial hygiene and talking about money more openly could help you reduce potential stress and tension when it comes to your family or partner, and better cope with its impact on your relationships. You may also be able to help others or share new experiences, strengthening these relationships in turn.
- Meaning: Financial wellness tends to be correlated with feeling one's life has meaning and worth. After all, many tend to view the ability to earn an income, provide for yourself and your family, support not-for-profits or other favourite charities, fund endeavours that speak to your soul and/or provide financial independence as an important element of the meaning of life.
- Accomplishment: Setting and meeting financial goals such as saving for a down payment on a house, paying down debt, or building a retirement fund – especially when you can track your progress and celebrate the achievement along the way – will help you feel more

accomplished and developed. Practising financial
hygiene will lead you to feel better.

So, when you cultivate good financial hygiene, you build
financial wellbeing, which contributes to the several pathways
to flourishing that Seligman enumerates. Financial wellbeing
is not separable from life; it is part of the emotional, social and
personal fulfilment that are its foundations. Thus, fostering financial hygiene is a critical part of any strategy for flourishing
and the good life.[3]

Behavioural economics and decision-making theories show
the crucial role of cognitive bias and shortcuts in financial decisions, too – such as present bias when prioritising short-term
over longer-term financial goals, or loss aversion when being
overly risk-averse when investing.[4] Understanding the psychology behind these will be important in nudging people into good
financial hygiene and maintenance.

Financial literacy and education can provide people with the
knowledge and skills necessary to make informed choices about
money matters.[5] For example, certain forms of financial education can help to engender responsible financial behaviours, such
as budgeting, saving and investing prudently, and this can lead to
good financial wellbeing.[6] How effective these programmes are,
however, can depend on how they are structured, the needs and
characteristics of the target audience, and other factors.[7]

Components of financial hygiene

Tracking your spending is a task within the larger field of financial hygiene which encompasses strategies to budget well and the
tools used to do so (e.g. making a budget, tracking spending and
prioritising expenses).[8] Many budgeting strategies exist, such as the
50/30/20 rule (spending 50 per cent of your money on needs, 30 per
cent on wants, and 20 per cent on saving and paying down debt).[9]

Saving can help with building an emergency fund, saving for retirement and for the high costs of such goals as paying for college or purchasing a home. Different saving strategies, especially automatic saving with goal setting, can support good saving habits, such as the 'Save More Tomorrow' programme that systematically increases retirement saving contributions when employees receive pay increases.[10]

Investment incorporates saving and investing, including the trading of stocks, bonds and mutual funds, which should reflect your financial life goals and future plans for accumulating wealth. Risk management, asset allocation, and the mathematical foundation of compound interest (which is magic) are critical concepts in this respect.[11] Diversification, rebalancing, and the power of time are important approaches to managing portfolio risk and maximising reward.[12]

Strategies for dealing with debt in a proactive and responsible way include debt consolidation, debt repayment solutions and avoiding debt traps where high-interest debt obligations grow to unmanageable levels over time.[13] *Voilà!* We have a well-rounded understanding of economic knowledge. Paying off high-interest debt first, negotiating with creditors, and talking to debt counsellors are all useful coping mechanisms to deal with financial difficulties and put your debts back in some sort of order.

Psychological aspects of financial hygiene

Financial stress harms mental health, with results such as feelings of anxiety, depression and reduced wellbeing.[14] Chronic financial stress, including living payslip to payslip, is also linked to outcomes such as sleep problems, headaches and heart trouble.[15] Coping strategies may include some form of mindfulness (such as meditation or prayer), social support, wise use of money without guilt, changes in employment or housing, effective communication with creditors, or use of cognitive behavioural techniques such as challenging negative thought patterns.[16]

Likewise, practising financial hygiene may have emotional benefits, such as reducing financial stress or increasing financial security.[17] By feeling that you're in charge of your money and making progress towards your financial goals, you may feel more at ease or have greater satisfaction with your overall quality of life.

Interventions drawn from positive psychology – focusing on strengths, practising gratitude and building resilience, for example – can encourage financial wellbeing. Being grateful for your financial resources, no matter how small, promotes a sense of abundance and fulfilment. Recognising your personal strengths and capabilities to budget, save and spend prudently boosts confidence in managing money.

Adopting and maintaining financial hygiene requires a specific mindset with several key elements:

- **Proactivity:** Financial hygiene involves a proactive attitude that you adopt where you take charge of your own financial hygiene by monitoring your financial situation, anticipating risks and preventing financial crisis by being prepared for unexpected financial shocks and self-correcting to prevent a crisis.
- **Delayed gratification**: Good financial hygiene often involves the ability to delay gratification to prioritise financial success far into the future. We choose to penalise ourselves today by saving, investing and paying down debt so we can pay ourselves with a strong financial future.
- **Discipline:** Financial hygiene is about discipline. It requires a willingness to stay committed to healthy money habits and practices including the regular use of a monthly budget, regularly saving and avoiding impulsive or excessive spending.
- **Resilience:** Financial problems and setbacks are part of life and require a resilient mindset – the ability to bend

with the changes, learn from failures and rebound from bad money habits with renewed focus and modified strategies.

- **Constantly learning:** Financial landscapes and personal circumstances are ever-changing, and that means effective financial hygiene requires a constant learning mindset. This means either learning about or staying up to date with what's going on vis-à-vis financial markets, regulations and best practices. It also means remaining open to learning and acquiring new knowledge and skills for improving your money management.
- **Being goal-oriented:** Financial hygiene works best when driven by specific, measurable, achievable, relevant, time-bound (SMART) financial goals. That means specifying what you want and when you want it, and systematically aligning your financial practices to achieve it.
- **A balanced approach:** Financial hygiene requires a calm and reflective style of self-regulation, and mindfully keeping a healthy perspective on finances and money matters, balanced with a recognition that other domains in your life also deserve attention and nurturing – not least in terms of personal relationships, health and wellbeing, and personal development.

By cultivating a mindset that embraces proactivity, discipline, delayed gratification, resilience, continuous learning, goal-orientation and a balanced perspective, you can effectively adopt and maintain financial hygiene practices, paving the way for long-term financial wellbeing and stability.[18]

Empirical evidence

Much research on financial hygiene has examined connections between financial hygiene behaviours (such as budgeting, saving and investing) and financial wellness indicators (such as a sense of security and satisfaction),[19] and found that good money management habits, like budgeting, saving and careful use of credit, correlate with higher levels of financial satisfaction and general wellness. For example, one study confirmed that good money management improves satisfaction and wellbeing.[20]

Financial education programmes can improve financial knowledge, foster beneficial money behaviour and strengthen financial wellbeing, although the degree to which they are effective in boosting financial wellbeing might depend on factors such as intervention design and mode of delivery.[21] Some big reviews suggest that although financial education programmes have a small positive effect on financial knowledge, they might have limited ability to change behaviour – in particular, if they are not comprehensive and client-centred.[22]

Challenges and barriers

We've noted above, and elsewhere in the book, several things that individuals can do to improve their financial hygiene, and handle some of the issues involved to create financial wellbeing. Some of these challenges also can be eased by general policy changes. In government or organisations or communities, policies and practices can implement research on the foundations of financial hygiene.[23]

Behavioural biases, such as the fear of loss and focusing too much on the present, can make it harder for people to build good financial habits. Simple strategies, like offering helpful suggestions and setting up choices in a smart way, can reduce these biases and encourage better money management.[24] For example, automatically enrolling employees in retirement savings plans (while still letting them opt out) has helped more people save for the future by overcoming their tendency to delay decisions.[25]

Socioeconomic factors, such as income, education and access to financial capital, can play a role in how well people are able to perform financial hygiene.[26] Low-income earners, for example, maybe less able to build up an emergency rainy day fund or access products that provide them with affordable banking services or limit the consequences of complex financial systems.[27] Improving the financial wellbeing for everyone should be a priority.[28] This would include policies and legislation on financial markets and lending, financial inclusion (or, as the Congressional Budget Office has said, promoting financial capability) and education for young people and adults that emphasise 'financial hygiene'.

Conclusion

Ultimately, financial hygiene is essential for overall wellness, and many characteristics of personal hygiene and its role in physical health are also applicable to financial hygiene. Conscious, considered, consistent and balanced behaviours of financial hygiene are the pathway to success in managing your money. When this success is achieved, it aligns with financial stability and security, as well as the positive emotions, engagement, relationships, meaning and accomplishment that are the building blocks of a happy and fulfilling life. This is according to the research findings of Martin Seligman, author of *Flourish*.

After all, many studies have shown that positive financial hygiene practices act as a facilitator of greater financial wellbeing. It is now widely recognised, by scholars working on financial education and financial literacy efforts, that there are also several active barriers and formidable challenges to the simple adoption of effective financial hygiene practices by some people – from deep-seated behavioural biases to socioeconomic factors. It's important to work through policy changes, clever design of financial systems, and better public education to reduce the barriers and challenges to hygiene along the spectrum of financial wellbeing so that all people, regardless of their family circumstances, income bracket, skill levels or racial identity, can achieve financial wellbeing.

In short, by making financial hygiene a major concern and understanding and appreciating its place among other wellness efforts, individuals and society can get on the path to building a better – more secure and prosperous – financial life. It is not always easy, but with the right attitude, tools and support, most people can begin their journey to better financial health. As with physical health, you are never too old to start building good habits and making changes that can help your financial life and, by extension, your happiness. Why not start today? Your future self will thank you!

In this section, we have delved into the significance of financial hygiene and maintenance practices in fostering financial wellbeing, thereby enhancing overall flourishing and life satisfaction. In the next section, you'll find numerous activities aimed at cultivating financial hygiene and maintenance habits.

Activities

To cultivate and uphold financial hygiene, theses activities are divided into two categories. The first set focuses on cultivating a mindset conducive to financial hygiene, while the second addresses practical financial management strategies to maintain it.

Activity 20.1

- **Mindfulness meditation:** Practise in one's everyday life to become more aware of financial habits and impulses, bringing issues to mind more thoughtfully and acting more consciously and in line with money intentions.

- **Gratitude journalling**: Write in a gratitude journal about financial blessings and successes to maintain a healthy positive outlook about money and counteract feelings of scarcity or inadequacy. (See Chapter 4 for more information.)
- **Daily affirmations**: This involves using positive statements to challenge negative beliefs about money, such as feelings of lack, worthlessness or helplessness. The goal is to instil a greater sense of self-worth, resourcefulness and sufficiency. The purpose is to help you prove to the universe, through your words and beliefs, that you are capable of attracting more cash and abundance.
- **Financial education**: Make time to actively educate yourself on money matters by reading books, taking a course, or listening to a podcast to learn about and apply basic personal finance principles, boosting your ability to make smart decisions about your finances moving forward. (See Chapter 16.)
- **Surround yourself with healthy people and aspirations**: Surround yourself with people who demonstrate positive and responsible financial practices and attitudes, whom you admire and who encourage you in your efforts.
- **Goals and visualisation**: Set goals clearly and vividly as a place to come back to. This gives you a sense of orientation through time, of purpose and direction that can create the desire for disciplined financial conduct. (See Chapter 18.)
- **Stress management techniques**: Deep breathing, exercise, hobbies – whatever you use to relieve financial anxiety and return yourself to psychological homeostasis, your tranquil 'zero point' of quietude and emotional equipoise that brings clarity and focus to

your thinking about money – and makes doing your financial hygiene at least marginally less unpleasant.

- **Financial self-awareness exercises:** Participate in self-reflection exercises about your attitudes, beliefs and behaviours around money so you can figure out if and where you want to change.
- **Personal practice:** Practice self-reflection, self-compassion and self-discipline to develop financial resilience, flexibility and a 'growth mindset'.

This is just a short list but it shows that there is a variety of solutions for people who struggle with money, and different opinions about what constitutes good financial wellbeing.

Activity 20.2

- **Budgeting and expense tracking:** One of the basic, daily routine activities is to develop and regularly update your budget which includes income and expense tracking, categorising your expenditures and allocating funds towards your financial goals. You can use budgeting tools, apps or spreadsheets to track and add up your expenses.
- **Saving goals and automation:** Specific savings goals should be set and contributions to these savings automatically be made (via direct to your savings account) as income comes in to establish the habit of saving over the long term. Automating your savings removes the temptation to spend and ensures that saving is prioritised.
- **Debt management plan:** Paying off debt, particularly high-interest debt, is an essential part of money hygiene, so if you're in debt, a plan should be created to pay it off. You should develop some kind of repayment

schedule, negotiate with creditors or consider consolidating some of your debts.

- **Financial tracking app:** If we have cash within our budget and are keeping any 'side funds' separate, then spending will be trackable, saving us from fee-intensive debt repayment.
- **Investment planning:** Selecting the right mix of investments for the right reasons, with an eye towards your personal risk tolerance and financial goals (think retirement accounts, mutual funds, or individual stocks and bonds) plus regular review, including periodic rebalancing.
- **Credit monitoring:** Monitoring a credit report, and checking a credit score on a periodic basis alerts credit report checkers to possible problems that can then be remedied to maintain a good credit profile.
- **Create an emergency fund:** Save a portion of your income in a dedicated savings account so it is available for unforeseen expenses or income interruptions.
- **Net worth calculation:** Net worth (total assets minus total liabilities) may be a more comprehensive measure to follow. It can be calculated periodically and used to track progress towards important financial goals.
- **Financial literacy:** Participating in activities such as reading books, participating in a seminar or workshop, or taking online courses boosts the ability of people to comprehend the financial nature of a different asset, thus contributing to a higher expected return.
- **Financial advice:** If you have complicated questions such as how to minimise tax during retirement planning, how to leave money to the next generation, or how to lower your mortgage, you can approach a financial adviser, an accountant or a planner.

Many of these activities are explained in detail in various chapters of this book.

After completing these exercises, revisit the financial hygiene and maintenance questionnaire introduced at the start of this chapter and assess any potential changes in your responses.

Resources

Here are some further resources to help you understand the influence of financial hygiene and maintenance on your overall wellness.

Books

Flourish by Martin Seligman, Atria Books, 2011
  A comprehensive exploration of positive psychology and the elements that contribute to human wellbeing and fulfilment.

The Happiness Advantage: How a Positive Brain Fuels Success in Work and Life by Shawn Achor, Crown Business, 2010
  Examines how cultivating a positive mindset can lead to greater success, productivity and happiness in various life domains.

Flow: The Psychology of Optimal Experience by Mihaly Csikszentmihalyi, Harper Perennial, 1990
  A seminal work on the concept of 'flow' – the mental state of being completely engaged and immersed in an activity.

The Psychology of Money: Timeless Lessons on Wealth, Greed, and Happiness by Morgan Housel, Harriman House, 2020
  An insightful exploration of the human behaviours and biases that shape our relationship with money and financial decision-making.

The True Cost of Happiness: The Real Story Behind Managing

Your Money by Stacey Tisdale & Paula Boyer Kennedy,
Wiley, 2014
Examines the emotional and psychological factors that
influence our financial choices and wellbeing.

*Spend Well, Live Rich: How to Get What You Want with
the Money You Have* by Michelle Singletary, Random
House, 2004
A practical guide to making the most of your financial
resources and aligning your spending with your values and
priorities.

*Why Didn't They Teach Me This in School?: 99 Personal Money
Management Principles to Live By* by Cary Siegel, Cary
Siegel, 2012
A straightforward, no-nonsense approach to personal
finance education for young adults and those seeking to
improve their money management skills.

The Total Money Makeover by Dave Ramsey, Thomas
Nelson, 2013
A comprehensive, step-by-step plan for getting out of debt
and achieving long-term financial security.

Apps

You need a budget (YNAB) – budget tools
Plum – money management and investment
Headspace – mindfulness
Wallet hub – reviews of financial products, credit control
Credit Karm – credit scores and improvements
Moneybox – money management
10% happier – mindfulness
Wally – worldwide money tracking

Websites

Michelle McQuaid: www.michellemcquaid.com
The Flourishing Centre: theflourishingcenter.com
Positive Psychology: positivepsychology.com
Calm Blog: blog.calm.com
This is Money: www.thisismoney.co.uk/money/index.html
Money Mentor: www.money-mentor.org
The Ascent by The Motley Fool: www.fool.com/the-ascent
The Motley Fool: www.fool.com

Blog/journal articles

What is flourishing in Positive Psychology: positivepsychology.com/flourishing
Seligman's PERMA+ Model Explained: A Theory of Wellbeing: positivepsychology.com/perma-model
How to Choose the Best Personal Finance Software and Apps: www.nerdwallet.com/article/finance/best-personal-finance-software
How to start meditating daily: blog.calm.com/blog/how-to-start-meditating-daily
The psychology of money: www.ramseysolutions.com/budgeting/psychology-of-money
The Psychology of Money: What You Need To Know To Have A (Relatively) Fearless Financial Life: www.forbes.com/sites/prudygourguechon/2019/02/25/the-psychology-of-money-what-you-need-to-know-to-have-a-relatively-fearless-financial-life
The psychology of money: www.moneyflamingo.com/the-psychology-of-money
Five ways to manage your personal finances: hbr.org/2022/11/5-ways-to-manage-your-personal-finances

Blogs

Get Rich Slowly: www.getrichslowly.org
Mind Over Money Matters: www.wearemindovermoney.com
Money Mentor: www.money-mentor.org
Money Crashers: www.moneycrashers.com
The Best Interest: bestinterest.blog
Good Financial Cents: www.goodfinancialcents.com
The Balance: www.thebalancemoney.com
Budgets Are Sexy: www.budgetsaresexy.com

Videos

Flourishing – a new understanding of wellbeing – Martin Seligman
Prof Seligman on PERMA
Interactive Personal Finance Dashboard with free excel template
How I manage my money: income , expenses , budget, etc – personal finance in my 20s
Personal finance: How to save, spend, and think rationally about money – Big Think
How To Buy Happiness
Saving For Tomorrow, Tomorrow
The Emotions Behind Your Money Habits

Podcasts

Michelle McQuaid's Podcast
The Science of Happiness Podcast: greatergood.berkeley.edu/podcasts/series/the_science_of_happiness
10% Happier: www.tenpercent.com/podcast
The Ramsey Show: www.ramseysolutions.com/shows/the-dave-ramsey-show

The Clark Howard Podcast: www.clark.com/podcast
The Martin Lewis Podcast: www.bbc.co.uk/programmes/
   p02pc9q4/episodes/downloads
So Money: podcast.farnoosh.tv
Financial Freedom

Appendices

APPENDIX 1

Common cognitive distortions

Cognitive distortions are irrational and biased thought patterns that contribute to negative emotions and behaviour. Here's a list of common cognitive distortions along with brief explanations for each:

1. **All-or-nothing thinking (black-and-white thinking): Perceiving situations in extreme terms without acknowledging middle ground or nuance.**
   Examples:
   - Thinking 'If I can't save £1000 this month, I'm a complete failure at budgeting' instead of recognising that any amount saved is progress.
   - Believing that if you're not a millionaire by thirty, you're financially unsuccessful, ignoring the progress you've made in paying off student loans and building an emergency fund.

2. **Overgeneralisation: Forming broad conclusions based on limited information or isolated incidents.**
   Examples:

- After one bad investment, thinking 'I'll never be good at investing' rather than seeing it as a learning experience.
- After one credit card application rejection, concluding 'I'll never qualify for any credit' without considering other factors or card options.

3. **Catastrophising: Anticipating and expecting the worst possible outcome, often exaggerating the importance of a situation.**
   Examples:
   - After a minor expense overrun, imagining 'I'll end up bankrupt and homeless' instead of calmly reassessing the budget.
   - Upon hearing about potential layoffs at your company, immediately assuming you'll lose your job, deplete all savings, and be unable to pay your mortgage.

4. **Mind-reading: Assuming you know others' thoughts, typically negative, without any concrete evidence.**
   Examples:
   - Thinking 'My friends must think I'm poor because I don't go out often' when they may understand you're saving for a goal.
   - Believing your coworkers are judging you for bringing lunch from home, when they might actually admire your frugality and financial discipline.

5. **Fortune telling (predicting the future): Anticipating negative outcomes without sufficient justification or evidence.**
Examples:
- Thinking 'I'll never be able to retire comfortably' without actually reviewing your retirement plan or options.
- Assuming a new business venture will fail before even starting, thinking 'I'll lose all my savings' without considering potential success or learning opportunities.

6. **Personalisation: Attributing external events to oneself and taking responsibility for things beyond one's control.**
Examples:
- Blaming yourself for a market downturn affecting your investments, rather than recognising broader economic factors.
- Blaming yourself for a joint financial decision with your spouse that didn't work out, taking full responsibility instead of viewing it as a shared learning experience.

7. **Filtering (selective abstraction): Focusing exclusively on negative aspects while disregarding any positive elements.**
Examples:
- Dwelling on a late bill payment while overlooking consistent savings in other areas.
- Focusing solely on a credit card debt while ignoring the value of your retirement account and the equity in your home.

8. **Discounting the positive: Downplaying or rejecting positive experiences, often attributing them to chance rather than personal effort.**
   Examples:
   - Reaching a savings goal but thinking 'It's not enough' or 'I just got lucky' instead of acknowledging your effort.
   - Downplaying a promotion and raise, thinking 'It's not a real achievement because the cost of living increased too' instead of recognising the career progress.

9. **Should statements: Maintaining inflexible rules about behaviour, often leading to guilt and frustration.**
   Examples:
   - Thinking 'I should never spend money on luxuries' can lead to guilt over occasional treats, rather than maintaining a balanced approach.
   - Believing 'I should have my student loans paid off by now', leading to unnecessary stress, instead of acknowledging the progress made within your means.

10. **Emotional reasoning: Believing that one's emotions accurately reflect reality, even when they may not align with objective facts.**
    Examples:
    - Feeling anxious might lead to thinking 'I feel worried about my finances, so I must be in trouble' even if, objectively, your finances are stable.
    - Feeling excited about a 'hot stock tip' and thinking 'This must be a great investment because I feel so good about it', without doing proper research.

11. **Labelling and mislabelling: Assigning negative labels to oneself or others based on specific behaviours or mistakes, rather than seeing them as isolated incidents.**
    Examples:
    - After an impulse purchase, thinking 'I'm a shopaholic' instead of 'I made a mistake but generally manage my money well'.
    - After forgetting to pay a bill once, labelling yourself as 'financially irresponsible', ignoring your overall good track record with payments.

12. **Blaming: Incorrectly assigning responsibility for problems to oneself or others, without considering all factors involved.**
    Examples:
    - Either blaming others entirely for your debt or taking full blame for shared financial issues in a partnership.
    - Attributing all financial struggles to the economy or government policies, without considering personal financial habits that could be improved.

13. **Control fallacies: Misunderstanding the extent of one's control over external events, either overestimating or underestimating it.**
    Examples:
    - Either thinking you can control market performance through sheer will, or feeling completely helpless about improving your financial situation.
    - Believing that frequent checking of your investment portfolio will somehow influence its performance, or conversely, feeling that your

financial situation is entirely at the mercy of
external factors.

14. **Comparisons: Evaluating self-worth through
    unrealistic comparisons with others, often leading to
    feelings of inadequacy.**
    Examples:
    • Comparing your starting salary to a CEO's
      compensation and feeling inadequate, rather than
      considering career stages.
    • Constantly comparing your financial situation to
      social media posts of friends on luxurious vacations,
      without considering differences in priorities, debts
      or income sources.

15. **Fairness fallacy: Expecting life to be consistently
    fair and feeling distressed when it isn't, without
    recognising the complexity of situations.**
    Examples:
    • Feeling it's unfair that others got a promotion or
      thinking 'I work hard, so I should be rich by now'
      without considering various factors affecting wealth
      accumulation.
    • Feeling it's unfair that you have to budget
      carefully while others seem to spend freely,
      without considering their full financial picture or
      potential debt.

Recognising these distortions in financial contexts can help
individuals develop a healthier relationship with money, make
more rational financial decisions and reduce money-related stress
and anxiety.

APPENDIX 2

Expenses checklist

Housing
Mortgage/rent
Buildings and contents insurance
Renter insurance or deposit
Property taxes
Utilities
  Water and sewage
  Gas
  Electricity
  Oil
  Telephone
House repair e.g. plumbing, electrical work
Household consumables e.g. washing liquids
Household durables e.g. washing machine
Garden maintenance e.g. fuel for mower
Gardener
Cleaner or maid

Food
Food shopping

Eating out
Coffees/sandwiches/snacks
Drinks for home
Meals at work

Clothes
New clothes
New children's clothes
Work clothes

Technology
Mobile phone
Internet
Computer

Travel expenses
Breakdown cover/roadside recovery
Rail/bus/coach/taxi
Car maintenance
Car insurance
Car tax or duty
Parking
Fuel
Cycling costs

Banking and debits
Bank account fee
Overdraft cost
Personal loan repayments
HP repayments
Credit card interest

Entertainment
Drinking out

Smoking
Streaming services
IT/computing (e.g. anti-virus)
Hobbies
Pet costs
Shopping for fun
Big days out
Books/music/films/computer games
Cinema/theatre trips
Family days out
Satellite/digital TV subscription
Newspapers and magazines

Childcare
Childcare/play schemes
Babysitting
Children's travel
Laundry/dry cleaning
Nappies/baby extras
Pocket money
School meals
School trips

Health and fitness
Fitness/sports/gym
Private medical insurance
Dental insurance
Healthcare cash plans
Beauty treatments
Dentistry
Hairdressers
Optical bills
Complimentary therapies
Shampoo, toothpaste, etc.

Education costs
Your courses
School fees
University tuition fees
Supplementary e.g. books, software

Insurances
Life assurance
Income protection
Personal accident
Critical illness cover
Pet insurance
Travel insurance
Gas and plumbing/boiler cover
Health and medical fees

Savings related
Regular savings
Lump sum savings
Bank deposits
Into tax relieved investments
Into gross investments
Charity donations

Occasions
Christmas
Summer holiday
Winter holiday
Birthdays
Wedding expenses
Funeral expenses

Taxes (if not listed in income)

For a full list of endnotes in the book, please visit
https://overcoming.co.uk/715/resources-to-download.

Index